Commend

This precious book may well be the b
available to the individual, the famil
Freemasonry. I cannot recommend it ...

As someone who has taught and ministered in ...
I can confirm that:

- When an individual willingly partakes in Christ-less prayers and Christ-less hymns within a Freemasonry 'temple' there are spiritual consequences.
- When an individual willingly partakes in the various secret oaths, curses and rituals associated with the many Freemasonry degrees there are spiritual consequences.
- When an individual seals those Freemasonry oaths and curses with the witchcraft oath of "so mote it be" while kissing a Bible set upon an altar within a pentagram there are spiritual consequences.

This well researched and well-written book is greatly needed within the Body of Christ. Too many people are unaware of the consequences that a family member's involvement in the secret society known as Freemasonry can have, and for several generations.

Ken Symington
Author, international speaker and founder of
Christian Restoration in Ireland

All who want to be free from the effects of Freemasonry in their life and that of their family will be deeply grateful to Otto Bixler for writing this book. It will also be an invaluable tool for all those involved in the ministry of healing. For this is not just a book about Freemasonry, but a practical workshop manual which first helps people identify the real source of problems, which can have their origin in Freemasonry, and then shows them how to overcome them, be healed and set free. I pray that through this book there will be many who discover the amazing truths in God's Word which point the way to freedom.

Peter Horrobin
Founder and International Director,
Ellel Ministries International

IT ISN'T FREE
and
IT ISN'T MASONRY

IT ISN'T FREE
and
IT ISN'T MASONRY

Otto Bixler

Published by Sovereign World Ltd
PO Box 784
Ellel, Lancaster
LA1 9DA

Published June 2016
First edition published by Zaccmedia

British Library Cataloguing-in-Publication Data
A catalogue record for this book is available from the British Library.

ISBN 978-1-85240-870-1

Zaccmedia aims to produce books that will help to extend and build up the Kingdom of God. We do not necessarily agree with every view expressed by the authors, or with every interpretation of Scripture expressed. We expect readers to make their own judgment in the light of their understanding of God's Word and in an attitude of Christian love and fellowship.

Front cover design by Angela Kovacs, cover photograph by Otto Bixler.
Typesetting by Zaccmedia

Printed and bound in Great Britain by Bell and Bain Ltd, Glasgow.

Acknowledgments

The first acknowledgment is to God Himself, who has encouraged me to write a self-help book for those wishing to be free from the effects of Freemasonry. Secondly, I wish to acknowledge my dear wife Sharon's patience and tolerance of the many hours of attention that this book has taken away from our personal intimacy and shared time. Thirdly, I wish to acknowledge all those who so kindly listened to me and encouraged me to write *It Isn't Free and It Isn't Masonry*. Finally, but not last on the list in my heart, are those who came alongside me in editing and preparing this work particularly for the relief of the many millions of living and yet-to-be-born descendants of those who were Freemasons and the current millions of Freemasons. In most cases these people have no idea what they are really involved in. The primary editors, in the order of their processing of the text are: first editor, Lynne Vick; second editor, Roger Bullard; third editors, Allen and Linda Fode.

Contents

Appendices

Foreword

The focus in this Freemasonry book is not darkness, but light. We are not bashing Masons, detailing all their materials and rituals for condemnation. Rather we seek to bring the light of the Gospel in place of the false light that Masons seek in their studies, oaths and rituals.[1,2]

Freemasonry has publically observable, natural impacts on the global community, but at its core it is spiritual[3] and is a "successor of the ancient Mysteries [religions],"[4] "the secret worship rites of the pagan gods. Each of the pagan gods had, besides the public and open, a secret worship paid to him to which none were admitted but those who had been selected by preparatory ceremonies called initiation."[5] "Every Masonic Lodge is a temple of religion and its teachings are instruction in religion (Royal Arch Degree)."[6] "It is the universal, eternal, immutable religion (Grand Elect, Perfect and Sublime Mason)"[7] and "propagates no creed except its own most simple and sublime one; that universal religion taught by Nature and Reason (Prince Adept Degree)."[8]

It is the spiritual effects on the individual that we wish to bring to light, while giving choices for a better life that people may not have known are theirs. As we will reveal in this book, Freemasonry takes us away from God, His ways, and the well-being that He guarantees to those who live in conformance with those ways. Therefore, we may conclude that our overall welfare is diminished by Freemasonry. To get to this point, we will have to examine some aspects of God and His ways to compare these with Freemasonry's ways and the gods it worships. As we look at the temporal effects of Freemasonry, we will also discover that descendants of Masons, those who have been or are Masons and their living families, are under various curses from which they and their yet-unborn descendants may escape.

Discovery, Healing, and Release

This book is a guided adventure of discovery, healing, and release. Don't look here for a deep discourse on all the rituals, oaths, clothing, jewelry, and regalia of Freemasonry. Rather, we will examine the physical, mental, emotional, financial, relational, and "spiritual" damages brought on by membership and participation in the fraternity of Freemasonry. These impact the individual and bring similar collateral damage to his family and descendants. We will discover that the keys to release are knowledge, the love of God for us, and the sacrifice Jesus made on the cross for us.

This book was written with the intent to make known to all, Christians and non-Christians alike, the way to freedom and healing, and to bring freedom to Christians from the personal, residual effects of Freemasonry worldwide. Christians will be assisted in bringing themselves and other believers into spiritual freedom. Understanding is helpful, but freedom from Freemasonry is available only to Christians and only in the name of Jesus Christ.

If you are not yet a Christian, please take a look at Chapter 7 or Appendix I to see a more detailed explanation. You may be surprised to find just how easy it is to give your life to Christ. Of course then, as a Christian, you would also be able to be helped into freedom by this book.

Ultimately, this is a Christian book applying spiritual truths to the cultural experience of the many millions of Freemasons, both living and dead, including those who have left the "Craft," for their wives and children and descendants. Since spiritual damage propagates down the family line, bringing trouble to the fourth generation, we are addressing a much larger population than the many millions of Masons living now. By looking both backward four generations and forward four generations, according to the Laws of Idolatry, to the millions and millions of individuals it can affect, we will see that individuals, whether or not they ever directly participated in Freemasonry, suffer loss.

We will show you some of the basic spiritual principles that undergird Freemasonry, and bring them into focus in a biblical perspective that exposes the fabric and framework of the spiritual construct holding the multitudes of unsuspecting Freemasons and their descendants in powerful bondage. It is a basic premise of this book that Freemasonry has the form and strength of a false (non-Christian) religion. You will discover the spiritual laws that allow any past family participation in Freemasonry to hold you in bondage in the present. More importantly, we will show you how to use God's spiritual laws to set you and your family free.

It Isn't Free and It Isn't Masonry is a "how-to book." It is more than informational; it's tutorial. As you read and enter into the written exercises presented, chapter by chapter, your journey will lead from discovery to discovery, eventually bringing you to a new personal understanding about God, yourself, and your family. Finally, through the guided prayer ministry in Chapters 7, 10, 11, and 12, you will receive a new level of personal freedom that you may never have dreamed possible.

As an aid to you who are not yet moving with confidence in the ministry of healing and deliverance, six tutorial appendices are included. They will help the less experienced to understand the undergirding principles which support the guided prayer ministry chapters.

Introduction

Perhaps you picked up this book because you had some questions regarding Freemasonry. Perhaps you are in a family where the husband/father is an active Freemason or was active in the past. Maybe it is you, yourself, who is or was in Freemasonry. Or perhaps it is somewhere in your generational line, a grandfather, great-grandfather, or even further back. The spiritual after-effects of participation in Freemasonry follow the family line down the generations.

So, just what is this thing called Freemasonry? When we ask our family members about Uncle Bob, or even when we directly ask our husband or dad, who is a member of the Freemasons, to explain, why are there never any satisfying, complete answers? Why don't we get answers when we ask a priest or pastor? You may have heard conflicting information about Freemasonry—that it is the greatest organization, with a history going back farther than the pyramids in Egypt. Perhaps you've heard that it is virulent and evil. So, just what is the truth, and why are there such disparate claims?

As you begin this book, you are embarking on an amazing voyage of discovery, probably unlike any other exploration that you have ever made. But any successful journey begins with some preparation, particularly when venturing into unknown territory. If you are to get free from the residual effects of Freemasonry, you will need both understanding and spiritual strength. The exercises in the first seven chapters are necessary to gain both.

Without some understanding of the spiritual realm, we cannot evaluate the subject of Freemasonry, since it is spiritual. Freemasonry itself claims to be a religion in its private literature (although claiming otherwise publically). As you read this book you will discover why that is so. All religion is spiritual in nature and bridges between the seen and unseen, the natural and supernatural realms. Therein lies the blockage to our ability to understand this thing called Freemasonry: most of us don't have the forensic spiritual tools to examine the corpus of literature, claims, and stories.

Without spiritual understanding we are extremely vulnerable to being misled, deceived, or coming to wrong conclusions when reading contemporary literature and publicity in regard to Freemasonry. Since Freemasonry is spiritual in nature, if we are to understand it we must look at it through spiritual eyes. The best spiritual lens that we can use to examine spiritual matters is the Word of God, i.e. the Bible. To get to the point of answering the questions we have, we must first begin to understand some things in the Bible that will equip us to weigh and evaluate the literature, practices, and claims of Freemasonry. We ourselves must be willing to go on a spiritual journey and be open to having our worldview adjusted a bit. We will then discover how to deal with the spiritual effects of Freemasonry.

As we develop this subject, we will do our best to make it understandable to both Christians and non-Christians alike. While being a Christian or attending church may aid you in some ways in your understanding of Freemasonry, since it is a religion, it is not a Christian religion, and therefore will not be familiar to most in its functioning. It is, in fact, idolatry by another name.

Across the face of the earth, within nations, cultures, and language groups, the schemes of Satan, the enemy of our souls, are in operation to enslave. There are three major afflictions that affect Masons and their descendants:

1. Breakdown of the family
2. Spiritual bondage
3. Physical, social, and economic damage.

As of this writing, there are about six million Freemasons across the world with nearly five million in the United States. They meet secretly, month after month, behind the guarded doors of their temples. There they perform occult rituals and form alliances that are sworn to be above or beyond the law of the nations in which they meet. Revealed in the US Senate Congressional record of September 9, 1987, Freemason members were accounted for in the following: Federal Judiciary (41), Senate Judiciary Committee (one-half membership), Senators (18) and House of Representatives (76).[9]

Britain's 800,000 Freemasons, meeting secretly in 8000 lodges in the UK, account for one in sixty adult males. Reportedly, they have formed a secret link between the most powerful institutions of the nation, infiltrating Parliament, the judicial system, newspapers, and fire and police departments,[10,11] with over 60 percent of the police chiefs being Freemasons.[12]

What are these occult rituals and alliances that supersede the laws of the land? How does the behavior of a father and husband in Freemasonry affect his family? What does his membership in the Freemasons do to him personally? Read on to find out.

It is not the objective of this book to provide a reference work on Freemasonry and all claims to its origin. There are many books, booklets and websites documenting the oaths, rituals, and indoctrination procedures. The purpose of this book is to examine Freemasonry from a Christian perspective, explaining in simple terms how membership in this occult society will bring problems, accidents, poverty, infirmity, and even death into your life. You will learn how it will compromise your walk with God, the God of

Abraham, Isaac and Jacob, and Jesus, the Christ, the only begotten Son of God, and separate you from the Holy Spirit.

This book is not an exposé of Freemasonry, but rather a path to freedom for those who have been members of this fraternity, and for those who are unfortunate enough to be born into family bloodlines with forebears who were Freemasons or its derivatives. The truth is that membership in Freemasonry, DeMolay, Rainbow Girls, Job's Daughters, and Eastern Star not only damages you, but opens up your family and future generations to many problems not of their own making. The freedom being offered here can only be obtained by Christians, those who know Jesus Christ as their Lord and Savior.

Knowing Jesus in this way assures us of entry into heaven. But even guaranteed salvation, as great as it is, does not remove Freemasonry's temporal problems from our life here on earth.

The Bible tells us that people, even God's people, suffer because of lack of knowledge. We need to know what the sins of Freemasonry are and how to use our relationship with God and the privileges we have as Christians to extract ourselves from the earthly curses of this covertly false religion.

Join in now as we begin to unravel the mystery of Freemasonry. God has redeemed the lives of thousands and given them a chance to make their lives count for something of lasting value. Read on to discover how He can do the same for you.

PART I
Stepping into Strength and Knowledge—Restoring the Family

CHAPTER 1

Symptoms without Cause

Unrecognized Symptoms

Brenda, aged fourteen, reached to take a piece of communion bread, but could not grasp anything. Her fingers scrabbled frantically around in the plate trying to grab one of the tiny pre-formed wafers while the long line behind her stopped its progression. As she fought to control her fingers, she finally managed to pick one up. Every Sunday, when she dipped her fingers into the plate, they went numb. It only happened at the communion plate and she had no sickness or other symptoms.

Walter and his wife Sarah were despairing. It seemed that Bobby, their four-year-old, would eventually burn the house down. Somehow, he always managed to find matches—or some other way to start fires in the house. In the last several months he had set fire to his bed three times.

John, a bread and pastry delivery truck driver, was a careful, professional driver, and yet he had violent accidents, one after the other. His family chalked it up to his long hours of work, but not so secretly worried that one day the large truck he drove would not be enough to protect him. His end came, not by a traffic accident, but from complications after being crushed by the fall of a tall pallet load of bread and pastries.

Mary suffered from stabbing pains in her left breast, but there was no medically detectable source of affliction. She lived in constant fear that she would have a heart attack and die.

William often got headaches that manifested as a tight band across his forehead, extending over his ears and ending behind his head. Aspirin or other pain relievers would hardly touch the affliction. This happened so often that he finally convinced his family doctor to order an MRI. Having no health insurance, William ended up with an expensive bill, and no relief except for the assurance that there was no brain tumor or other observable cause.

For each of these people, the source of their trouble was attributed to Freemasonry, coming down through the generations from family members who had been participants in this fraternal order. While it proved to be too late to help John, who died as a result of his spiritual vulnerability to accidents and death, freedom was made available to the others through the understanding and help which is available in this book. While the girl with the finger affliction, as of this writing, has yet to receive prayer ministry, the others were set free from their generational afflictions and healed.

Most of us would never consider that we might have a spiritually rooted affliction. Perhaps we've seen a film about adventurers or missionaries in Africa, or tomb raiders in Egypt, coming down with maladies that they did not realize resulted from curses. There are many sources of spiritually rooted affliction that can affect those not overseas or in culturally primitive societies. However, we with "Western mindsets" seldom become aware of their roots and may suffer our entire lives with their effects. Below are a few more specific areas where individuals, Christians and non-Christians alike, may suffer but never realize that they are experiencing spiritually rooted symptoms often seen in Masons, their families, and their descendants. Therefore, they may never seek and obtain relief through the spiritual means available. Some may even go to an early grave because of the causes behind these symptoms.

SOME TYPICAL SYMPTOMS SUFFERED BY MASONS AND THEIR DESCENDANTS

- Accidents and injury—frequent (thematically in life), head injuries, falling, etc.
- Death, miscarriages, and stillbirths; early deaths in family
- Poverty and financial difficulties
- Headaches (migraine), or tight bands around head, particularly at the forehead
- Throat problems
- Bowel problems
- Heart problems, even leading to heart transplant
- Head or neck problems
- Allergies and breathing problems
- Mental confusion and learning difficulties
- Infertility in women
- Eye and vision problems—including problems with Bible reading
- Speech problems, including mouth, tongue, and vocal cords; resistance to receiving the spiritual gift of tongues
- Blasphemy, cursing, and foul language usage
- Hand usage difficulties
- Walking difficulties—feet, legs and knees
- Stiffness and paralysis
- Hearing problems, including an inability to hear God speak or to comprehend church sermons/preaching
- Lack of spiritual growth in Christianity, including a lack of intimacy with God

- Difficulty in entering into worship at church
- Falling asleep in church
- Fascination with fire
- Mockery of Christianity or Christian leaders, including faultfinding and disappointment
- Lack of intimacy with your father—experienced lower levels of love, nurture, support, modeling, and instruction from father
- Divorce, personal or your parents'
- Resistance to the Gospel and receiving Jesus as Savior.

The Freemasonry Connection

Perhaps some of the above are your symptoms. But until now you never realized that these afflictions are experienced by many others and that there may be a common cause: Freemasonry. This news is stunning! Even better news—there is a way of escape from your suffering, poverty, propensity towards accidents, marital discord, and more. If Freemasonry is the cause, then there is logical, progressive, permanent deliverance from the symptoms we've listed. Many have gone before you in receiving this freedom. That's the subject of this book: making escape from this previously undetected source of bondage available to you.

Freemasonry, as practiced since the early to mid-1800s, has the form of a false (non-Christian) religion. Membership carries with it the possibilities of material reward through cooperative efforts among its practitioners as they favor each other, even illegally, over non-initiates—primarily in politics, law, and business. In actuality, membership brings with it a guaranteed spiritually induced disaster—first in the immediate family, and then proceeding down the generations. Since the basis of membership is spiritual, giving oaths of recognition and fidelity to pagan gods and ultimately to Satan,[13] the remedy for those seeking relief must also be spiritual.

Initiation into Freemasonry is easily begun by the initiate. Participating in an indoctrination ritual in a room dedicated to the ancient gods of Egypt, making proclamations, swearing allegiances, and wearing some strange clothes, can be accomplished by any person. But, unlike removing an unwanted program from your computer, indoctrination into Freemasonry is a one-way process, which does not include an "uninstall program" tool with an icon that you just click on. Once begun, the initiate and his family have entered into a contract that includes only death, ruin, and curses as penalties for default.

A practical example may help you understand this spiritual trap. One summer we took our fourteen-year-old son on a camping trip in the High Sierras, where he and a friend went out fishing on Lake Mary. They returned to shore with a very vexing problem: somehow, his friend's number 16 gold-plated fishhook became embedded in our son's arm. Fishhooks have a small, backward-facing barb at the tip that prevents them from releasing from the mouth of any fish foolish enough to swallow the bait-laden hook. The hook, meant for catching a fish, was now firmly and painfully implanted. Any attempt to pull it back out would result in severe tearing of the flesh. Cutting it out with a razor blade would also make a rather large wound. Our son came to me, his father, for help. Using a small wire-cutter, I released the line by removing the eyelet to which it was tied. It was then a simple matter to use needle-nosed pliers to push the curved hook further through his skin, causing the barb to emerge, and then pull out the hook, barb first. Freemasonry is like a barbed hook, with a line attached to the powers of darkness. Only with the help of our Heavenly Father can we be set free without serious damage.

For many readers this will be a new experience. The only hope of escape from Freemasonry without severe penalty is an appeal to a spiritual entity of greater power than the gods of Freemasonry (some being the gods of Egypt that Moses battled). Our remedy comes from One higher than Satan himself. Only God can set you free. We will show you how to obtain freedom from Freemasonry as you progress through this book. In the remaining sections of this chapter, we will examine a brief history of this false "religion" and begin to look at the biblical consequences of worshiping pagan gods.

A Brief History of Freemasonry

THE BEGINNINGS AND EARLY CHRISTIAN INFLUENCE IN FREEMASONRY

Although much of the following may be confirmed in other references, what is documented in this section is drawn from David Barton's book, *The Question of Freemasonry and the Founding Fathers*.[14] This carefully researched book, containing over 300 references, is based upon historical documents predating the American Revolution.

Over a thousand years ago, across Europe, the primary building material for cathedrals, abbeys, churches, castles, fortresses, and other large structures was stone. The craftsmen who cut the stones and assembled them into buildings were known as stonemasons. Some masons were permitted by the nobility to travel from one country to another across Europe. These were called freemasons. Most of these people belonged to guilds or lodges (something like today's union halls) in which they shared their craftsmanship secrets, obtained help, and generally supported each other. The lodges were Christian in nature and had several levels of membership available to individuals depending upon their skill level. Novices were classified as Entered Apprentice. With a number of years' experience, the apprentice could be advanced to the Fellow Craft level. Finally, masters of the trade could become Master Masons.

Freemason guild members were first governed by the "Old York" Constitution, established in AD 926, then by the "Old Charges" of AD 938. There were four areas regulated by these resolutions:

- The relationship of a mason to God and religion
- The professional craft of masonry, particularly the conduct, training, and behavior of masons
- The comprehension of geometry to know both the scientific and mathematical basis necessary for architectural design and subsequent construction
- Understanding of protocol in regard to dealing with royalty, since most of what was being built was sponsored by the rulers of nations—monarchs, nobles, and, for the church, popes, bishops, and other high-ranking church officials.

Starting in AD 926, the Old York Constitution required that "Every mason shall cultivate brotherly love, the love of God and frequent holy church." At each meeting masons were required to pray heartily for all Christians. Although the guild requirements officially changed over the years, they remained Christian in nature. Although things evolved as time passed, by 1582, the masonic guiding documents proclaimed, "The might of the Father of heaven, and the wisdom of the glorious Son, through grace and the goodness of the Holy Ghost, yet being three persons and one God, be with us at [our] beginning." By 1686, masons were required to be "true men of God and the holy church." By 1722 the masonic documents declared that a mason, if he understood the craft of his profession, would "never be a stupid atheist" nor an immoral and ungodly person.

But, by the end of the eighteenth century and going into the nineteenth century, as construction techniques and materials changed, less and less stone was being used to construct buildings and fewer and fewer masons were working and being trained to carry on the profession. In an attempt to maintain the stonemason guilds, a rescue plan was launched, allowing non-masons to join the guilds as honorary members. In 1703, the masonic codes that governed membership in the guilds proclaimed that membership would be opened to men of other professions. The guilds then began to be called lodges of Accepted Masons since they were accepting non-stonemasons into their ranks.

MURDER AND A SPIRITUAL TURN FOR THE WORSE

By 1717, with the floodgates open to non-stonemasons, the ranks swelled, leading to speculation and spiritualizing of the early symbols and rituals. In this year, four independent London Accepted Masons lodges joined together to reform the old standards and practices in a "Grand Lodge," which was codified by 1723. This reform planted the seeds for current-day Freemasonry, a stepping away from Christianity into reverence for pluralistic pagan deities, with a philosophical framework of beliefs. In Europe, these roots continued to spiral downward into paganism and secularism. But in America, masonry, while open to other professions, remained faithful to Christ and required orthodox Christian doctrinal instruction as part of its functioning. This orthodoxy persisted until 1813, when English Freemasonry teaching and practices, which allowed non-Christian membership, began to infiltrate. It should be noted that George Washington, the father of the United States, and indeed most of the American founding fathers, were Christian Freemasons, active during Freemasonry's Christian period. They had died before the occult infiltration took place. Thus, the United States was founded by Christian fathers, not by Freemasons of the current pagan ilk.

By 1825, Freemasonry in America had radically departed from the Christian practices that prevailed during the formation of the country, embracing both paganism and a disregard of the laws of the nation. An alleged murder[15] attributed to a group of Freemasons in that year caught the attention of the nation. The deceased, Captain William Morgan, was planning on publishing his exposé of the pagan rites of Freemasonry when his life was cut short. In the uproar and controversy that followed, the public began to see Freemasons as being far from Christianity and conspiratorially outside of the laws of the nation. Court justices (Freemasons themselves) were seen to favor their fraternal brothers. The result was that Christians fled the lodges and there were numerous state laws passed suppressing Freemasonry. The fervor against Freemasonry lasted about ten years, and began to reduce by 1835.

In 1879 Albert Pike, the father of modern Masonry, published his now infamous work, *Morals and Dogma*, which changed the face of Freemasonry, not only in the United States, but around the world, bringing a powerful blend of paganism, the occult, spiritual mysticism, and pluralism (multi-deities). Scottish Rite Masonry remains essentially as Albert Pike shaped it and continues to this day.

Preparation for Receiving Freedom: "Like Preparing to Climb Mount Everest"

If we were going to climb Mount Everest, or run a marathon, we would need physical conditioning, technical training, and healing for any bodily impairment to be equal to the task ahead of us. Prior to 1990, those escaping from the Soviet Union had to believe that there was a better life. They needed to overcome the mental confusion of propaganda in order to plan and execute their bid for freedom. Release from Freemasonry is a bit like that—there is a need for preparation and spiritual understanding. Without these, there is a strong possibility that you will not escape with your whole life. We are going to spend the next six chapters in spiritual training and exercise to prepare you for your escape from Freemasonry. Then you will be in condition, ready to execute God's escape plan for release from its effects.

Modern Freemasonry, at its root, is spiritual in its reverence of false gods. Unfortunately, many churches will not have adequately prepared you for this spiritual task. Let's take another, deeper look at some of the problems and symptoms that Freemasonry brings into families and individuals. Much of this negative fruit will not only bring physical problems, but spiritual and emotional damage. These wounds, problems, and our resultant coping mechanisms can interfere with our getting free, but with diligence you will succeed in your escape.

A Further Look at Freemasonry's Influence

While there might not be a stereotypical family or individual that has been influenced by Freemasonry, here are some factors that are shared by many:[16]

- Family breakdown and divorce
- Fatherlessness (by neglect or leaving the family household), and abuse by fathers (physical and sexual)
- Anger, violence, and verbal cursing
- Physical and spiritual afflictions, disabilities, sicknesses, and infirmities
- Alcoholism
- Sexual impurity
- Poverty, financial reversals and failures.

Freemasonry, when entered into wholeheartedly, can consume much of a man's non-working time. The husband's and father's attentions are turned away from family and the knowledge of God (by swearing allegiance to false gods), and towards the friendships, activities, and goals of Freemasonry. The result is that children, in particular, are damaged.

My people are destroyed for lack of knowledge.
Because you have rejected [the] knowledge [of God],

I also will reject you from being My priest.
Since you have forgotten the law of your God,
I also will forget your children.

Hosea 4:6

To those of us who are children of fathers (and mothers) that walked away from God, this scripture sounds hopeless. But we must not lose sight of the meaning of the Hebrew name for the prophet who spoke these words. Although he had to bring a difficult message, confronting the nation, the life message of Hosea, whose name means "salvation," was to bring help to a suffering people. Even though they were suffering because of their rejection of the knowledge of God and His ways, salvation was theirs. So it can also be for those who have rejected God and His ways under the influence of Freemasonry.

In Hosea's prophetic book, chapter 2, verses 14 and 15, God said He would speak kindly to Israel even in the wilderness of her trouble, which she brought on by her own sinful behavior. He declared His intention to bless the nation again, and was providing a doorway (a door of Achor, i.e. pain) back to God and His blessings via the pain of her condition.

Therefore, behold, I will allure her,
Bring her into the wilderness
And speak kindly to her.
Then I will give her her vineyards from there,
And the valley of Achor as a door of hope.
And she will sing there as in the days of her youth,
As in the day when she came up from the land of Egypt.

Hosea 2:14–15

Pain is given to mankind as a warning that something is wrong. When we are plagued by pain, physical, mental and / or emotional,

13

we seek to find and fix what is broken. Israel had pain but was unaware of the cause. That's why the nation needed the prophet Hosea, to direct her to the problem. God's message is timeless and is not only for historic Israel, but also for all nations and all peoples. That means He is speaking to all of us, including those influenced by Freemasonry. He does not want us to suffer in ignorance. He offers us hope of restoration through His prophetic Word.

As we proceed through this book, we will be highlighting certain problems whose origins may be rooted in Freemasonry. We will look at the spiritual reasons for these problems and then provide basic prayer ministry guidelines that lead to freedom and healing from these afflictions. This freedom and healing is only available in and through the name of Jesus Christ. You are reading a Christian book that shows how to apply your faith through understanding the causes and remedies for your troubles, as explained in the Bible. If you do not know Jesus yet, don't be discouraged. Have a look at Appendix I near the end of the book; getting to know Him is not as difficult as you might imagine.

Already, thousands of individuals who were in Freemasonry, as well as the descendants of Freemasons, have received God's mercy and healing in public meetings and in Bible schools, through application of the principles we present here. We are so pleased to make this mercy, healing, and restoration available to you through the printed word.

Restoration and Hope

This book is about restoration and hope. The Lord has compassion and mercy for the afflicted. The Lord's heart is for healing wounds and setting right the wrongs of the past. There is hope. There is healing. The heart of the Lord is not a fire without warmth, or a promise without hope. He gives to all who are without; and for all who are burdened and heavy laden who cry out to Him, He lifts their loads. The scripture below explains what God wants to be for you.

> *A father to the fatherless and a judge* [one who executes justice] *for the widows,*
> *Is God in His holy habitation.*
> *God makes a home for the lonely;*
> *He leads out the prisoners into prosperity,*
> *Only the rebellious dwell in a parched land.*

Psalm 68:5–6

The Lament of Some

What was it that killed our family? Who destroyed our father's ability to be a father and husband? Was he just an evil, thoughtless man seeking only his own desires? It certainly seems that way.

Somehow we want to break away from what has happened to us. But we cannot see how. It is as if we were beaten, robbed, and thrown down along the roadside. No one stops to help us. It seems that we need to save ourselves, take care of ourselves, and somehow arise and limp along life's road until death or the oblivion of alcohol brings relief. Even as Christians we've heard about the "Father's" love and yet it seems elusive or infrequent. What is keeping us in this condition? If God is who He says He is, where is our comfort? Where are His promises of provision and family restoration?

As we look at the church today in our nations, we see more women than men, and many of those are married to husbands who are without genuine interest in God, who are more interested in their work, baseball or football, or Freemasonry than their family. We ask ourselves, "Why? Is it that God's Word is not true?" Or is there something keeping us from His blessings?

I believe it is the latter. Something is holding back the blessings of God from those influenced by Freemasonry. I would like to share with you what we've experienced in our own lives and through personal contact with hundreds and hundreds of God's people since 1990. That is when God began to give me the keys to releasing people from the influence of Freemasonry. What has happened since, as we've met and prayed with so many, forces us to write about it, believing that God's love and power will come to set you—and your children, family, and friends—free.

It is not religion or church that will set us free; it is knowledge of ourselves, of our condition, and of God and His spiritual laws that govern our lives. We need to know Him personally, not just know about religion. We need to know Him intimately. We need to know how to gain His favor by working within His spiritual laws, which govern the whole world. God is a God of justice. When we, as individuals, families, cities and/or nations, continually violate His commands and statutes, we begin to lose favor, well-being, and peace. Our physical, spiritual, and emotional condition reflects the long-term level of godliness we have maintained, either individually or as a people. For those who have turned away from Him, God continually holds open a doorway to return as individuals, families, and nations.

Then why are so many still in such bad condition? Our problems lie in two areas. First of all, we are unaware that our condition is a result of spiritual behavior. Then, secondly, we don't know the way back to the blessings of God from which we migrated. Those of us who were born into the influence of Freemasonry particularly suffer from these problems. Seven centuries before Christ, the prophet Hosea addressed this very same issue in the nation of Israel, which had seriously strayed from God's ways and was now suffering tremendously.

❧ LIFE IMPACT ❧

How to Receive Freedom

The path to healing and freedom is taken one step at a time. In the following chapters we will examine some of the spiritual laws and principles that provide protection to God's people. When we step outside of these protective borders, we also step outside of God's blessings. The way to freedom and blessing is to step back inside these boundaries. The problem is that most of us are unaware of these boundaries and therefore have stepped over them without knowledge. It is more like we stepped on a land mine and never heard the explosion. We just woke up in a hospital filled with damaged people, whole nations full of them, all who suffer with similar conditions. Culturally, there are so many of us in this condition that our wounded lives almost seem to be normal; but our spirit tells us they are not. It seems that we are afflicted, but we have no idea why.

Some of us blame the government, society, our parents, the educational system, global warming, the ignorance of others, God, etc. But the truth is, we and/or our families have crossed spiritual boundaries, stepping from blessing into curse. As we read in the last section in Hosea 4:6, even if it wasn't us, but our ancestors who crossed God's boundaries, He would turn away from favoring us.

So just what are these boundaries that separate the territory of blessings from the land of adversity and curses? How do they work and where are they explained? And further, if they exist, then how can I cross over into blessings? These are all good questions and they will be explained as we progress through the chapters of this book. We begin in Chapter 2, "Spiritual Laws That Govern the World," by discovering four amazing biblical principles guaranteed to make us more successful, peaceful, and happy as we faithfully apply them to our lives.

First, though, let's remind ourselves—the way back from trouble and adversity is through knowing God and His ways. Entering into fellowship with Him and walking along His prescribed paths brings blessings. May we bring you the same promise and strategic plan for blessings that Hosea gave to the people of Israel in the midst of their troubles?

Come, let us return to the Lord.
For He has torn us, but He will heal us;
He has wounded us, but He will bandage us.
He will revive us after two days;
He will raise us up on the third day,
That we may live before Him.
So let us know, let us press on to know the Lord.
His going forth is as certain as the dawn;
And He will come to us like the rain,
Like the spring rain watering the earth.

Hosea 6:1–3

If you are not yet a Christian, please take a look at Chapter 7 or Appendix I to see a more detailed explanation. You may be surprised to find just how easy it is to give your life to Christ. Of course then, as a Christian, you would also be able to be helped into freedom by this book.

Something about *It Isn't Free and It Isn't Masonry*

- The book is divided into two parts: Part I, "Stepping into Strength and Knowledge—Restoring the Family," and Part II, "Spiritual Prisoners—Getting Free." The first part examines basic spiritual principles that govern our well-being and relationship with God. The practical application of these truths to our family and interpersonal situations will show

---

the origins of many of our problems, and lead us into God's promised blessings.

- In the second part of the book, we will be examining how the idolatry, self-cursing, and blasphemy of Freemasonry brings suffering and loss. Applying some of the principles that we learned in the first half of the book, we explain God's provision for restoration from these sinful practices.

- The Appendices at the back of the book give information about salvation, the Lordship of Jesus in our lives, basic Christian doctrine, and ministry practices that support the process of moving from adversity to blessings.

Prayer Journal

IMPORTANT NOTICE TO THOSE SEEKING GOD'S HELP

- Don't miss the summary and personal questions at the end of each chapter. They remind us of the main chapter points and prepare us to step from adversity into God's blessings.

- This is a self-help book intended to both inform and bring the reader into a series of life issue interactions with the living God. Self-help means that the reader intentionally participates in a process. Reading is not enough! It is important for the reader to make a journal (small notebook or diary) of personal responses from each chapter. Using the reader's journal responses, Chapter 7 provides a guided prayer ministry to resolve the life issues discovered in the first six chapters.

Receiving Freedom

Receiving freedom in our lives is a process. Although it will come from God, we must participate with Him. Part of the formula for receiving freedom is knowledge, some of which you will obtain as you read on in this book. But simple knowledge is not enough—we must respond! Without an active response, we should not expect to be saved from the sins of our family and our past, nor healed. As a self-help book, information is made available to you, but there is also guidance towards essential action.

Two action phrases are included in the preceding scripture, Hosea 6:1–3: "Come, let us return to the LORD" and "Let us press on to know the LORD." God will heal, but we need to take action.

This contemporary story about a Christian man whose house was caught in a flood illustrates the importance of action:

> As the waters rose, a man came by with a boat and offered to save him. He refused, saying "God will save me." The waters continued to rise and now the man took refuge in the second story of the house. Another boat came by and again the man refused to be rescued, saying, "God will save me." The waters rose and he was forced to climb on the roof where a helicopter came to rescue him. He refused saying, "God will save me." Finally, the waters closed over him and he drowned. Upon reaching heaven he demanded of God, "Why did you not save me?" God replied, "I sent you two boats and a helicopter."

The point of the story is that many look passively to God for healing and improvement. The Scriptures present a different model. God gives us opportunity, but expects us to intentionally press on towards Him.

Most of us do not know how to press on and into God. We're like the man in the flood expecting some supernatural miracle, but God wants us to get into the boat with Him. The man in the flood died from passivity, not from God's failure to save. In the same way, just reading this book will not be enough to set you free.

To get the full benefit of the book, you will need to consider carefully how the issues you have discovered in the text impact your life, and then bring these to God with the appropriate response. The summary and questions section at the end of each chapter is designed to help you get into the boat with God. One way of using this feature is to respond through a Prayer Journal (see the box: "Using a Prayer Journal"). In Chapter 7 you will find out how to receive prayer ministry for the personal issues you discovered and to which you responded in writing in the first six chapters. Chapter 7 gets you ready to receive the promised freedom in the second part of the book, Chapters 8 through 12.

Using a Prayer Journal

At the end of this and each teaching chapter, you will find a "Key Concepts" section that summarizes the information just presented. After refreshing ourselves in this overview, we can begin our walk towards God's rescuing, healing presence using the "Key Personal Questions" section that follows. If you've never journaled before, here are a few suggestions that have helped many others to begin:

- Choose a small, bound notebook, similar to what a student would use to take notes or write compositions.
- Do not use the notebook for other purposes.
- Date each entry.
- Keep the notebook in a safe place where others will not be tempted to read what you've written.
- Somewhere near the top of the first page write the title, "Key Personal Questions from Chapter 1."
- Write (copy) the first question from the chapter in your journal.
- Take a moment and ask the Lord to help you bring a truthful, factual answer to that question.

- Write your answer/response to each question directly below the question that you copied.
- Take another moment and ask the Lord if there is anything more that you should add, and then respond appropriately.
- Use as much space as you need before going on to the next question. Write well enough that you may read it later when you get to Chapter 7, the ministry chapter. Your journal responses will help guide you personally in beginning to receive your healing from God.
- Take your time. You don't have to answer all the questions at one sitting. But please do be faithful and address all the questions and anything else that the Lord brings up from the book.
- Follow this same procedure at the end of each chapter for all of the questions.

Key Concepts from Chapter 1

- Today, there is worldwide instability in our families and in society in general. It is not just your family situation. It is also not what God has planned and purposed for you. For many, one not-so-obvious contributor to these conditions is the ungodly practices that are prevalent under Freemasonry.
- God is a God of justice, and when individuals and nations continually violate His commands and statutes, they begin to lose favor, well-being, and peace. Many of our difficult issues are a result of wrongful spiritual behavior.
- With spiritual understanding of the social and individual practices under Freemasonry, we can begin to see some of the major causes of our problems. Basic prayer ministry, along with spiritual understanding, leads to freedom and healing

from these afflictions. This freedom and healing is only available in and through the name and person of Jesus.

Key Personal Questions from Chapter 1

Please answer the following in your Prayer Journal:*

1. Do I know the Lord Jesus Christ as my Savior and Lord? Have I ever prayed a salvation prayer? When and how did I receive salvation? Have I ever made Jesus Lord over my whole life? (See Appendix I, "Salvation and Lordship," for more information.)

2. Do I come from a broken family? How and why did this happen? Whom am I holding responsible for this? How has this affected me?

3. Has my marriage/family broken down? What caused this and whom am I holding responsible?

4. Am I willing to trust Jesus Christ to restore my life? What's keeping me from coming to Him in a deep way?

* See preceding box, "Using a Prayer Journal," for help in answering the above questions. We don't want you to be surprised when you get to Chapter 7. Your strengthening, cleansing and healing prayer ministry will use these responses. Without these, Chapter 7 will not bring the blessings you wish.

CHAPTER 2

Spiritual Laws That Govern the World

The Freemasonry Fish Hook

In Chapter 1 we shared a story about Freemasonry being like a fish hook. The indoctrination rituals established after the mid-1800s are similar in form to those used in witchcraft and Satanism—two spiritual cultures which claim that you can never get free, once initiated. The powerful, secret, spiritual bonds established cannot be easily broken (without help) by today's average churchgoer and are impossible to overcome for those not believing in Christ. This statement is not meant to frighten you, nor to publically vilify Freemasons, many of whom are unaware of the truth about their involvement. Those who have entered into Freemasonry have entered into a society that has a very charitable public face but ultimately reverences Satan.[17]

While it is good to renounce any personal or familial involvement, that will not be enough to bring freedom or healing to an individual. Beyond salvation, there are several considerations that will help you escape the collateral damage of membership—yours or that which is inherited: 1) spiritual strengthening/cleansing, 2) a basic understanding of how the spiritual world functions, and 3) a knowledge of the spiritual agreements with darkness into which every Mason has entered.

In this and the next five chapters we will be preparing you with biblically based spiritual knowledge and cleansing to prepare you for release from Freemasonry and its effects. In the last chapters of this book we will be helping you receive the freedom possible only through Christ Jesus.

Rooftops, Stoves, and Land Mines: Hidden Things Governing Life, Death, and Happiness

At an early age, we learned not to touch a hot stove lest we be burned, and not to step off the roof of a building, or we would fall to our death. This survival knowledge about the natural laws of the world helps preserve our life and well-being. Far more important, though, are the spiritual laws that so few of us know. They affect our daily lives and impact our ultimate destiny of heaven or hell. These spiritual laws govern life and death, as well as the degree to which we either enjoy blessings or suffer curses in our lives. As we progress through this chapter we will discover some of these fundamental spiritual truths. With this knowledge we can avoid many of life's problems, have more peace and prosperity, and even escape the problems of the past.

It is my hope that you will begin to get excited enough about God's spiritual truths to want more and begin to mine them out of the Scriptures for yourself. There is a hidden wealth there just waiting for those who seek God's wisdom and knowledge. Without this knowledge, we are prone to repeating our mistakes over and over again, suffering needlessly in our ignorance.

Ignorant Suffering

As we discovered in Chapter 1, the Lord spoke through the prophet Hosea saying,

My people are destroyed [or perish] *because of lack of knowledge.*

The apostle Paul wrote in his letter to the church at Ephesus that many are

darkened in their understanding, excluded from the life of God because of the ignorance that is in them ...

Ephesians 4:18

Most of us are in this condition. We can see our problems, but can't see the cause of them. We suffer in, and because of, our ignorance. In fact, the idea that there might be spiritual causes to our problems is surprising to many of us. Let's return to this theme from Chapter 1 and dig a little deeper to see if we can discover why trouble has overtaken us. We need information and understanding or we will continue to step on these hidden spiritual land mines again and again with the same results: areas of our lives will continue to be destroyed.

Let's examine this issue from another viewpoint. As I write this, I believe our Heavenly Father is saying there are things in our lives that are like the edges of the rooftops, and that we must spiritually avoid. Some spiritual things are as hot as the top of a cooking stove, too hot to touch. We must let go of them. The difficulty is that we don't know what these things are. We're missing the perception of cause and effect. If we are going to take advantage of this idea, we need instruction from our Heavenly Father. In the next section we'll dig deeper yet.

Spiritual Laws—the Keys to Freedom and Happiness

HOW THEY WORK

Many of the spiritual guidelines that direct us towards blessing and away from adversity are actually written in the Bible in the form of spiritual laws. No, these are not parental controls by God who seeks to limit our enjoyment and fun, although many have been told just that. They are, rather, impartial principles, just like the law of gravity, that tell us what will happen if we spiritually step off a cliff or the edge of a roof. They can be like land mines, blowing us up, taking our lives and those of our families, when we unknowingly step onto them. These spiritual laws are the heavenly undergirding that governs the whole earth. They are similar to the laws of chemistry and physics, but these laws are not about the physical things of the natural realm. Instead they affect our lives, our happiness, and our ultimate destination when our body dies. They are written in the Bible, which is God's instruction book for life.

Although there are many spiritual laws, we're only going to examine a few of them in this book, key ones that can hold us in spiritual bondage. When we disobey God's commands these key laws come into effect. They have the power to hold us in isolation, in hopelessness, and under curse, or they can set us free depending upon how we act. The operative concept here is, "depending upon how we act." These spiritual laws are immutable, unchanging principles that were in place before the world was formed. They are the pillars that support life here in God's created universe. If we wish for the condition of our life to change, we must realize that the spiritual laws will not change. What we do and think must change. To neglect these laws, to walk in the ungodly culture we learned from our parents, virtually ensures that our lives and those of our children will continue to mirror what we see in our nations today!

THE BIG FOUR

These four laws were written centuries ago in the Bible, yet they are still available today. You can use them to change your life. They are tried and true. As we have learned to obey them over the past twenty-five years, God has set us free, prospered us, and used us to help release thousands from bondage. We will examine these primary laws and then see how they can be used to our benefit. I invite you to join the free and blessed who have crossed over from ignorance, bondage, and pain.

The Law of Forgiveness

The first law we will examine is recorded in the book of Matthew, in chapter 6, verses 14 and 15 (NIV):

> ... if you forgive men when they sin against you, your heavenly Father will also forgive you. But if you do not forgive men their sins, your Father will not forgive your sins.

This law is strengthened and clarified in the parable that Jesus told at the end of Matthew 18 about a man who refused to forgive someone. As He finishes the story, Jesus explains that when we willfully refuse to forgive others, God removes His protection around us and turns us over to demonic torturers, giving them free access to us until we change our mind and forgive.

When someone hurts or damages us several things happen. First, we feel the damaging impact (i.e. the hurt that happened to us). Second, there are our reactions—feelings of loss, pain, hurt, embarrassment, etc. And third, we desire justice—wherein the one who hurt us should suffer, perhaps even more than we have suffered.

Holding on to the second and third items gets us into trouble. In our hearts we hold the perpetrator responsible for his or her action. We may be angry and want to hurt the person in return; this intention is called vengeance. But God requires us to release the matter (and persons) into His hands. It is God's job to bring your injury claim into the heavenly courts to weigh the matter and execute any punishment required.

> *Therefore, thus says the LORD,*
> *"Behold, I am going to plead your case*
> *And exact full vengeance for you ..."*

> Jeremiah 51:36

When we hold on to a matter (the pain, the accusation, and the desire for vengeance), we are in sin. We are not to handle the matter, other than to release it to Jesus. Our pain, distorted vision, and personal sense of righteousness do not reflect Jesus' ability as the mediator of righteousness and justice.

You may ask, "What about the pain, hurt, embarrassment, etc?" These things we must give to Jesus immediately following the injury so that He can comfort us. Emptying our heart of the pain and hurt is part of the process of forgiveness; it makes room for God's comfort and healing and helps us stop our blaming, faultfinding, and accusation. Without the fuel of pain and emotions, the fire of our desire for vengeance will go out and it will be easier to trust God for His justice. Forgiving someone does not mean that we must trust them in their areas of weakness, the places where they have not changed. In forgiving, we have released our claim of revenge to Jesus. It does not mean that the person who hurt us has been processed or changed through our personal transaction with God. There is a huge difference between being forgiven and being trustworthy.

In the Law of Forgiveness, we are introduced to the concept that our rewards and punishment come from the heavenly realm, based upon what we do or think in the earthly realm. For many of us, we are so earthly bound in materialism, science, history, medicine, psychology, and even traditional religion that we never consider the possibility that earthly suffering could be a manifestation of the spiritual consequences of our earthly behavior. In many churches, the primary focus has been evangelism, because of the need for salvation leading to eternal life. But those who have been converted and added to our church have needs and problems in their lives that have spiritual origins. Many of their difficulties are a result of others sinning against them. Unforgiveness over the wounds and betrayal they suffered is very often a key issue. One of the major difficulties Christians face is unforgiveness towards those who have hurt them.

Let's look at an experience we had in a church setting to see one way the Law of Forgiveness might work in a person's life.

Not long ago a young woman missionary came up to us for prayer at the end of a church service. She was suffering with a large tumor on one of her ovaries which was causing her much discomfort. Her doctors had informed her that she needed immediate surgery as it was developing into a life-threatening situation.

As we began to pray for her, right there in the church, God gave me some questions to ask her that began to unwind the bonds of infirmity that were holding her in sickness. The ministry went something like this: "Tell me about your self-esteem. Do you like yourself?" A deep hurt began to surface as she took these issues to the Lord for His help to deal with them. The presenting symptom was the life-threatening tumor, but attached to this physical condition were low self-esteem and a dislike of self. As we followed the root downward, an unresolved childhood issue of sexual abuse by a close family member came up. This act severely devalued her as a person and led to self-hate.

Finally, the root of unforgiveness towards her abuser had to be faced. In this case, as she released her abuser to Jesus for judgment or forgiveness, she also expressed all her anger and pain to Him, telling Jesus just how she felt. The effect was immediate: she was released from the self-hate arising from Satan's accusation that she was responsible for being abused. Self-hate invited the tumor to grow.

As self-hate left her life, the enemy had no more rights to maintain the tumor. When she returned to the doctor a few days later to review her surgery options, the tumor was discovered to have reduced in size so dramatically that she no longer needed surgery.

Chapter 3, "Forgiveness: A Deeper Look," further develops this subject.

The self-hate and retained anger living in this young woman's unforgiveness tormented her emotionally and physically, resulting in a life-threatening affliction. The pain drove her to Jesus and His answer to her problem, as it is so clearly seen in the Law of Forgiveness. With a change of heart, she was set free through forgiving her attacker and being forgiven herself for her sin of unforgiveness.

Unforgiveness can often lead to judgment as we begin to denigrate the character and personality of the person who damaged and offended us. Let's explore this concept further in the next section.

The Law of Judgment

Righteousness and justice are the foundations of God's governmental administration for His creation (Psalm 89:14). Judgment involves comparison with a standard of acceptance, quality, or righteousness. When God judges, He has all the facts, including knowledge of what is/was in our heart (Proverbs 2:2). He puts the attitudes and intent of our heart in His balance against the weights/standards of righteousness. He deals with us accordingly.

In Daniel 5, God writes on the palace wall that the king has been weighed in the balance (scales of God) and found deficient. When God does this weighing, He does it righteously and considers everything. Jesus is the rightful Judge of all (Acts 17:31). When we weigh and judge, there are four major problems:

1. We do not have all the facts.
2. We are not impartial.
3. We don't fully understand God's standards.
4. In judging at all, we have taken Jesus' place as judge.

When we weigh and judge, we are in sin.

The functioning of the Law of Judgment is similar in principle to the Law of Forgiveness that we looked at in the preceding section: supernaturally, trouble will come upon us for our transgressing God's commandment. (See Appendix II, "God's Commandments and Spiritual Laws," for a deeper treatment of these principles.) The Law of Judgment tells us the legal punishment that will happen when we disobey Jesus' command, recorded for us by Matthew:

Do not judge so that you will not be judged.

Matthew 7:1

The apostle Paul echoes this command in his letter to the Romans, referring to all who pass judgment on others:

... in that which you judge another, you condemn yourself ....

Romans 2:1

As Paul continues, he explains that while we may feel we are more righteous than those whom we are judging, truthfully there will be areas in our lives where we are making the same kind of mistakes. The problem is that as we condemn others, we are, in fact, speaking the same judgment upon ourselves without seeing it. And he tells us that the judgment of God rightly falls on those, including ourselves, who practice these things. Jesus clarifies the issue as He explains just what will happen to us who judge others:

For in the way you judge, you will be judged; and by your standard
of measure, it will be measured to you.

Matthew 7:2

As prayer counselors, my wife and I continually see the results of
judging in people's lives. It is like a self-curse come true. The only
escape is to renounce the judgment and ask God to forgive us for
our words and for the internal score sheet that we've kept against
the people whom we have judged. We can only be set free through
the name of Jesus and by His precious blood, which not only
opens the doors of heaven for us, but releases us from earthly
captivity.

Let's see just how this works in a person's life. This story is one
that I'll never forget, as it is from my own life. The problem we
have in recognizing cause and effect in our transgressions is that
often our disobedience happened many years in the past; perhaps
it occurred even in our childhood and has been long forgotten. So
it was in this case.

We had not been married very long when I noticed an unwelcome
change in my wife's behavior: she was becoming increasingly late in
being ready to go somewhere with me.

Before we married, I remembered, she was as precise as a Swiss
watch in her appointments. But now, it seemed that she could not be
on time no matter where we were going. As a recently born-again
Christian with only a few years' experience in godly communication
and living, I was struggling with how to communicate my displeasure
to her. At this point, I had only managed a few gentle reminders
about the time that we needed to be somewhere. But my wife had
noticed "her problem" and had already begun to take responsibility
for her increasing tardiness. Unknown to me, whenever we were
going somewhere together, she had systematically begun to get
ready earlier.

Over a period of time she began correcting the situation by starting to prepare fifteen minutes earlier, but she was still late. So she began to get ready a half-hour earlier, but she was still late. As the months rolled by, it seemed that nothing could get her out of the house on time to go somewhere with me.

As time passed, I became more and more intolerant of her lateness. It was really causing me and our relationship a problem. Finally, one day, I could stand it no longer, watching her slowly dressing and going through her clothes deciding what to wear. It was clear we were going to have another "late experience." I exploded in anger, "Can't you ever be on time? You're just like my moth...e...r!" The last word sort of squeezed its way from my mouth as I attempted to stop it. I was so startled at what I was saying, and instantly I recognized that a judgment from the past had just surfaced.

In a split second, my face turned crimson with embarrassment, as my sin lay exposed for us both to see. We knew full well what a judgment is and there was instant recognition that afternoon in our bedroom. Our eyes locked on each other, and the expression of guilt and shame on my wife's face for being late one more time transformed into something like that of a trial lawyer as he cross-examines a witness in the courtroom. Glaring at me, she stepped closer, hands now on her hips. A slightly superior smile began to form on her lips as she demanded, "Tell me about your mother!"

I instantly knew that I was a dead man: tried, convicted, and sentenced, all in the space of a few moments. The "condemned" one was exonerated and her accuser now stood guilty.

A dawning social awareness happens to most teenagers, making them overly sensitive towards embarrassment. This sensitivity manifests when real or imagined differences are perceived between us or our family members and others outside the family. At that age, we desperately want to be the same as everyone else.

So it had been with me. Earlier in my life I had begun to notice that my family was often late to social functions and it embarrassed me. As I looked to see why this might be, I began to believe that it was my mother's fault for not getting ready quickly enough. We continued to be late as a family, and I began to judge my mother. I can still remember the day that I finally verbalized it and walked out of the family home as preparations to go somewhere were progressing too slowly for me. I slammed the door behind me, exclaiming, "I don't know about the rest of you, but I'm going now and I am going to be on time!" The words were dripping with judgment, accusation and self-righteousness as I stomped out the door.

My sin caused my wife to be late. As she later recounted, "It was like walking through glue each time we tried to go somewhere together. I just could not move faster and things always happened to delay me." The transgression of God's commandment not to judge puts the Law of Judgment in motion, and the sentence under this law is often amazing in the way it mirrors the sin itself. It is not that we are going to be excluded from heaven by the sin, but rather that we will suffer here on earth (see Appendix V, "Temporal versus Eternal"). In this case, judging my mother resulted in punishment through my wife; but it came years later. As we will see in the next law, God is not mocked; what we do will bring a consequence. Our difficulty is, we often don't recognize suffering as punishment because it may occur years after the sin.

As I confessed and repented of my sin of judgment that afternoon, God set my wife free of being the just implement of my punishment. She is no longer chronically late. Now, more often, I am the late one!

The negative rewards for our sin of judgment are not always carried out through our spouses, but it often happens as a result of judging our parents. When a man complains about his wife to us, we usually ask him, "What was your mother like?" It's amazing how many overweight wives have an overweight mother-in-law and how many alcoholic husbands have an alcoholic father-in-law! God's laws never fail, but the time and way in which they work are up to God.

Perhaps now you are seeing some patterns in your own life, marriage or family. In Chapter 7 there are some model prayers to help you escape from the consequences of the Law of Judgment through the only remedy possible, the blood of Jesus applied to your sin of judgment. In receiving Jesus as our Savior we receive the right to enter eternity as a child of God; but through confession and repentance of sins, we are enabled to put the blood of Jesus over the doorways of trouble into our lives here on earth, just as was done to prevent death entering at the Passover.

The Law of Sowing and Reaping

> Do not be deceived: God cannot be mocked. A man reaps what he sows.

Galatians 6:7 NIV

(see also Hosea 10:12–13; Exodus 34:6–7)

If we plant weeds, how could we expect to reap corn or watermelons? Yet, many of us are surprised when trouble comes our way and we have forgotten or never realized that an earlier sin is responsible. Again, the timing between our sin and the judgment of God is often great enough that we miss making the connection and we continue to suffer, not realizing a remedy exists.

The Law of Sowing and Reaping is similar to the Law of Judgment in that the temporal sentence we receive—punishment or disfavor—will have an essence of, or similarity to, our transgression. The difference between this law and the preceding one is that it is not specifically linked to judging others. It is a legal principle that helps us understand what comes upon us, because our sentence will often have discernible similarities to the sin. Simply put, the seed (sin) that you plant will result in a growth that looks similar to the seed (original deed of disobedience).

Let's first take a look at how this law works, with an illustration from the book of Judges in the Bible. In this story, the Hebrew tribes are continuing the conquest of Canaan following the death of Joshua.

> *Judah went up, and the* LORD *gave the Canaanites and the Perizzites into their hands, and they defeated ten thousand men at Bezek. They found Adoni-bezek [the king] in Bezek and fought against him, and they defeated the Canaanites and the Perizzites. But Adoni-bezek fled; and they pursued him and caught him and cut off his thumbs and big toes. Adoni-bezek said, "Seventy kings with their thumbs and their big toes cut off used to gather up scraps under my table; as I have done, so God has repaid me."*

Judges 1:4–7

In this case, the king was aware of his wrongdoing and immediately understood what had happened to him. But many of us are suffering with symptoms or consequences of sin, and we have not recognized the source of our problems. When God shows us our transgression, why we are suffering is frequently as obvious to us as it was to this pagan king. In most cases, when God has made evident the source of our suffering we may agree with Him, confessing our sin, repenting, and receiving forgiveness in the name of Jesus. This process begins to release us from the consequences prescribed by God's law for that particular sin.

Some years ago, a man, let's call him Peter (not his real name), came to us seeking relief from chronic headaches. We prayed a simple prayer for healing, but nothing happened. As we began to question him, we learned that he also experienced frequent head injuries, even around the home. But there seemed to be no point of origin for his condition.

As we asked the Holy Spirit to show us the cause, suddenly Peter remembered a family story. Several generations back, in a rural farming area, a severely deformed baby was born into his family. Not knowing what to do with this baby, the father took it out to the barn area and, using a piece of wood, killed it by a blow to the head. The sin was murder.

We led Peter through a prayer of repentance for the murder carried out by his family and a prayer of forgiveness towards them for opening up this spiritual doorway of punishment into his life. As we ministered to him again, proclaiming freedom through the name and blood of Jesus, Peter was instantaneously healed. When we saw him again, months later, he reported having suffered no more headaches and was no longer receiving head injuries. He was set free from the consequences of the Law of Sowing and Reaping.

In telling this story, we've introduced another element: the concept of generational sin and its consequences in the present day. (See Chapter 4, "Sins of the Family," for a more complete explanation of generational sin.) We've seen many set free as they repented of both their own sins and those committed by their families who came before them.

It is important to know that we are responsible for all of our sins.

For we must all appear before the judgment seat of Christ, so that each one may be recompensed for his deeds in the body, according to what he has done, whether good or bad.

2 Corinthians 5:10

One part of Jesus' work on the cross was to make it possible for us to have eternal life, but the other part was to make it possible for us to be healed and set free from the consequences of sin in this life. We've prayed with many over the years who have been set free from present-day problems as they have repented of their sins of the past.

Interestingly, our present suffering may be the result of sins we committed, either before or after receiving Jesus as our Savior. There is no difference in the punishment for sin, whether its origin was before or after our salvation. It is surprising to many that our salvation, while it assures our entrance to heaven, does not prevent our suffering for prior sins while we're here on earth. Further, these same sins, if not confessed and repented for here on earth, will have to be accounted for at the doorway to heaven and will cost us something (see 2 Corinthians 5:10 above and 1 Timothy 4:8).

All three of the laws we've examined in this chapter tell us that our destiny and the benefits we can enjoy here on earth are related to how we think and act towards both God and others. Taken together, these spiritual laws show us how important it is that we forgive others, not holding their faults against them; we will either receive goodness or difficulty in our lives depending upon how well we do in our hearts and actions. It's very simple. Much of what we receive or experience in our lives can be influenced by what we think, say, and do.

These three spiritual laws or governing spiritual principles sound simple, but understanding how they apply to our lives and our culture is a process of successive revelation in our personal relationship with God.

The Law of Idolatry

You shall not make for yourself an idol, or any likeness of what is in heaven above or on the earth beneath or in the water under the earth. You shall not worship them or serve them; for I, the LORD your God, am a jealous God, visiting the iniquity of the fathers on the

children, on the third and the fourth generations of those who hate
Me, but showing lovingkindness to thousands, to those who love Me
and keep My commandments.

Exodus 20:4–6

The Law of Idolatry is found in the second of the Ten Commandments and is linked closely to the First Commandment. Those who
worship idols will be visited with trouble, both those who are personally involved in idol worship as well as those whose families worshiped idols in previous generations. As we study how idolatry
works and who may be ensnared in it, we begin to see why God
began the Ten Commandments by dealing with idolatry; it seems to
be the number one thing that separates people from God.

Let's be careful as we examine this law. First, God gives us a
command not to worship idols. What follows is the law telling us
what will happen if we do. The law is the legal prescription for
punishment for those who violate the commandment. As we
examine this law and how it works, you may begin to discover some
idolatry hidden in your own life. In the second half of this book, we
will look at the idolatrous roots of Freemasonry that affect our lives.
The process of being freed from the curses of idolatry will be
explained in Chapter 7, "Praying Our Way to Freedom."

In its most basic form, the Law of Idolatry tells us that if we look
to someone or something other than God, to get what God wishes
to give us (see Appendix IV), or to other gods like the many that
Hindus worship (e.g. Brahma, Shiva, Vishnu, Krishna, the Monkey
God), or any of the various ancient gods like Diana / Artemis (Queen
of Heaven), Zeus, Sofia, Thor, etc., then we and our families will be
under the curse of idolatry. That is, we will be under the prescriptive
punishment of the Law of Idolatry.

The question is: how can I recognize idolatry in my life and see
its effects? The best way to recognize idolatry is through experience

and an understanding of the Scriptures. A couple of prayer ministry examples will further illustrate how the Law of Idolatry functions.

One evening while we were in England, my wife and I were praying with and counseling a woman who had come to us with a problem. As we invited the Holy Spirit to enter the situation, something amazing happened: she seemed to go into a catatonic trance. Her eyes remained open, but she could not see us. All her muscles locked up and she became rigid like a statue. Her breathing became so shallow that it was impossible to detect and her face took on an appearance something like carved wood or stone. Nothing that we did seemed to break her out of this state. We became more and more alarmed (in our ignorance) that somehow we had ruined her life by praying for her. As we cried out to the Lord, He very quickly told us to look in Psalm 115, which says,

> Their idols are silver and gold,
> The work of man's hands.
> They have mouths, but they cannot speak;
> They have eyes, but they cannot see;
> They have ears, but they cannot hear;
> They have noses, but they cannot smell;
> They have hands, but they cannot feel;
> They have feet, but they cannot walk;
> They cannot make a sound with their throat.
> Those who make them will become like them,
> Everyone who trusts in them.

Psalm 115:4–8

We were so relieved. It was just an evil spirit named Idolatry! Somehow this woman or her family who came before her had been involved in some form of idolatry, and the lawful punishment for that sin is outlined in Psalm 115. With this knowledge, we took authority over the spirit of idolatry (see Appendix VI) and bound it up, forbidding it to act while we were praying for the woman. Immediately she returned to normal and we were able to ask her some questions that led to our understanding of where the idolatry had entered her life. With that knowledge, and our explanation of why she had this problem, she repented of the specific sinful practice that was in the form of idolatry. In our following prayer ministry with her, she was healed and set free from this spirit through God's mercy and power and our courage to command this spirit to leave. All praise and glory to His precious name!

For our next teaching example, let's go to the subcontinent of India.

We were ministering in a church setting when God began showing us various infirmities that some of the people at the meeting were suffering from. Usually, when the Lord does this, what He wants is to heal the people in such a public setting. So our practice has been to call forward those who have those conditions, either to the front of the meeting or to the speaking platform. Those whom God tells us to pray for, we see Him heal. He loves to bring His compassion and mercy to each person who is suffering and He loves to demonstrate His kindness and power to all so that they might believe and come to seek and know Him better.

We did what we usually do: we invited the people whose illnesses God identified to the front of the meeting and prayed for them. It was shocking what happened next, or better said, what did not happen—no one was healed! We were so surprised and not just a little worried. Where were God's mercy, love and power?

We were silently crying out to God as we stood before the meeting with a large group of unhealed people whom we had invited forward. At times like that, you begin to ask yourself, "Did I really hear God?"

Quickly the answer to our prayer entered our hearts from heaven. But it was more in the form of a question: "What kind of people were these before they became Christians?" The answer was, of course, that they all were formerly Hindus! As we questioned each person, we discovered that none of them had ever renounced the gods that they and their families had worshiped. Although they had received Jesus as their Savior, they had never repented of their idolatry and renounced their former idols.

The Law of Idolatry was preventing them from being healed. That was what God wanted everyone at the meeting to know and understand. Their past sins were keeping them from the blessings of God. We led everyone gathered there in prayerful repentance for their own and their families' sins of idolatry, and had each renounce the gods that they formerly worshiped. After binding up the spirits of idolatry and commanding them to leave (casting these spirits out), we were able then to pray effectively for healing to each person who had come forward. God did not disappoint: each one was healed immediately!

While the form idolatry takes can vary from country to country and from culture to culture, it is present everywhere. It blocks what God wants to do in our lives, prevents us as Christians from reaching our full potential in Christ, and keeps us from enjoying the blessings that He has for us as we follow Him. In Appendix IV the subject of idolatry is examined further to reveal some of the things that are common in many cultures and nations, things that replace God in our lives and as such fit the definition of idolatry. We need to repent of these things. In Part II of this book, called "Spiritual Prisoners—

Getting Free," we will also revisit this subject, but with a special cultural emphasis for those of us who were Freemasons or grew up under Freemasonry, or whose family did so.

Good News

While much of this chapter seems like bad news, it is not. We all have been raised in ignorance and live in societies which do not recognize the Living God, His statutes and precepts. Therefore, we all have areas of our lives that are outside of God's boundaries for living a blessed and fruitful life here on earth. As we close this chapter, let's focus on the Good News, that through confession, repentance, and being forgiven in the name of Jesus, we can be set free from our past sins. Then we can come back across the boundaries of God's commands and laws and enter the territory of His blessings. In 2 Chronicles 7:14, God makes a promise to us about the territory of our lives:

> ... and [if] My people who are called by My name humble themselves and pray and seek My face and turn from their wicked ways, then I will hear from heaven, will forgive their sin and will heal their land.

2 Chronicles 7:14

(see also Leviticus 26:40–43)

❧ LIFE IMPACT ❧

Catching Our Breath

This chapter has been a very deep and powerful one, opening so many possible sources of trouble in our lives. Before you're overwhelmed, let's take a moment to catch our breath and look to God for some peace and stability.

Let's stop and thank God for this new information and submit it all to Him. He is both the Lord of revelation and the Lord of our healing and deliverance from the effects of our sins. He has an order to our healing and will meet us in His kind way, in His timing.

> Holy Spirit, we ask that You would come, bring Your peace, and meet us as we pursue You in these matters.

As we finish the teaching portion of this chapter let's not miss the upcoming review section, which condenses what we have just studied. In the previous pages we discovered how the spiritual laws work practically in a person's life. Now we are in a position to get personal and begin to see just what and how God wants to deal with us in our own lives.

Doing My Part—Prayer Journal Entries

The final part of this chapter begins the process of becoming set free from the unwanted effects of disobeying God's commands. Let's prayerfully and patiently seek the Lord to help us complete the next entries in the Prayer Journal we began in Chapter 1. It might be helpful to return to Chapter 1 to review the guidelines for starting and maintaining a Prayer Journal.

In preparation for Chapter 7, "Praying Our Way to Freedom," you will need a foundational list of personal issues from each chapter. The Prayer Journal, based on your response to the "Key Personal Questions" from each chapter (see the box), will form this list. Again, be reminded that this is not a race. Take your time to answer the questions. Dedicate the time for your Prayer Journal to the Lord and seek both the hour and place where you will be undisturbed.

Key Concepts from Chapter 2

There are spiritual laws that govern life on planet earth. Knowledge and use of them will lead to our success and happiness. Ignorance of them will open us up to failure, curse, and unhappiness.

The Big Four (primary) spiritual laws are:

- Law of Forgiveness—If I don't forgive others, then God will not forgive me. Simply said, I will not find favor with God when I have unforgiveness in my heart.
- Law of Judgment—The way we judge others is the way that God will judge and treat us.
- Law of Sowing and Reaping—If we do good, good comes back to us; and if evil, then evil comes back to us, always in multiplied form, just as seed when planted multiplies itself.
- Law of Idolatry—Those who worship idols or are involved with idolatrous things will become as dead and disfunctional as a wooden idol in many areas of their lives. Worse yet, curses will travel down our generational line for three to four generations. Appendix IV expands the definition of idolatry, going beyond carved images and false gods to include anything that takes the place of God in our lives.

Key Personal Questions from Chapter 2

Please answer the following in your Prayer Journal:*

1. Forgiveness—Whom have I not forgiven? List them. What am I holding against them? Why have I not let it go?
2. Judgment—Is there a familiar pattern of trouble in my life or my spouse's? What is it? Is this trouble similar

to something I saw in someone else? Did my husband become an alcoholic just like my dad? Have I become just like my father or mother in areas of bad habits or character? Name them. Has my marriage fallen apart like that of my parents did? Whom did I blame for those failures? Whom have I judged and why?

3. Sowing and Reaping—What have I sown against God's ways that is now producing bad fruit in my life?

4. Idolatry—Are there any roots of idolatry in my life from my personal involvement with false religions: Hinduism, Islam, Jehovah's Witnesses, Christian Science, etc., or occult practices: witchcraft, fortune-telling, water witching, tarot cards, horoscopes, yoga, psychic healing, hypnotism, acupuncture/acupressure, etc.? (We will revisit this subject again in Chapter 4 to see how idolatry from your family's previous generations affects you today.)

5. Fleshly idols—What things have become idols in my life: cigarettes, alcohol, narcotics, pornography, masturbation, etc.? (Read Appendix IV to help you answer this question.)

*See "Using a Prayer Journal" at the end of Chapter 1.

Forgiveness: A Deeper Look

Forgiveness is something near and dear to the Lord's heart. The concept of forgiveness appears in the first book of the Bible and continues as a theme throughout the whole of the Scriptures. But many of us are unclear about the concept and held in bondage by the spiritual laws undergirding God's requirement to forgive. We want and often expect God to forgive us, but somehow we neglect to forgive others.

The Forgiveness of God towards Mankind

Privilege comes through right relationship with the one who can grant favor. When we do something to damage or step outside of the boundaries set by the one who grants privilege, we can expect to suffer loss of the benefits enjoyed in right relationship. The one who has been transgressed against or damaged by us holds the right to restoration through forgiveness. If, as transgressors, we somehow come to our senses and confess that we were wrong, perhaps even making compensation to the injured party, it still lies within their power to hold us in unforgiveness, and the relationship will remain unrestored.

In the case of our pre-conversion sinful condition, we are barred by God, who grants this privilege, from entering heaven. Here's the problem we have:

- Heaven, God's home, is a place where the sinful are never allowed.
- We are sinful and the punishment for sin is spiritual death (Romans 6:23)—not earthly death, but eternal separation from God who lives in heaven. So, when our earthly body dies, we don't get into heaven. Instead, we go to a place of torment.

Here's the Good News:

- Jesus, who lived on earth as both man and God, never sinned, but died for our sins on the cross and was temporairly separated from both Father God and heaven.
- He paid the price for our sin—separation from Father God.
- Through our contrition and receiving Jesus as our Savior we can enter heaven when our earthly body dies—see paragraph below.

Only through our repentance, and recognition of Jesus' deity and His substitutionary death on the cross, can we access the ransom from death. Our pardon (God's forgiveness for our sin) is free, but it requires a change of heart: our entering into an allegiance to God Himself. Coming to God through Jesus His Son is not merely an intellectual assent to what He did, dying for us, but it includes entering into our Father's family, coming under His authority and entering His plan for our lives. We are no longer "free agents," captains of our lives, but are bondservants to the One who saved us from death.

Many who have come to the revelation of Christ have failed to understand that the right to eternal life comes with an obligation towards the One who gave us the life. While salvation is free, a gift of grace from God, it requires a shifting of purposes from living for ourselves to living for God. Without this understanding, we can find ourselves at cross-purposes with God and, if we continue willfully in this condition, we could eventually find ourselves outside of the grace into which we entered.

Interpersonal Forgiveness

One of the most urgent needs that we have is to forgive. It is a matter of life or death, but many do not realize it. In the New Testament we discover that only forgiven men and women enjoy earthly privileges from God, and that only men and women forgiven through the blood of Jesus can enter heaven. Jesus makes a startling statement quoted in Matthew 6:14–15, which ties our status of being forgiven by God to our heart towards others. He said that if we do not forgive others, then His Heavenly Father would not forgive us. How many unforgiven men and women are in heaven? The answer, of course, is none! God is serious about our forgiving one another. Let's take a further look at the process of forgiving.

The word "forgive" makes its first appearance in the Bible in Genesis 50:17 where Joseph's brothers are trying to influence his heart to spare their lives. Forgiveness begins in our heart; we need to decide within ourselves to forgive. Then we must take some action. But forgiveness is not necessarily an interpersonal transaction, although in many situations we may need to express our forgiveness one to another to restore a broken relationship.

First, forgiveness is something God has commanded us to do both in our heart and as a transaction with Him. Ultimately, it is our response to Him.

There are four primary elements involved in forgiving:

1. Releasing the person and the situation to Jesus for Him to work out what should be done
2. Releasing to God all our thoughts about it
3. Releasing our decisions about the person and situation of hurt to God
4. Giving Jesus our feelings of outrage, rejection, pain, embarrassment, shame, vengeance, etc.

These four steps entail forgiving with our whole heart (mind, will, and emotions—see Appendix I, Section 8.0) in response to Jesus' imperative expressed in Matthew 18:34–35. Let's look at a real-life example of how such forgiveness might work. Perhaps you will see some elements of your own life in this example.

Tanya came to us with serious problems in her life. She was a single mother who ran away from home to escape her father's drunken violence. She thought that she had found the perfect way out in her boyfriend Sasha, who listened to her with sympathy. However, before long she was pregnant and Sasha left. Now Tanya was rebellious towards every authority figure, couldn't keep a job, and was experiencing various aches and pains in her body. As we talked with her, it became apparent that she needed to forgive her father. But she exploded in anger when we suggested this. She refused to forgive him, whom she viewed as the source of all her problems. She felt that her unforgiveness was like a knife in her hand cutting her father's throat, punishing him for all he did to her. What she couldn't see was that spiritually she was holding a knife to her own throat, cutting herself off from the peace and healing of God through unforgiveness. She protested, "He hurt me. He ruined my life. He should have been a better father. What he did has cost me everything! I'll never forgive him!"

But forgiveness doesn't say that it didn't hurt, that it didn't matter, that you didn't care, or that it didn't cost you something. Of course it did, but that's not what forgiveness is about. Amazingly, it isn't about our feelings towards the person. In our hearts we might even want to kill the person that wronged us!

As we explained these things to Tanya, she began to be curious. "What then is forgiveness about?" she asked.

We explained, "Forgiveness is about releasing those who hurt us, as well as all of our feelings about the damage, to Jesus—for Him to decide what to do about what happened. The problem is that we don't know everything in the person's life that led them to do what they did. Only Jesus knows and can justly judge the matter." We told her, "Perhaps a little story might help":

"Let's imagine there was a young man who lived in Kiev and was blessed to have a twenty-year-old, Russian-made Lada automobile. He imagined that someday he would be a great racing car driver and compete internationally. So each day he would practice going as fast as the car would go around corners and through traffic. One day he got into a bit of a road competition with a mafia man in a BMW and was run off the road. The young man was so angry at the poor performance of his car that he took a huge sledgehammer and smashed the car into a mass of broken glass and metal. Now, with his dreams shattered and in much bitterness, he walks or takes the bus and metro. You see, his old car had many miles on it before he got it, and it was never designed to be anything but a Lada."

We continued, "Sometimes, when someone lets us down, hurts us or does not meet our expectations, we judge them and hold them in unforgiveness for not performing as we wished or expected. It's something like our friend from Kiev who expected racing car performance from his well-used Lada. Perhaps we have hatred, judgment and murder in our hearts towards someone, based upon our expectations, but not on the knowledge of that person's abilities or previous hurts. These hurts and injuries make them unable to meet our wishes. The problem is that our unforgiveness results in our struggling through life, just like our friend in Kiev who now walks almost everywhere."

As we talked more with Tanya, she recalled a number of stories about her own father's childhood and how he had been damaged and hurt by his alcoholic parents. She began to understand why her own father was unable to meet her needs and expectations. She released her judgments and anger towards him, giving them to Jesus. She then asked Jesus to forgive her for her unforgiveness and judgments. As we prayed for her, she was healed.

We must be realistic though. Our forgiveness does not heal or transform those who hurt us, so we must not expect that the persons who hurt us are now trustworthy in those areas of previous failure.

❧ LIFE IMPACT ❧

Preparing to Step into Freedom

Our second look at forgiveness helps us understand just how important it is to God. We also begin to see how neglect of this process can deeply affect both our earthly life and the heavenly life we will enjoy after our body dies.

Let's next take some time to review the main points of Chapter 3 in the "Key Concepts" section in the box. This review will help prepare us to work on our personal Prayer Journal entries in response to the questions in the following section, "Key Personal Questions."

Now that we have some of the keys to forgiveness, we are in position to work these concepts into our lives a little deeper. The next step is to prepare a new Prayer Journal page with the date and title: Chapter 3, "Forgiveness: A Deeper Look." If it would be helpful, review the guidelines for starting and maintaining a Prayer Journal presented in Chapter 1. As we develop our journal entries, we're getting ready to work through our personal issues with God. These personal issues will be the main subject of Chapter 7, "Praying Our Way to Freedom." In that chapter, you will be using the information that you develop in the Prayer Journal as a basis for life-changing prayer, healing, and cleansing.

Take a few moments and pray. Ask God to come close to you and help you work through the "Key Personal Questions" in the box. Be relaxed and take your time, first writing out each question, then answering it in the space following before proceeding to the next question and answer. Don't rush. Include God in your answer by asking Him to help you write the truth, reminding you of facts about yourself and others, and to help you see the circumstances through His eyes. Remember, you don't have to answer all the questions in one sitting, but discipline yourself to complete the task. It will be well worth it.

Key Concepts from Chapter 3

- We can lose favor with God because we have not forgiven someone.
- Unforgiveness is a sin. God has commanded us to forgive.
- The penalty for sin is spiritual death—eternal separation from God (following our natural death).
- Forgiving someone does not mean that we need to like the person. Nor does it mean that we were not hurt.
- When we forgive someone it is a spiritual transaction. We release the person and all of our unforginveness and judgment towards them, giving it all (including our feelings in the

matter) to Jesus. We ask Him to judge righteously. Then we are eligible to receive forgiveness from God.

Key Personal Questions from Chapter 3

Please answer the following in your Prayer Journal:*

PREPARATORY QUESTIONS TO DEEPEN UNDERSTANDING

- If Jesus asked you personally, "Do you want to be forgiven?" what and how would you answer? What do you think it means?
- Matthew 6:12 speaks of our sins and forgiveness. Copy this verse into your journal. What does this verse mean to you? What are you asking for and what conditions are attached to receiving this gift God is offering?
- Evaluate and explain the word "as" in Matthew 6:12. What does it mean? Examine the concepts of quality, depth, sincerity, and completeness that are carried in this comparative word.
- How then do I want to be forgiven and how then must I forgive others if I want to receive that kind of forgiveness from God?
- Do you feel that you need God to assist you in this kind of forgiving? If so, how would you get His help?
- Matthew 6:14–15 tells us how God will treat us. Copy these verses into your journal.
- Read the parable on forgiveness in Matthew 18:21–35. Copy verses 34 and 35. What is Jesus saying will happen to those who are unwilling to forgive?
- How and when should I respond to the above scriptures?

MINISTRY QUESTIONS TO BE PRAYED THROUGH IN CHAPTER 7

1. Whom have I not forgiven? Name them and list the issues requiring forgiveness.
2. Are there things in my own life for which I need to forgive myself? List them.
3. Is there anyone to whom I need to go to tell them I am sorry for what I did to them? List the names and issues for each person you hurt.
4. Have I damaged anyone in such a way that I need to make restitution? Ask God what He thinks about each situation; then write out your response.

*See "Using a Prayer Journal" at the end of Chapter 1.

CHAPTER 4

Sins of the Family

Let's take a look at a dramatic, contemporary example of how the sins of our ancestors can affect our life. With the real-life drama recounted below in mind, we can examine what God's Word says about ancestral sins. We will then be in a position to evaluate the effects on our own lives from the collective, generational sins of our family.

While in Cairo, Egypt, for a pastors' conference, we were scheduled to meet with the elders of a church that wanted to introduce the ministry of healing into everyday congregational life. The elders wanted to discuss the possibility of presenting a training class later in the year on how to perform the healing works of Jesus.

On the day appointed for our discussion, we were informed by phone that the elders had changed their minds and canceled our appointment. Instead, they wanted us to pray urgently for a member of their congregation. This was a young woman in her early twenties who had been in the hospital for some months and was now in a coma. Her life was rapidly ebbing away. The situation was desperate and the whole church had been in intercession, with people praying at the hospital every day. How could I say no?

As I put the phone down, however, I realized two things. One, I had never prayed for a person in a coma, and two, the outcome of that prayer ministry would influence the church elders to either receive or reject the healing ministry. This was a test. I fell on the bed and wept before the Lord for the comatose woman, the church, and the nation. It felt as if the enemy (the devil) was contesting the introduction of the healing ministry into Egypt. I did not have the slightest idea of what to do.

The Lord spoke gently. He asked me to pick up an Egypt tour book I had been reading. Then he directed me to find the names of the various gods of Egypt mentioned in the book, and to match them up with the plagues He brought upon Egypt when Moses went before Pharaoh. He explained that the plagues were not just to show His power, but they were a demonstration that would embarrass and shame both the Egyptians and the gods they worshiped.

The reason, God showed me, that the Egyptian Christians had not been successful so far in praying for the young woman's healing was that they had never repented. The nation has continued, generation after generation, to honor the Pharaonic gods. To this day, these principalities hold sway over this land and this people. As their images and statues are restored in the name of tourism and archeology, these gods are gaining power once again! God was telling me this lovely Christian woman did not just have an undiagnosed illness; she had come under the power of the gods of Egypt and was slowly being killed.

I took a list of these gods into the Muslim hospital where the young woman lay in intensive care, tubes and wires attached to her body. Accompanied by a translator, I entered the ward where a number of Egyptians barely hung on to life. As I read from the list and bound up each of the spirits from their assignment against this young woman, God had me call her back to life and consciousness in Jesus' name. Her eyes fluttered open for the first time in many weeks. The nation's death-bringing spirits were forced to break off their attack in the mighty name of Jesus Christ. She was rescued from death, her healing made complete, although her recovery took some time. When we saw her again, months later, she was restored, laughing, vibrant, and full of activity and life.

The sins which our family and nation committed, even before we were born, can and do spiritually and physically affect us. In this chapter, we will look more closely at what and how the effects of the sin of past generations can come upon us. Even though we're not Egyptians, we need to realize that the past sins of our family and our nation can be affecting us here and now. In the second part of this book we will look at the effects Freemasonry brought to your life.

Living in Enemy Territory

Be encouraged. We are close to stepping out of the curses affecting our lives and into the blessings God has promised us. In Chapter 2 we were introduced to the concept that past sins of our family can follow our bloodline from previous generations on down, to damage our lives today. In a spiritual sense, many of our predecessors crossed God's boundaries of righteousness into enemy territory, becoming sons of disobedience, dwelling in the land of cursedness. Unknown to us, we and our family may be living deep in enemy territory. To enter the land of God's blessings, we may need to escape the spiritual place where our ancestors left us. Examining the life of Abraham will help us understand this concept.

We have been speaking about the spiritual and physical condition of our lives resulting from the sinful practices of our families. In

Genesis chapter 12, the spiritual conditions of Abraham's life are mirrored in his physical situation. Born in an idol-worshiping culture, he had to physically walk out of his nation, across boundaries, and into the land of God's choice and promised blessings. Similarly, if we are dwelling in the spiritual territory of our ancestors' sins, it is more difficult for us to receive God's blessings. We must walk away from these sins.

Families: The Vehicle for God's Purposes

As this chapter unfolds, we will be examining further the spiritual laws regarding how God's judgments against our ancestors for their sins pass down the generational bloodline to us. We then look at how the outworkings of these judgments may appear in the present-day lives of ordinary people. But before we begin, it will be helpful to know how God works to accomplish His purposes through families. If we can understand His ways, then we can begin to agree with God, rather than resist Him in our ignorance.

Let's gain some insight through examining Abraham's life a little more closely. We'll see how God worked to develop the most powerful family line in history. The key issue here is relationship. God initiated such a deep relationship, first with Abraham and then with the fathers of Israel, that they in turn imprinted their whole households, particularly their children, with that godliness. Here is what God said about Abraham:

> For I have chosen him, so that he may command his children and his household after him to keep the way of the LORD by doing righteousness and justice ....

Genesis 18:19

Ultimately, then, God's plan was that each child would grow up to teach their future families to know God. Having introduced this concept here, it will be further developed in Chapter 5, "Where Have All the Fathers Gone?" Let's return now to Abraham and see how God set about this enormous, but delicate task.

Family: The Origin of Our Spiritual Inheritance

In one of the most dramatic stories in the Bible, we meet a man named Abram. The son of idol-worshiping parents living in ancient Mesopotamia, Abram is called into God's plans and purposes out of the depths of idolatry and the other sinful practices in which his family and culture engaged. As the story opens, we find Abram (his original name, before God changed it to Abraham) living in the land of the Chaldeans, married to his half-sister Sarai. But God had an amazing plan. Beginning with Abraham, He would set aside a people group for Himself through whom He would reveal Himself to the whole world.

> ... Abraham will surely become a great and mighty nation, and in him all the nations of the earth will be blessed ....

Genesis 18:18

As God began this project, the people group He wanted did not even exist, except in the plans and purposes of His heart. To accomplish this global task that would span all future generations of mankind, God starts with a solitary man and his barren wife somewhere in the plains of Mesopotamia. He then spends the better part of 100 years establishing a relationship with this man and developing his character before He allows him to begin having children. God spoke to Abraham through the spiritual realm, guiding and encouraging him. Every now and then He took on the form of a man and dropped in for a personal visit, sometimes with a couple of His angels in tow.

From the beginning, God has been intent on reproducing His image in mankind through and in the midst of family. Somewhere along the way, this image was distorted through sin and the works of the devil. Through Abraham, God would begin to bring restoration to families and His creation. But a lot of work on Abraham's character and faith were needed before Abraham could begin to father God's planned people group. That way, when his family began to grow, they would have a godly father living with them—loving, encouraging, correcting, and, most importantly, modeling the character of God. Abraham would imprint their lives with the image of their heavenly Creator. To accomplish this imprinting, it would take a man who had a lifelong relationship with God. The man would have to be faithful, with character proven beyond doubt. This man, Abraham, who risked his life in obedience to God, was visited time and again by God Himself.

God's plans center in the family, where He intends to bless us and develop our relationship with Him. But it is in and through the family where we are attacked the most. God's laws provide the mechanism to pass blessings and godliness down our bloodline, giving us our spiritual inheritance. However, because of the impartiality of these laws, both the good and bad effects of our family's behavior pass down to us. At the start of this chapter, you may have realized that you lack information about some aspects of your spiritual inheritance. This ignorance may be keeping you from enjoying God's blessings for your life and from walking in His plans and purposes. Let's look more closely now at how disfavor passes through family bloodlines to affect our own lives.

Spiritual Law Governing Inheritance of Blessings and Curses

The concept that family sin has a powerful effect on our lives is no longer common knowledge, although it was a clearly understood principle in biblical times. Examining a present-day tragedy can give us some spiritual insight. When the nuclear reactor at Chernobyl, Ukraine, failed in 1986, children born to families that were exposed to uncontrolled radiation were often deformed. In the natural realm, we can understand that radiation produces birth defects, a result of where the parents were living and what they were doing. And yet, it is surprising to many of us when we discover that the spiritual wrongs of our parents and ancestors can also affect us. Both physical and spiritual inheritances come to us in the same way—from the activities of our families, either good or bad.

In reference to His commandment about idolatry found in Exodus 20:3–5, God also gave us this spiritual law, bound up with a commandment:

> … I, the LORD your God, am a jealous God, visiting the iniquity of the fathers on the children, on the third and the forth generations of those who hate Me, but showing lovingkindness to thousands, to those who love Me and keep My commandments.

> Exodus 20:5–6

Since this principle is not often taught in churches around the world, many are surprised. Their first reaction is that this law must have ceased in New Testament times. But this is not what Jesus taught.

> Do not think that I came to abolish the Law or the Prophets; I did not come to abolish but to fulfill. For truly I say to you, until heaven and earth pass away, not the smallest letter or stroke shall pass away from the Law until all is accomplished.

> Matthew 5:17–18

The prophet Isaiah wrote, at God's direction, very strongly about how our own sins and those of our families would affect our own lives:

"Behold, it is written before Me,
I will not keep silent, but I will repay;
I will even repay into their bosom,
Both their own iniquities and the iniquities of their fathers
together," says the LORD *....*
"Therefore I will measure their former work into their bosom."

Isaiah 65:6–7

Generational Sexual Sin

There are three main sources of sexual sin in our lives:

1.   Our own lust and weakness, encouraged by the lies of the world (contemporary society) and helped along by our lack of knowledge. (The church has not brought spiritual understanding of sexuality.)
2.   Our judgment of family, in particular our parents (see "The Law of Judgment" in Chapter 2).
3.   The effects of the sexual iniquity of our predecessors.

Let's get some insight into these issues by looking at the life of David in the Bible. You can read the underlying story in 2 Samuel, chapters 11, 12, and 13.

King David decided to stay home from battle one spring when he should have been leading his army. In stepping away from his duty as king, he was in disobedience to God's commission. In this sin-weakened condition, David went up to his rooftop and watched Bathsheba taking a bath nearby. As his lust grew, it culminated in adultery.

But the story did not begin there. It started in David's bloodline about 900 years before, in Jacob's family with his son Judah who also was being disobedient to God. In the midst of his disobedience, Judah ended up committing sexual sin with his daughter-in-law

Tamar (the wife of his deceased son), producing two illegitimate sons, Perez and Zerah (see Genesis 38).

As we count the generations from Judah to David we find that there are exactly ten (Matthew 1:3–6). In Deuteronomy 23:2 we discover in the Law of Illegitimacy that the curse of sexual sin can pass down the family line ten generations.

Apparently, all three influences towards sexual transgression were operating in David's life as he sinned with Bathsheba. By this he opened the spiritual doorway of sexual immorality into his family for another ten generations. Interestingly, it is recorded that David's son Amnon displayed this same sin with David's daughter Tamar, the namesake of Judah's daughter-in-law (2 Samuel 13).

We have seen the inherited curse of illegitimacy bring two main results into the lives of many to whom we've ministered. There is a propensity to sin sexually, and a tendency not to be able to come close to God, in hearing Him, knowing Him or experiencing Him in a deep way. Many forms of rejection also seem to be prevalent in the lives of those with illegitimacy in their bloodlines.

Although we have been discussing the effects of sexual sin leading to illegitimacy, sex outside of marriage is only one kind of sexual sin. All forms of sexual sin result in generational curses descending through the bloodlines. Therefore, all these areas will need to be considered when receiving ministry into our lives, as we will see in Chapter 6.

Contradictory Scriptures?

Although the Bible makes many references to the effects of ancestral sin on our own lives (see "Additional Scriptural References Concerning Generational and National Sins" later in the chapter), some confusion can arise when reading two particular passages that seemingly contradict both our contemporary experience and other scriptures. Rather than leave these questions unanswered, let's examine them now. The first scripture is found in Jeremiah 31, starting in verse 27:

"Behold, days are coming," declares the LORD *....*

> *"In those days they will not say again,*
> *'The fathers have eaten sour grapes,*
> *And the children's teeth are set on edge.'*

But everyone will die for his own iniquity; each man who eats the sour grapes, his teeth will be set on edge."

Jeremiah 31:27, 29–30

First, we need to recall that Jeremiah is a prophet. He is speaking prophetically, not of the present, but of future days. As we read on in chapter 31, he begins to help us know more about these future days when all of Israel will know the Lord. As we look at both historical and contemporary Israel, we realize that this condition has not yet been fulfilled. Jeremiah is not discussing the effect of generational sin on your life today in this passage.

There is a similar set of scriptures in Ezekiel 18, again talking about the fathers eating sour grapes and the children's teeth being set on edge. But in these passages, Ezekiel picks up on and brings further light to an additional theme introduced in Jeremiah 31:30 that states:

But everyone will die for his own iniquity; each man who eats the sour grapes, his teeth will be set on edge.

Jeremiah 31:30

As God, through the prophet Ezekiel, further explains Himself, it becomes clear that He is speaking here, not about the generational effects of sin, but the eternal consequences of our own sin, spiritual death.

Behold, all souls are Mine; the soul of the father as well as the soul of the son is Mine. The soul who sins will die.

Ezekiel 18:4

As we think about this, we realize that all of us will die, so the passage is nonsense if we are thinking only about the death of our body because of sin. Here, God is talking about our eternal soul and clarifying that we will not go to hell because of His judgment on our fathers.

God is not talking in Jeremiah 31 or Ezekiel 18 about the present effect of the spiritual laws that allow us either to receive blessings or to suffer in this life here on planet earth because of the sins of our ancestors. He is clarifying the difference between the eternal and temporal effects of sin (see Appendix V, "Temporal versus Eternal").

❧ LIFE IMPACT ❧

Walking Like Abraham

Earlier in the chapter, we talked about Abraham walking out of Mesopotamia, the land of his forefathers' idolatry. He traveled to the land of God's promise. In this chapter we are taking you on a spiritually similar journey. But at the beginning of any journey, first we must prepare. We need to evaluate the place where we and our ancestors have been dwelling spiritually and prepare to move from there.

This chapter, "Sins of the Family," covers a lot of new material that is not often taught in today's contemporary church. If we are going to walk out of the entanglement of the enemy, we will need to have a good grasp of the material and concepts from this chapter. Below, we've provided a list of scriptures in addition to the ones we have already looked at. Since the concept of generational sin may have been unfamiliar to some, these verses will encourage you in God's Word.

When looking at the "Key Concepts" section at the end of this chapter, we'll see in condensed form the truths that lie at the core of what we've been discussing. Understanding these will help us to examine our own lives and family history.

Prayer Journal

Finally, we need to walk out of the iniquities of our family. We will address this process in Chapter 7, "Praying Our Way to Freedom." Like Abraham, if we are going to enter the land of our blessings we must begin to choose what is worth taking with us and recognize what we must leave behind. The trip to a spiritual position of personal godliness will be too difficult if we do not leave our family sins behind.

The Prayer Journal will help deepen our understanding of this chapter, and help us to discover the family sin areas that we need to leave behind through the prayer ministry of Chapter 7. Please write out each question from the "Key Personal Questions" in the box at the end of the chapter and beneath each question write your answer or response. Take your time, and ask God to help you write sincerely with as much detail as is appropriate. If you have not yet begun your Prayer Journal or need refreshment in the concept, review the guidelines for starting and maintaining a Prayer Journal presented at the end of Chapter 1.

Additional Scripture References Concerning Generational and National Sins

- Lamentations 5:7—*"Our fathers sinned and are no more, and we bear their punishment."* (NIV)
- Leviticus 26:40–42—*"If they confess their iniquity and the iniquity of their forefathers, in their unfaithfulness which they committed against*

Me, and also in their acting with hostility against Me ... so that they then make amends for their iniquity, then I will remember My covenant with [Jacob, Isaac, and Abraham]...."

- Jeremiah 16:11—*"It is because your forefathers have forsaken Me,"* declares the LORD, *"and have followed other gods and served them and bowed down to them; but Me they have forsaken and have not kept My law.'"*
- Jeremiah 14:20—*"We know our wickedness, O LORD, the iniquity of our fathers, for we have sinned against You."*
- Exodus 20:5–6—*"... visiting the sins of the fathers on the children, on the third and the fourth generations of those who hate Me, but showing lovingkindness to thousands, to those who love Me and keep My commandments."*
- Deuteronomy 23:2–3—Illegitimate birth, and also those who hate Israel to the tenth generation. (Look for anti-Semitic roots in your family and nation.)
- Nehemiah 1:6—*"... let Your ear now be attentive and Your eyes open to hear the prayer of Your servant which I am praying before You now, day and night, on behalf of the sons of Israel Your servants, confessing the sins of the sons of Israel which we have sinned against You; I and my father's house have sinned."*
- Nehemiah 9:2—*"The descendants of Israel separated themselves from all foreigners, and stood and confessed their sins and the iniquities of their fathers."*
- Daniel 9:16—*"O Lord, in accordance with all Your righteous acts, let now Your anger and Your wrath turn away from Your city Jerusalem, Your holy mountain; for because of our sins and the iniquities of our fathers, Jerusalem and Your people have become a reproach to all those around us."*

Key Concepts from Chapter 4

- The spiritual effects from previous family generational sins can be visited upon us.
- It is more difficult to receive God's blessings if we are living under curses that came from the sins of our ancestors (those in our direct bloodline).
- God's spiritual laws prescribe how the wages of both disobedience (sin) and obedience will be passed down our generational bloodline.
- There are two major areas of ancestral sin (curse) that affect many, if not all, of us—sexual sin, which can be passed down ten generations, and idolatry, which can come down three to four generations.

Key Personal Questions from Chapter 4

Please answer the following in your Prayer Journal:*

PREPARATORY QUESTIONS TO DEEPEN UNDERSTANDING

- Write out the Bible verse Exodus 20:5. How many generations could be affected directly by this sin?
- Now read Appendix IV, "Idolatry," for a basic core definition of idolatry. When responding to the last item in the Ministry Questions below use this core definition of idolatry.

MINISTRY QUESTIONS TO BE PRAYED THROUGH IN CHAPTER 7

1. Ask the Holy Spirit to remind you of family stories about the wrongdoing of ancestors in your direct bloodline.

List the sins, such as unforgiveness, bitterness, hatred, feuding, violence, dishonesty, alcoholism, stealing, immorality, anti-Semitism, etc. Next to each sin note who did this—father, mother, maternal grandfather/grandmother, paternal grandfather/grandmother, etc., for each sin. Find a Scripture verse that speaks about each family sin that you know about. Write out the Bible verse after your listing of it.

2. Are there sin areas of your life which you have confessed and repented of, but cannot get victory over them? Name them. (These areas could be powered by the sins of your family.)

3. Who in your family was conceived when their parents were not married to each other? Consider yourself, either or both of your parents, grandparents, and any others in your direct bloodline.

4. What forms of idolatry did your ancestors practice? Name the religions other than Christianity which were practiced by your ancestors. When answering, consider the contemporary (your parents) and historical idolatrous practices of your people group.

5. What other things became idols in your family line—cigarettes, alcohol, narcotics, pornography, masturbation, etc.? (Read Appendix IV to help you answer this question.)

*See "Using a Prayer Journal" at the end of Chapter 1 for assistance.

CHAPTER 5

Where Have All the Fathers Gone?

We have become orphans without a father,
Our mothers are like widows.

Lamentations 5:3

Across all the nations we've ministered in, we see the same pattern—fathers are missing from families. Chapter 1 explained how our families were robbed of fathers. Chapters 2 and 3 began to explain why we are not being blessed as we would like. But still, we need an answer to the question, "Exactly how did we lose our fathers?" The answer comes out of two areas of influence we are examining in this book: first, the worldwide plans of Satan to separate mankind from God; and second, the social, cultural, and spiritual context of the lives of those who have lived in Freemasonry-influenced families.

God's Plan for Governing the Earth

Let's first examine God's worldwide plan to settle and subdue the whole earth, placing it under godly government. Surprisingly,

His plan is centered in the family, as revealed in the Genesis 1 Mandate:

God created man in His own image, in the image of God He created him; male and female He created them. God blessed them; and God said to them, "Be fruitful and multiply, and fill the earth, and subdue it; and rule over the fish of the sea and over the birds of the sky and over every living thing that moves on the earth."

Genesis 1:27–28

When God gave this mandate to Adam and Eve, He intended, through successive generations of godly children (families), to extend His rule over the face of the earth. But Satan's worldwide plans always resist that which God is doing. In this chapter, we're looking at fathering's influence on the doorways to God's rewards. These are rooted in God's ways and mandates for families. Knowing of the devil's schemes and the purposes of God will aid us in stepping out of the enemy's ways and into God. Let's now take a closer look at God's plan for raising children in the context of family, an area that Freemasonry damages.

Children are not born into this world automatically in relationship and obedience to God. God's plan for children is for them to come to know Him through the love, nurture, and acceptance of their parents. By their behavior, parents represent God and thereby introduce Him and His nature to their children. In this godly plan for families, two planes of relationships are developed. In the horizontal, each child relates first to those inside the immediate family and then to those further out. As the child grows, the parents can teach him or her about God. Eventually, a vertical relationship is developed between the child and God. Through these two planes of relationship, the family is designed to extend God's dominion around the world. It should come as no surprise that Satan concentrates his efforts against families! Because of our ignorance, he has had worldwide success.

Unpacking the Genesis 1 Mandate

How are we to regain the ground that we've lost to the enemy over the centuries? To answer this question, we will need to understand more about God's plan for us. Then we can begin to stand against Satan's work in our own lives, as well as in our families, churches, and nations.

Let's take a closer look at the Genesis 1 Mandate as presented in chapter 1 of the first book of the Bible. It is here that God unfolds His plan to rule His creation, planet earth.

> *God created man in His own image, in the image of God He created him; male and female He created them. God blessed them; and God said to them, "Be fruitful and multiply, and fill the earth, and subdue it; and rule over the fish of the sea and over the birds of the sky and over every living thing that moves on the earth."*

Genesis 1:27–28

Let's examine the language in these two verses to understand something of God's plan. First, we see that God created man and woman in His image. The word translated as "image" is:

> *selem*, from an unused word; translated in this passage as image but variously in the Old Testament, as [with number of occurrences]: form (1), image (5), images (6), likenesses (3) and phantom (1).

Strong's catalog number 6754:
the root word is "shadow"

God intended that man would be a reflection of His form even as a shadow represents something of the person to whom it belongs. But a shadow reveals yet another aspect of a living person: the shadow does what the person does, in perfect concert with their actions. In John 14:9, Jesus told Philip, *"He who has seen Me has seen the Father."* And in John 5:19 Jesus said, *"whatever the Father does, these things the Son also does in like manner."*

Jesus came to show the world what His Father in heaven is like; He is God's shadow onto the earth. He came, both as the Son of God preparing the way to the Father, and as the second Adam to model the Genesis chapter 1 image of God's role that we are to fulfill in our own lives. In committing to be Christians, we are setting our hearts to walk as Jesus did in God's plan and purpose for our lives, as God's shadows, looking like Jesus and, therefore, our Father, and only doing what He is doing. The Father's shadow does what the Father does. Shadowing the Father is God's plan for our lives: *"to become conformed to the image of His Son"* (Romans 8:29), so that like Him we would reflect the image of our Heavenly Father.

God's Dynamic for Fathering

In this section we will examine God's plan for fathering. By this, we will gain understanding to aid us in being healed from damages to our character and our ability to parent. Most people who were raised in Freemasonry-influenced families suffer in these two areas.

Let's begin by looking more closely at the directives that God gave to us in Genesis 1:27–28, where fathers are commanded to be fruitful and multiply. In godly families the role of fathering is intended to fulfill these two imperatives; within them lie the keys to unlock the knowledge of God's plan for fathering. But to get these keys, we must understand the two terms: "fruitful" and "multiply."

Unlocking God's plan for fathering will give us a standard of comparison. By this we can then evaluate the fathering we received and that which we gave or are presently giving. We can even appraise the cultural performance of fathering in our nation. The proper measure, the "gold standard," if you will, is not to be found in some psychology text or popular book about raising your family. We need to look carefully at the Bible for our answers.

FRUITFULNESS

In pursuit of the keys to fathering, let's now examine the processes described by the words "fruitful" and "multiply." Originally Adam and Eve were vested with something of God the Father; they resembled Him. God revealed His plan to govern the whole earth through many people just like Adam and Eve. But He didn't intend to personally make any more people after He made the first two. The job of reproducing was given to Adam and Eve. We are to make more of our own kind through the capabilities He has formed in us. Part of the process of replication is being "fruitful." Fruitfulness, biologically speaking, indicates that we can produce babies—just as an oak tree will produce acorns that will sprout and grow into trees.

MULTIPLICATION

But what about the word "multiply"? Does it not express the same idea as fruitfulness? Let's look a bit deeper. We've not yet examined character and personality, two of many things that distinguish mankind from plants. A tree or other plant wraps up in its seed the essence of what it is—its characteristics, which will always be the same. But character and characteristics are not quite the same. A person's character can be influenced for good or bad, but a tree lacks moral character, only having characteristics.

God invested another kind of seed, something of His character, into Adam and Eve. Biological reproduction is not enough. Character is formed through relationship; this process initiates in the womb. It is intended to come from parents interacting with and training their children, giving of that which was invested in them. God invested in Adam, spending quality time educating and developing his character in the garden. There Adam learned practical things like farming, but he also experienced fathering by God. In His fathering role, God brought every bird and animal that He made to Adam. He entrusted him with the authority to name every one of them as he observed them. It must have been a very long process considering the nearly endless number of species of animals and birds (many of which are now extinct), and all of this Adam did with his Father God.

Adam's character developed through instruction, observation (modeling), and relationship with his Maker, "Father God." Within the limitations of his experience and humanity Adam would have come to reflect something of God's image. The Bible also records that God spent time with both Adam and Eve, coming to walk in the Garden with them. But He only did this with these two who didn't have earthly parents to learn from.

Goslings learn to be geese from their parents; puppies learn how to be dogs from their parents, and even more so human children learn the same from their parents. God sets our biological form in nature, but a large part of who we are and how we behave comes out of relationship with our parents. He has called us to be fruitful, reproducing the biological form He gave us, but God gave further instruction: to replicate (multiply or imprint) the image of Himself in our children. He stepped out of heaven to instill the image of Himself in the first man and woman, visited Abraham face to face to do the same, and finally He sent His Son Jesus to show us the Father.

Let's examine for a moment just how parents produce a copy or reflection of themselves (or what they believe in) in their children. It happens by example—not so much by instruction as by what is done in the child's presence and that which is done to, with, and for the child. As Christian parents, particularly fathers, we are called to represent the characteristics of Father God to our children even before they can speak, and certainly before they can understand or reason in an adult way.

There are two aspects to this imprinting. One part of the imprinting has a training element that prepares our children to know God Himself, both what He is like and how to have a relationship with Him, through practice with us, their earthly fathers. The second aspect of imprinting is to instill in our children God's character so that they mirror Him who first made man in His own image. This is the multiplication mandated in Genesis chapter 1.

God intended that the whole world would be filled with His image and reflect His character. He has commanded us to join Him in the task of multiplying His image by instilling it in each child, as the inherent biological fruitfulness that He established in mankind produces offspring according to His plan and command. This is the system as God intended it to be.

Like Father, Like Son

By now we should be bursting to know, just what are these character attributes of God? What should our parenting instill in our children, so that they may reflect the image of God? If we have these attributes, or could attain to them, then we could expect to easily see and enter into the things our Heavenly Father is doing here on earth now. We would be doing what the Father is doing, just as Jesus did.

> *Therefore, Jesus answered and was saying to them, "Truly, truly, I say to you, the Son can do nothing of Himself, unless it is something He sees the Father doing; for whatever the Father does, these things the Son also does in like manner."*

John 5:19

It is this relationship between Jesus and the Father that God holds up as a standard for us to see. With proper fathering, we find ourselves shadowing what our Heavenly Father is doing. The problem is that when we have not been fathered according to God's standard by our earthly fathers, we do not have instilled in us the godly character values we need, and we don't even know when we're off track. The point of this discussion is not to encourage hopelessness, but to make us aware of why we are unable to fulfill our Heavenly Father's desires for our lives. Let's make this whole discussion personal now.

Let's take a look at what we think God is like and then examine our beliefs to discover how sound they really are.

⮞ LIFE IMPACT ⮜

Discovering What God Is Like

Jesus said, *"you will know the truth, and the truth will make you free"* (John 8:32). In this section we are going to take a look at fifty-two qualities of God attested to in the Scriptures and use them to begin to set our lives free from our problems of the past. God wants to bless us and add to us some of His character that we missed getting as we were growing up. If our earthly fathers were imperfect, God stands ready to help us now; we can be re-fathered by God. To be fathered by Him means that we have become His children. We need to be born again (see Appendix I) to become His children. If we are baptized in the Holy Spirit (see Appendix I) we will have the power of heaven behind us as we enter into a deeper relationship with our Heavenly Father. As we submit to His ways, He will develop our character so that we are complete, lacking in nothing (James 1:4).

Let's familiarize ourselves with the table "Qualities of God the Father" starting on page 86. We will be using this table in our Prayer Journal exercises at the end of this chapter.

- In the first column are listed some of God's character values manifest in His behavior.
- In the second column are the Scripture references for the character traits listed in column one.
- We will be using column three to list our own impressions of God that correspond to the same character trait listed in column one. We are going to be a little bold and brave here, and dare to look at those perceptions of God that came from imperfect modeling by our earthly fathers, or other experiences in life that have led

us to perceptions of God that perhaps do not match up with the Scriptures.

- In column four, we will again be using the column one "character trait of God" as a reference. But in this new column we will list how we have seen our own father in relationship to this reference (i.e. how he represented God as Father to us). For example, in the fifth line, God is portrayed as just, but if our father was unjust with us, then our entry in column four would be "unjust."

- Let's use the last column to qualitatively list our own manifestation of the column one qualities and see how we measure up. For example, if in the fifth line we also have been unjust, then we would write "unjust" in this last column.

The point of this exercise is to discover where we've not known God for who He really is, so that we can begin to do something about it. If we begin to set things right, there are two obvious and direct benefits: we will open the door to a better and more fruitful relationship with God, and we will begin to change more into the image of Jesus. Let's see how this change could happen.

Here is an interesting line of reasoning: Jesus tells us that He is an exact representation of the Father and that if we've seen Jesus, then we've seen the Father (John 14:9). Therefore, as we confess that we want to be like Jesus, we are also saying that we want to be like His Father and our Father. So, in the first column of the following table, we can identify qualities of God's character and, therefore, how He wants us to be. The problem is, we were raised with imperfect parenting and our understanding of what God is like will be influenced to a great degree by the circumstances of our early lives.

Perhaps we've not known God as He is described in the first column. Some of these characteristics are outside our experience. In fact, we might protest and say that He has not treated me and my family as the Bible says He would. Fair enough, but let's take a look at *why* our experience could indicate a relationship with God that is different from the kind we would expect from the Bible references we've examined. There is an astonishing set of scriptures that give us insight into having a relationship with God:

> *With the kind You show Yourself kind;*
> *With the blameless You show Yourself blameless;*
> *With the pure You show yourself pure,*
> *And with the crooked You show yourself astute.*

Psalm 18:25–26

Somehow, God treats us according to our behavior! As we act according to His ways, we experience Him as He claims to be. But as we act outside of His ways, plans, and purposes, we are treated in response to how we act. Culturally we say, "What goes around (the results of our behavior) comes around (to us);" or biblically, what we sow, we reap (Galatians 6:7; see Chapter 2, "Spiritual Laws That Govern the World"). In the parable of the talents, one of the servants believed the master to be a hard man and buried the money that he was given to invest (Matthew 25:24). Interestingly, as he believed the master was, that is how he was treated.

Perhaps we've not known God as He is because we've behaved in ways influenced by how we thought He is (or is not), based upon our parenting. This behavior has prevented Him from meeting us in the ways that both He and we would wish. So, while God is wonderful in so many ways, it is possible that the spiritual principles of relationships we've just examined have prevented our experiencing Him as He would wish for us.

Prayer Journal Entries

We're now in a good position to press forward to know God better than we did before. Please begin a new entry in your Prayer Journal for Chapter 5, "Where Have All the Fathers Gone?" If possible, photocopy the table, "Qualities of God the Father," and paste it into your journal—otherwise, hand copy it into your journal. You can then safely begin to fill in the blank columns for each quality of God, following the reference Scripture. To get the most value out of this exercise, please follow the directions in the next few paragraphs for each column. Before you begin, please take some time to ask the Holy Spirit to come and lead you into the truth about your life experience and condition.

Having prayed for God's help in this exercise, start in column three, putting in what you feel or have experientially perceived about God the Father. We have to be careful here because it is easy to "spiritualize" our belief system, just to give a proper, acceptable and safe answer. As we honestly and prayerfully fill out this third column, we may begin to recognize where some worldly influences have robbed us of our understanding and knowledge of God the Father.

Now, as our courage builds, let's fill out the fourth column, writing in the character trait that our earthly fathers brought into our lives in correspondence to the qualities of God indicated in the first column.

The final entries that we will make in the table refer to ourselves. Let's now ask the Holy Spirit to help as we fill in the last column of the table. What is required is a healthy, honest evaluation of ourselves to see how we currently measure up to the qualities of God shown in the first column. His qualities are the ones that He wants us to mirror or express in our own lives as His child.

As we complete this exercise, we may see some interesting parallels, both in how we view God and how we view our earthly father. Further, as we then refer to the fifth column we may realize how the fathering we've received has influenced and shaped us. To the degree that we've been honest and made some discoveries here, we then have a basis for working on bringing positive changes into our lives. In the next chapter we will find out how to move forward, but first we have a little more work to do before we're finished here.

This has not been the easiest of chapters. Let's take a few moments to examine its core ideas. They are reviewed in the "Key Concepts" section located in the box at the end of the chapter. As we've refreshed ourselves in these, we're now in a position to begin to draw together the work done in completing the table we just made in our journal.

To finish this chapter's study, continue in your Prayer Journal by answering the questions under the title "Key Personal Questions" in the box. These questions are designed to help you begin to use the information that we've gathered by working through the "Qualities of God the Father" table. Again, write out each question and answer it in your journal before going on to the next.

Qualities of God the Father

God's Attributes	Reference	How Have I Perceived God?	How I Viewed My Father	My Own Attributes
God is love	1 John 4:8			
Generous	Romans 8:32			
He justifies, not condemns	Romans 8:33			
Nothing can separate us from His love in Christ Jesus	Romans 8:34–39			
No injustice with God	Romans 9:14			

God's Attributes	Reference	How Have I Perceived God?	How I Viewed My Father	My Own Attributes
God is kind	2 Samuel 9:3			
Kindness, tolerance, patience	Romans 2:4			
Gives you rest	Joshua 1:13			
Gives you strength and power	Psalm 68:35			
Gives you grace and mercy	Psalm 48:11			
Gives perseverance and encouragement	Romans 15:5			
Gives grace, mercy and peace	2 John 3			
Gives peace	Hebrews 13:20			
Gives hope, joy and peace	Romans 15:13			
Compassionate	Jeremiah 16:5			
Gives counsel	Job 15:8			
Will never leave us	Hebrews 13:5			

God's Attributes	Reference	How Have I Perceived God?	How I Viewed My Father	My Own Attributes
Will never forsake us	Hebrews 13:5			
Does not show partiality	Deuteronomy 10:17; Acts 10:34			
Against all unrighteousness	Romans 1:18			
His will is good and acceptable and perfect	Romans 12:2			
Faithful	1 Corinthians 1:9			
Holy	1 Corinthians 3:17			
Not of confusion, but of peace	1 Corinthians 14:33			
Is not mocked	Galatians 6:7			
Not unjust	Hebrews 6:10			
God is light and has no darkness in Him	1 John 1:5			
Does not lie	Numbers 23:19			
Executes justice for the orphan and widow	Deuteronomy 10:18			

God's Attributes	Reference	How Have I Perceived God?	How I Viewed My Father	My Own Attributes
Gracious and compassionate	2 Chronicles 30:9			
Favorably disposed to those seeking Him	Ezra 8:22			
A righteous judge	Psalm 7:11			
Our refuge and strength, a present help in trouble	Psalm 46:1			
Is for me	Psalm 56:9			
His way is holy	Psalm 77:13			
Righteous in all His deeds	Daniel 9:14			
Patient*	1 Corinthians 13:4–7*			
Kind*	1 Corinthians 13:4–7*			
Not jealous*	1 Corinthians 13:4–7*			
Doesn't brag*	1 Corinthians 13:4–7*			
Is not arrogant*	1 Corinthians 13:4–7*			
Doesn't act unbecomingly*	1 Corinthians 13:4–7*			
Does not seek His own*	1 Corinthians 13:4–7*			

God's Attributes	Reference	How Have I Perceived God?	How I Viewed My Father	My Own Attributes
Is not easily provoked*	1 Corinthians 13:4–7*			
Doesn't take into account a wrong suffered*	1 Corinthians 13:4–7*			
Does not rejoice in unrighteousness*	1 Corinthians 13:4–7*			
Rejoices with the truth*	1 Corinthians. 13:4–7*			
Bears all things*	1 Corinthians. 13:4–7*			
Endures all things*	1 Corinthians 13:4–7*			
Disciplines His sons	Hebrews 12:7–11; Deuteronomy 8:5			
Reproves those He loves	Revelation 3:19			
Will not leave (abandon) us as orphans	John 14:18			

* Qualities of love from 1 Corinthians 13:4–7, where we remember that God is love.

Key Concepts from Chapter 5

- The battle for dominion over the earth is being waged against families.
- God intends for parents to imprint their children with His image.
- God's character is modeled first by our parents, second by Scripture, and third through how He treats us and others.
- If we want to know what we should be like, we can look in the Bible to see what God is like. That's how we should be.

Key Personal Questions from Chapter 5

PREPARATION EXERCISE*

Carefully and prayerfully (i.e. ask the Holy Spirit to help) examine your completed "Qualities of God the Father" table that is now in your Prayer Journal.

- Look for patterns to discover where your impression of God does not match what the Scriptures say about Him.
- Now look at the places where the fathering/parenting you received does not match the character of God very well.
- Finally, look for places where your own character does not strongly match God's wish for you to be a mirror or shadow of Himself.

MINISTRY QUESTIONS

Please answer the following in your Prayer Journal:*

1. List the character areas from the table in which your experiential impressions of God do not match what He says about Himself. Are you willing to know God as He

says He is in the Bible? For each place where you've found a difference, write out a short prayer to God asking Him to reveal Himself experientially to you, to establish a history with you that verifies the biblical claim.

2. List each item where your parents gave you a wrong impression of God. Are you willing to forgive them?

3. List the areas where you can see that you have become what you disliked (the ungodliness) in your parents. Can you forgive yourself? Write out a short prayer for each item, asking God to help you be like Him in that character area.

* See "Using a Prayer Journal" at the end of Chapter 1 for assistance.

CHAPTER 6

The Family: God's Building Block for Society

In the previous chapter we began to grasp the importance of fathers in the family: they shape our image of God the Father. As we studied the Genesis 1 Mandate, we discovered that God's plan for families is for them to increase in number so they may bring order to and supervise the affairs of the world (Genesis 1:27, see Chapter 5). Now, let's examine the role of fathers in the family from another viewpoint.

In his book *Husbands and Fathers*, Derek Prince presents three primary roles for fathers in the context of family: prophet, priest, and king. In his role as prophet, the father communicates God's wishes and truths to the family. In his role as priest, the father brings his family and their needs to God. And finally, in his role as king, the father leads his family as they fulfill their earthly assignments. With this in mind, let's examine two major techniques the enemy of our souls uses to damage families through fathers. Satan's first strategy is to damage the father's character and his ability to love and lead in the family context. The second line of attack is to remove the father's presence from the family, either physically or by neutralizing him. In either case, the father's God-given family roles are negated or greatly reduced.

In Chapter 5 we saw how our image and understanding of God is affected by our father's character. We also saw that our own character is affected by what our father was like. Now we will examine how the enemy has removed the presence of our fathers and their influence from our homes.

Where Have All the Fathers Gone? (II)

Satan removes the godly influence of fathers from the family by capturing their hearts with business, sports, leisure, charity, or even God's work. Let's take a look at a modern-day parable to see how such a thing could happen, even in a Christian setting:

John's father was an amazing man of God, a pastor to pastors, a supreme Bible teacher. He was much in demand to speak and minister at churches all over the country and even abroad. To raise awareness of the Gospel around the world he regularly visited nations whose prosperity was less than his own nation. When traveling in his own nation he was usually not gone for more than a week at a time. But when on missions trips, he could be gone for more than a month at a time, and would return completely exhausted. It seemed as if John's father was gone all the time, either physically or emotionally.

The family maintained a wonderful "Christian" exterior. Pastor Goodman was respected and honored in his own church, throughout the whole country, and abroad. But at home, although the proper familial respect and honor for father was present in the home, it was merely a formality. Family life had no vibrancy. Relationships were strained, stiff, and distant. Pastor Goodman only had time for his God, Bible study, and sermon writing, plus the myriads of visitors seeking his wise counsel and prayer ministry. Finally, late in the evening, long after the rest of the family was asleep, he would fall into bed for a much too short, exhausted, dreamless sleep. In effect, Pastor Goodman was never at home for his family. They suffered immensely as the man was never able to be a functional father: a prophet, priest, and king to his own family.

John, over time, became surly, argumentative, and finally absent in the home as well. He found the male affirmation he desired in a street gang, where he gained status by acting out his frustration and anger through stealing, fighting, and finally comforting himself in illicit sexual relationships that were available to the tougher gang members. Satan had succeeded in stealing John's father from the home and family and now had a firm grip on John himself. The family teetered on the brink of destruction.

The story does have a happy ending, although it took a near tragedy before Pastor Goodman sought and heard the Holy Spirit on behalf of his own family. It was not until John lay in a hospital bed, on the edge of death from a knife wound he received in a gang fight, that Pastor Goodman woke up.

He began to realize how far his son had drifted away, from him, the family, and most of all from God. As he cried out to God at his son's bedside, asking for his very life, he began to question the reason for this catastrophe. It was as if the Lord said to him: "I have been waiting for you to ask me!" Then in a gentle, tender way, God began to reveal how Pastor Goodman had abdicated his responsibilities as a father and had made ministry something of an idol, to the neglect of his family.

John recovered miraculously after his father repented of his neglect and tearfully asked both his son and family for forgiveness. It was a long path back to intimacy with his eldest son. But as he began to turn his eyes towards John, to speak to him, and be more present in the home, the father–son relationship began to flourish. This change meant that he had to carve out quality time from his other activities to invest with John.

As time passed, the two began to share more openly with each other. Today, Pastor Goodman still has a church and a national/international ministry, but he weighs each speaking invitation before the Holy Spirit, turning down those engagements which God has not called him to accept. Now, when traveling, he often takes one or more family member(s) along, even abroad. Within two years' time, John returned to God, entered a theological seminary in Cleveland, and on weekends began helping his father develop a growing and exciting new youth ministry in the church.

Worldwide Parental Abductions

All over the world, fathers and mothers are being abducted (for all practical purposes) from their nuclear families with similar results: fathers become football addicts, sitting transfixed before televisions whenever they are home; mothers work to help support the family and are gone all day from their pre-school-age children. Those fathers lucky enough to be employed often work extra hours or overtime without pay to keep their jobs. Or, as they climb the ladder of "success," they spend more and more time away from home. Fathers are addicted to alcohol, often spending long hours away from home drinking, and even becoming involved with women other than their wives.

Amazingly, experiences similar to Pastor Goodman's are not uncommon even among ordinary church members, since many churches are so full of "required" activities. These extra commitments also steal parents away from their children in the name of God. Whether it is struggling to make a living in an outdoor market stall, over-activity in church, or drinking and football games, the net effect is the same. Fathers' (parents') eyes are turned from their children, who then miss proper parental love, instruction, and family stability.

Children are easy prey for the enemy of our souls when parents are not guarding their nest and their offspring.

The Freemasonry Way

To advance in Freemasonry, maintain relationships, and engage in the lodge and organization's activities requires both time and money. Active, zealous members end up spending both their time and money, which should have been spent on the family, on the plans, purposes, and activities of Freemasonry.

Members are not at home, but either are engaged in local lodge activities or are traveling to various regional or national conventions and seminars, where liquor and female entertainment are reportedly part of the program.

As a result, children's hearts are turned away from their fathers. Without proper fatherly influence, they effectively become orphans. The mothers become, for all intents and purposes, widows. Divorce may be—and often is—the result. The children's hearts are captured by the culture of the worldly environment in which we are all immersed, preventing them from being invested in their nuclear family's (parents') homes and God. Divorced, or effectively divorced, mothers are unable to cover both the father's absence and dereliction of duty. This leads to inferior parenting and the subsequent loss of potential in the children.

The Curse of Malachi

God planned that the world would be populated and ruled by His children, Adam and Eve, and their offspring. All would become God's children. He first commanded this assignment in Genesis 1:26–31 and then restated it to Noah after the flood in Genesis 9:1, 7. The only way God's plan could be realized would be through the cooperation of individuals, both with each other and with God (see

Appendix I). And God designed the foundation for this cooperation to be laid within the boundaries of a godly, loving family. That's another of the reasons God places such a high value on families. Within the family, God develops our abilities to cooperate with Him and each other to subdue and rule over (i.e. administrate His rule over) the world.

Freemasonry focuses only on the husband/father chasing after more revelation (more "light") through teachings in the lodge and increased development of relationships in which his family cannot participate, since lodge activities are secret in nature. This design is in direct opposition to the plans and purposes of God.

So treasured by God is the family unit; so close to His heart; so important to the development of each individual is the nuclear family, that God has made it clear: any culture not promoting family will be cursed in their land.

> *Behold, I am going to send you Elijah the prophet before the coming of the great and terrible day of the LORD. He will restore the hearts of the fathers to their children and the hearts of the children to their fathers, so that I will not come and smite the land with a curse.*

> Malachi 4:5–6

After speaking these words that end the Old Testament, God was silent for nearly 400 years. Referring to John the Baptist's harbinger ministry, God was saying that He would curse any nation which obstructs His plan for families. This is a core issue with God; ultimately, He will not allow perversion of His plan. He has commanded us to be fruitful and multiply (His image, see Appendix I, Section 5.0, "Purpose of Our Life on Earth," and "God's Dynamic for Fathering" in Chapter 5). For those who go against this plan, there is curse. The Hebrew word for "curse" appearing in Malachi 4:6 is חֵרֶם (*cherem*). When we examine the nations who have opposed God's plan for families, we see their lands are cursed in many ways.

Freemasonry, which by its nature and function opposes God's plan for families, turns the hearts of men towards its own gods and principles.

The Way Back to Blessings

If the preceding seems like bad news, it's not. While not a good report, it is an accurate spiritual assessment of the Freemason's family. For us to choose to walk out of a bad situation, first we must be aware that something better exists. In addition, we need a spiritual map to blessings. To use a map, we must know both our current position and where we want to go. We have already discussed our current position: curse, and the journey's end point—that "something better"—is blessing. The map we need, then, will enable us to travel from curse to blessing. The Good News is that such a map exists for those who have been damaged through the Freemasonry system— or under any other curse, for that matter: God through His Son Jesus Christ is the way out. God provides a way to travel from the curses upon us, through the lands of confession and repentance of the sins that gave the curse a right to exist, into the land of blessing.

> Like a sparrow in its flitting, like a swallow in its flying,
> So a curse without cause does not alight.
>
> Proverbs 26:2

According to this scripture, when we remove the cause, a curse will not stay upon us. The cause, or doorway, to the curse of Malachi is the collective sin of families where parents are not involved with their children and the children's hearts are not open to the parenting process. Therefore, to remove the Malachi curse, mothers and fathers need to restore the parenting process within the nuclear family group and children need to submit themselves to their parents. Where this curse originates in national sin, for the nation to be restored, those spiritually representing the nation need to repent on behalf of their people. Notice in Jonah 3:5, when God sent Jonah to Nineveh, the whole city-state repented and God did not bring the destruction upon them that they deserved from their collective sin.

The scriptural model for removing national curses is clearly outlined in God's word to Israel in 2 Chronicles 7. In this passage, we see God providing a way back from the curses He would bring upon Israel for their disobedience to His will and wishes:

> *If I shut up the heavens so that there is no rain, or if I command the locust to devour the land, or if I send pestilence among My people, and My people who are called by My name humble themselves and pray and seek My face and turn from their wicked ways, then I will hear from heaven, will forgive their sin and will heal their land.*

2 Chronicles 7:13–14

It worked for the pagan culture of Nineveh and it worked time after time for Israel, the people of God. It will work for you as an individual family and it will work for your nation. We need to realize, however, that our personal repentance, unless we are the king or president of our nation, will not be expected to produce noticeable national results. However, God can bless us even in the midst of adversity or among a sinful people.

Stepping Out of the Curse of Malachi

In the next chapter we will examine how we may escape the problems brought on by our individual and familial disobedience to God. We will explore the ways to freedom, not only from the curse of Malachi, but also from other family and personal problems we have discovered in the first six chapters of this book. The second half of the book takes us deeper into spiritually induced problems brought on by our and our family's direct involvement with Freemasonry.

❧ LIFE IMPACT ❧

In this chapter and in Appendix I, Section 5, we've studied God's plan for families to be led by fathers. If we desire God's blessings, we must return to Him, the source of all blessings. Let's now review this chapter's central teaching in the "Key Concepts" box. With these ideas firmly in mind we will be ready to answer the questions that turn our learning experience into a life-changing opportunity.

Prayer Journal

This journal section is the last one we will work on in preparation for the prayer ministry of Chapter 7, "Praying Our Way to Freedom." We began our personal Prayer Journal back in Chapter 1. We've come a long way since then, but there is a little more work to do. It's time to start a fresh section in your journal. Please respond to the questions and exercise topics listed in the "Key Personal Questions" section in the box at the end of the chapter.

Take some time and pray, asking the Holy Spirit to help you answer the questions in a way that will prepare you to step into God's plan for your life. The way to freedom is only through Jesus Christ. Let's now see how this chapter touches your life. First write out a question and then answer it before progressing to the next one. Remember to take your time. This is not a race or competition. It is okay to work through the questions over a period of time, even at more than one sitting.

Key Concepts from Chapter 6

- God intended fathers to represent His wishes and truths to their families, to bring the needs of their families before Him and to lead in the families' earthly assignments.
- Families begin to disintegrate when fathers do not spend enough time and energy on them.
- Satan's worldwide plan is to turn the hearts of the fathers away from the children and the hearts of the children away from the fathers.
- A curse comes upon families and nations when fathers' and children's hearts are turned away from each other (Malachi 4:6).
- The curse of Malachi can be broken through confession, repentance, and forgiveness through the blood that Jesus shed on the cross.

Key Personal Questions from Chapter 6

Please answer the following in your Prayer Journal:*

PREPARATION EXERCISE

- Explain in your own words the roles of prophet, priest, and king in the context of God's assignment for fathers in a family.
- Write an objective assessment, without criticism, of how your father carried out the roles in the family of prophet, priest, and king.
- Are you willing to completely forgive your father for his failures?
- Have you forgiven your father for the ways in which he failed you and the family? Name these failures.

MINISTRY QUESTIONS

1. List the areas where you need to forgive your father/mother for not spending enough time with you and the family. Examples include TV, sports, work, church, Freemasonry meetings, drugs, alcohol, sexual affairs (adultery), etc.

2. In what ways, or to what degree, did you become an orphan, and your mother a widow?

3. From your assessment above, which of the three paternal roles were not modeled well for you by your father? How has this influenced your ability to build and develop family? If you have children, has your parenting been negligent in the same areas?

4. To what degree was your heart turned away from your father and mother through other activities, such as drugs, immorality, or sports? Are you ready to ask God to forgive you for your lack of respect and attention towards your mother and/or father as you focused on your own activities?

5. Did you despise your family for their neglect, activities, and attitudes?

6. Which of your ancestors sold their hearts to Freemasonry? Make a list of those whom you need to forgive for participating in these kinds of activities.

* See "Using a Prayer Journal" at the end of Chapter 1.

CHAPTER 7

Praying Our Way to Freedom

Preparation for Prayer Ministry

In this chapter we are going to begin stepping out of the personal bondages we discovered in the first six chapters. The process involves getting things right with God. If we want things to go well with us, then we must consider where we are in conflict with God and His ways. We've spent six chapters examining our lives and relationships, finding out where we are within God's boundaries for blessings and where we are outside of them. Let's take a look now at how we may enter the land of blessings.

WHO MAY ENTER THE LAND OF BLESSINGS?

While the doorway to blessing is open to all, we need to understand a little more to help us get through that door. In 1 Timothy 4:8 the apostle Paul writes, *"godliness is profitable for all things, since it holds promise for the present life and also for the life to come."* We see from this scripture that there is an earthly realm of blessings and a heavenly realm of blessings.

Earthly blessings

Anyone has the option to turn from disobedience to God's commands and enter into His blessings here on earth. However, without the help of the Holy Spirit, it is impossible to completely obey God. Without Him, by ourselves, we simply are not strong enough. Therefore, without a relationship with God, we will not be able to enter into the fullness of His blessings here on earth.

Even if we stop doing wrong, our past disobedience (sin) remains as an open doorway, still allowing curse to flow into our life (see "The Law of Judgment" and "The Law of Sowing and Reaping" in Chapter 2). For example, if we robbed a bank in the past, even though we have stopped being a criminal, there is still an earthly penalty due for our past behavior: this sin will also have spiritual consequences that will continue bringing earthly problems. Finally, doorways of curse opened by our ancestors' sins cannot simply be closed by present or future godly behavior (see Chapter 4, "Sins of the Family").

Heavenly blessings

While good behavior in this life has the potential to bring heavenly blessings, without our repentance (receiving Jesus' atoning death on the cross), we will not even get into heaven after our body dies. Therefore, we will be unable to receive any reward there that might be coming to us for good behavior here on earth. We will only receive earthly blessings that may be a result of our behavior, without knowing Jesus. For those who have received salvation, our good behavior on earth can result in blessings both temporally and eternally (see Appendix I, "Salvation and Lordship").

CLOSING THE DOOR TO SIN'S REWARD

The previous two sections are not very encouraging. You may be wondering, "What hope is there for me?" Since the wages of sin is death (Romans 6:23), how can we ever escape the cumulative effects of our past and present sins? Don't give up; we're right on the threshold of freedom. Let's now explore how to close off the curse of sin from our lives and to enter into God's blessing.

There are five major steps that we need take to get away from the effects of sin and enter into the blessings of God:

- Receive Jesus and His atoning death for our sins (Appendix I, Sections 1 and 2).
- Make Jesus Lord over every area of our lives (Appendix I, Section 3).
- Be baptized in water and the Holy Spirit (Appendix I, Section 4).
- Bring our individual past sins before the Lord in confession and repentance, and receive forgiveness in the name of Jesus (Appendix II, Sections 6 and 7).
- Remove all demonic influences/bondages that used our sin and our family's sin as a right to trouble our lives (Appendix VI, Sections 3.4, 3.5, 5.1, and 5.2).

STEPPING INTO GOD'S BLESSINGS

Power in the process

The process of stepping into God's blessings begins with drawing near to Him and joining His family through Jesus' sacrifice on the cross. Many of you who are reading this may already know Jesus as Savior and be advanced in your walk with God; for others this may not be the case. In prayer, let's now begin our journey towards God and His freedom. (If the Lord leads you to skip over some of the first steps because you've done them already, that's fine.)

Prayer is talking to God and involving ourselves with Him in the process. Without directing ourselves to God in this chapter, all these steps will be without His power to rescue us. They would be a meaningless exercise!

Foundational steps

Salvation

If you wish to know God and walk in His goodness, please pray the Salvation Prayer provided in the box on the next page (from Appendix I). It is important that you speak out this prayer declaration with your mouth (or if you can't speak, to write it out). If at all possible, you should have a person witness your declaration to God. See Appendix I, Sections 1 and 2, for a more detailed explanation.

Lordship

If we are to walk out of the effects of our past sins, and continue on to enter the behavioral land of God's blessings, we will need help. We need God to be Commander and Chief over all that we think and do. We do not know the way, nor do we know how to walk. We need someone to guide, direct, protect, and lead us. We need Jesus in the position of Lord (Adonai or Master) over our life. Of course, when we receive Jesus as our Savior, God becomes our Father, but we need to acknowledge His total Lordship. To be successful in our Christian walk, we need to bring our whole soul and body (Appendix I, Sections 3 and 8) under His direction. See Appendix I sections for further explanation.

The model prayer provided in the box on page 110 will help you enter into submission to the Lordship of Jesus. If at all possible, when you pray this prayer to God have a person witness your declaration. You need to give audible assent to God. If for some reason you cannot physically speak, a written declaration in your own handwriting will also work.

Baptism

The Kingdom of God overcomes the kingdom of darkness. Our personal troubles originate in the kingdom of darkness. If we are to overcome our earthly troubles, we ourselves need to enter the Kingdom of God, i.e. enter into God's light.

Salvation Prayer

If you have come to a belief in Jesus Christ as Lord and Savior, the next step is to use these salvation keys to acknowledge your belief in audible testimony and prayer. Enter the doorway to salvation by praying the following model prayer aloud:

Dear Heavenly Father, I come to You now in the name of Your only begotten Son, Jesus.

- I acknowledge that I have not known You and have not lived my life according to Your righteous ways. Therefore, I have been headed on a course away from You and towards hell.
- I ask that You would forgive me for my sinful ways.
- I choose to change my ways and live my life according to Your ways.
- I confess today that Jesus is God and choose to make Him my Lord.
- I gratefully accept the work Jesus did in suffering the penalty of my sins in His body and dying on the cross, that I might live.
- I believe that You, Heavenly Father, raised Jesus from the dead.
- I ask that You would receive me now as Your child, through the precious blood that Jesus shed for me.
- I ask that You would reveal Yourself to me further, and that You would strengthen me to be able to walk in Your ways, Amen.

In John 3:5 Jesus tells us to be baptized in both water and Spirit for entry into the Kingdom of God. The Bible does not say that we need baptism to know God or receive a healing or deliverance from bondage. Nor does it say we must be baptized in order to go to

Lordship Prayer

Lord Jesus, I acknowledge my need of You and I accept You as my Savior, my Redeemer, my Lord, and my Deliverer.

I invite You to be Lord of my whole life:

- Over my spirit—my prayers, my worship, my spiritual understanding, my creativity, and my conscience
- Over my mind—my thoughts, my memories, my dreams
- Over my emotions—my feelings and emotional expressions and responses
- Over my will—all my decisions and purposing.

I invite You to be Lord over my body:

- Over my eyes: all that I look at and over every look that I give outward
- Over my ears and all that I listen to
- Over my nose and all that comes into it
- Over my mouth and all that goes into it and every word that comes out of it
- Over my sexuality
- Over all my physical activities.

I invite You to be Lord over all my relationships: past, present, and future.

I invite You to be Lord over my resources: time, energy, finance, property, and all that I have.

I invite You to be Lord over the time and manner of my death.

Come, Lord Jesus, and take Your rightful place in all the areas of my life.

Thank You that Your blood was shed that I might be set free from the influence of selfishness and Satan.

Amen.

heaven. However, to enjoy a continuing experience of God's presence (His Kingdom manifestation here on earth), being baptized in water and Spirit increases our availability to Him. If we are going to operate in His spiritual gifts, the baptisms are God-recommended (see Appendix I, Section 4). In Matthew 28:19, Jesus commands us to baptize all of our disciples (the converts whom we are training). This means every Christian is to be baptized.

Water Baptism

Our progress in and towards God is aided by being water-baptized in the name of the Father, the Son, and the Holy Spirit. This procedure is to be done by immersion (see Appendix I for a discussion of the original Greek word, baptizo), wherein we are put completely under the water. We do not baptize ourselves; another baptized Christian must baptize us.

Frequently the local church will be present and a pastor or elder will administer this sacrament to us. The biblical record shows that baptism was performed by those who had given their lives completely to God and were operating as His representatives (see Ephesians 4:11–12; Romans 12:6–8; 1 Corinthians 12:4–11). Those helping Jesus equip new converts are recognized as qualified to baptize others. If you have not yet been baptized in water, and you are in or near a local church, please ask them to perform this sacrament for you. In an area where there is no church, then a qualified servant of God, e.g. evangelist, local believer who led you to the Lord, etc., should be asked.

Baptism in the Holy Spirit

The next step following water baptism is baptism in the Holy Spirit. Sometimes God does this baptism for us where and when He wishes, all by Himself. (One of our friends was baptized in the Holy Spirit while riding public transportation going to work. I was baptized in the Holy Spirit while sitting in church during my first visit to a charismatic service.) Sometimes it happens immediately following water baptism, even as the person arises from the water. Another way is for someone already baptized in the Holy Spirit to "lay hands" upon us and invite Jesus to baptize us in the Holy Spirit. Often, we will begin to speak with the gift of tongues as the Holy Spirit comes upon us in power, but this is only one of the gifts listed in 1 Corinthians 12 that God may be bestowing on us through this baptism.

Baptism in the Holy Spirit is often a strong experience. It is not something that will go unnoticed, where we will need to exercise our faith to believe, or "claim it" after someone has ministered to us. If we did not have a notable, supernatural experience with God, we are not yet baptized in the Holy Spirit. In much the same way, if your body did not go under the waters of baptism (all at once, becoming submerged and wet) you were not baptized in water—you may have been christened or dedicated to Jesus, but not yet have had the full sacrament that Jesus commanded in Matthew 28.

For some, the presence of Freemasonry in your life may have prevented baptism in the Holy Spirit, but don't worry; God will help you anyway. For some Christians, the denominational beliefs of your stream of Christianity may not support water baptism and/or baptism in the Holy Spirit. While these are recommended, please don't despair. These beliefs should not prevent you from obtaining the release from Freemasonry that you are seeking. (Please see Appendix I for a further discussion of baptism in water and the Holy Spirit.)

Closing the Door to Sin and Receiving Cleansing

In this section we will begin to pray through our own life's issues that we discovered as we explored and prayed through the information presented in Chapters 1 through 6. The process of closing the door to sin is addressed in Appendix II, Sections 6 and 7. God has provided the way out of our sins through confession of our sins, one to another; repentance from each of these sins individually; and receiving forgiveness through the shed blood of Jesus. This procedure removes the right of the enemy to bring punishment upon us. We may also need to command a tormenting enemy to leave our life, once we have prayed through this process (see Appendix VI, Sections 3, 4, and 5).

Let's now begin praying through the issues from Part I of the book that we discovered and wrote of in our Prayer Journal. We will need the freedom and release obtained through these prayers to more effectively work through Part II of the book.

Please remember that we recommend staying within the biblical model of James 5, confessing our sins to one another.

RECEIVING HELP FOR YOUR PRAYER JOURNAL ISSUES: RELEASE FROM ISSUES RESULTING FROM CHAPTER QUESTIONS

Chapter 1, "Symptoms without Cause"—prayer ministry

First set of questions—foundations

In the previous section of this chapter, "Preparation for Prayer Ministry," we discussed and prayed through the first set of Prayer Journal questions from Chapter 1. Let's now turn to the last three sets of questions.

Second and third sequence of questions—parental divorce issues

Turn in your Prayer Journal to your responses to the second and third set of questions from Chapter 1.

If you come from a broken family, where your parents stopped living together (divorce, separation, abandonment, death of a parent, etc.) while you were still living at home, an important question is: Who am I holding responsible for this loss? As we learned in Chapters 2 and 3, unforgiveness can be a major source of trouble in our lives. Another problem that arises from unforgiveness is judgment. Here, the Law of Judgment (see Chapter 2) assures that trouble will come to us as we judge the failures of our parents or those who caused our parents' marriage to dissolve.

Coming from a broken home, first we need to forgive those who hurt us and those whom we love. Now is the time for you to pray a release over those who caused your parents' marriage to break. Please find a suitable prayer partner and pray through this first ministry prayer for forgiveness. Use the names appropriate to the situation.

MODEL PRAYER FORGIVING SOMEONE WHO DAMAGED US

Your prayer:

> Dear Heavenly Father, I come to You in Jesus' name. By an act of my free will, I choose to forgive my (mother and/or father) for (causing divorce/separation/my abandonment) (i.e. what they did). When my (mother and/or father) did that, I felt so (angry, hurt, ashamed, unclean, afraid, embarrassed, lonely, vulnerable, etc.). I now give You these feelings; I don't want to keep them any longer.
>
> Lord God, I also give You all my thoughts and decisions in regard to this (damage, hurt, and/or loss that I received).
>
> I now ask that You would separate me from any ungodly connection with my (mother and/or father) (i.e. the person(s) who hurt you) that was established in their sin.
>
> I now release (my mother and/or father) to You, as I forgive (him and/or her). In my complete release, I renounce my

judgment(s). I trust You to judge or forgive according to the truth, and by Your mercy and justice to treat each of them as You see fit.

I also choose by an act of my own free will to forgive (my father's girlfriend/mistress and/or my mother's boyfriend) who contributed to the divorce. I completely release (name of the girlfriend/boyfriend) to You to judge or forgive according to the truth and by Your mercy and justice for what they did. I renounce my judgment of them.

Fourth sequence of questions—setting your heart for restoration

As you examine this last set of questions from Chapter 1, please realize that you have made tremendous progress in leaving the land of curse. To progress into all that God has for you, it is necessary to trust Him with your restoration. The following prayer will help you enter into that trust relationship.

Your prayer:

> Dear Lord Jesus, thank You for my salvation and for entering my life through Your Holy Spirit, to help me change my way of living and thinking. I now ask You to come into my life with restoration. Please restore my relationships, internal peace, physical health, mental health, and cleanse me from the devil's influence that I may receive spiritual health. I now ask You to help me come close to You in a deep and meaningful way, to know You as my Father and Daddy.

Chapter 2, "Spiritual Laws That Govern the World"—prayer ministry

Examine your Prayer Journal responses to the questions from Chapter 2. Look for things in your life that can be expected to bring you trouble via the four spiritual laws that we examined. Please pray through each issue with a trustworthy prayer partner. It is possible to have multiple issues (spiritual problems) with one person. You will need to pray through each issue separately. It is also possible to have the same type of problem with a number of people or in a number of similar circumstances. Be sure to pray into each issue separately. Let's now proceed into the prayer ministry.

Question sequence one—unforgiveness

Your prayer:

> Lord Jesus, please forgive me for holding unforgiveness towards (person's name or group's name). I now choose by an act of my own free will to forgive (him/her or them) for (identify or explain what they did to you). I now release to You all my thoughts about this situation, any ungodly decisions I have made because of the hurt and damage I received from them, and all the feelings that I have stored up inside me regarding what happened to me because of their hurting me. I specifically give You all my hurt, feelings of vengeance, all my stored-up and unprocessed anger, etc. Lord, I was so (angry, hurt, embarrassed, etc.). I now ask that You would release me from all these things, in the name of Jesus and through His precious blood that was shed for my sins. I ask that Your Holy Spirit would come cleanse and empower me to continue in my choice to forgive. [Please note: You need to work through this process for each person on your "Unforgiven List" that you made in your Prayer Journal.]

Prayer partner speaks:

> In the name of Jesus, I speak forgiveness to you for your sin of unforgiveness towards (name of the person being forgiven).

116

Lord Jesus, please help my (brother/sister) release his/her feelings over this issue to You. In the name of Jesus, I speak healing into your human spirit. Holy Spirit, please come and heal and comfort my (brother/sister) from all the wounds suffered in this issue into which we are now ministering.

Question sequence two—judgments

This sequence of questions was designed to help you discover judgment cycles in your life—places where you have judged someone and now the effect of this is coming back on you. The distinguishing mark of a judgment cycle is that the thing from which you suffer somehow mirrors that which you judged in another.

Examine your Prayer Journal responses to the second question sequence. Identify problems that presently impact your life which are similar to those you saw and disliked in another. Perhaps you judged your father for alcoholism and the man you married has become an alcoholic, or the slim wife that you married has become overweight, just like your mother whom you judged for being fat, or any one of many possibilities. More examples might include anger, violence, unfaithfulness, divorce etc., where the very thing that you judged has come upon you. The consequences may have affected, afflicted or damaged your spouse, another family member, or could even be manifesting directly in you.

Let's now use the following model prayer for each judgment issue that you have discovered.

Your prayer:

Dear Heavenly Father, I now come to You in regard to my sin of judgment. I confess that I have judged (name the person or group) and have found (this person or group) to be inferior or insufficient in my eyes. I believed that I am superior to them and would not behave as badly or be like them if I was in the same position as they have been. Lord, this is the sin of judgment. I renounce this sin and choose by an act of my will to let go of this judgment in my heart. I proclaim that only You are the true judge. Therefore, I release (name the person or group) to You for forgiveness or judgment, as You see fit. Only You as God could know all the facts and the condition of their heart(s) to make a proper decision about their behavior. I now claim the blood of Jesus over my sin of judgment and ask that You would set me free from the consequences of this sin.

Prayer partner speaks:

In the name of Jesus, I speak forgiveness to you for your sin of judgment of (name of the person being released from judgment). Lord Jesus, please help my (brother/sister) release his/her feelings over this issue to You. In the name of Jesus, I speak healing into your human spirit. Holy Spirit, please come and heal and comfort my (brother/sister) from all the wounds suffered in this issue into which we are now ministering.

Question sequence three—sowing and reaping

Now look in your Prayer Journal for the third question topic from this chapter. The idea here is to examine problems in your life and ask the Holy Spirit to show any sin sources for them. For those sin sources brought to light, you can then confess them, repent, and receive forgiveness. This will effectively stop the ongoing development of new trouble from this source.

You must realize, though, that the Law of Sowing and Reaping functions to multiply whatever you do. If you were blessing others, then more blessings will return to you. If you were troubling others by your behavior, then you will receive more trouble than you troubled others with. Just like planting seed, you will get a crop of whatever you plant. However, even though you stop sinning (sowing trouble), your old crop of trouble may continue to come up in your life even after you stop (repent). You may not see immediate relief, but eventually you will be better off. Use the following prayer for each of the Sowing and Reaping areas you discovered in your Prayer Journal time with the Lord.

Your prayer:

> Dear Heavenly Father, I come to You now in the name of Jesus. Lord, I confess that I have sinned by (tell God here what you did wrong—where, when, with whom or to whom, etc.). Lord, I am sorry that I did this because it is against You and Your ways. I choose to turn from this sin and not to do this again. Please help me, Holy Spirit, to walk away from this sin in my life. Heavenly Father, please forgive me in the name of Jesus and through His precious blood. Amen.

Prayer partner speaks:

> In the name of Jesus, I speak forgiveness to you for the sin of (name the sin) that you just confessed. In the name of Jesus, I command every spirit from (the practice of this sin) to leave (name of the brother/sister) now. [Wait a moment for God to do this. Repeat this last command for each sin renounced. Check with the Holy Spirit to be sure that any deliverance that was necessary has taken place.]

Question sequence four—idolatry

In this section of your Prayer Journal we are dealing with false religions that you practiced. There are several key elements involved in removing the influence of these religions from your life: 1) Confession and repentance from your involvement (renouncing the religion, its doctrines, and each of the gods (idols) you served); 2) Commanding every evil spirit associated with this religion and its gods to leave you in Jesus' name (see Appendix VI); 3) Removing all materials from the false religion/cult from your life and releasing you from soul ties to those in that religion/occult practice.

The prayer ministry for Chapter 4 covers the generational effects from idolatry. Again, we remind the reader that it is important to have a prayer partner during the ministry sessions. This person is particularly needed when evicting evil spirits.

A typical prayer ministry for getting free from false religion is as follows:

OBTAINING YOUR FREEDOM FROM DIRECT PERSONAL INVOLVEMENT

Your prayer:

> Dear Heavenly Father, I come to You in Jesus' name. I confess my sin of being involved, believing, and practicing the false religion of (name the religion or cult). I now repent and turn away from this false religion. I now name (name the false gods or deities of this religion). I renounce all the doctrines and gods (idols). I renounce any and all dedications and indoctrination ceremonies (name each that you were involved with). I renounce all special names or identities received as a result of my involvement with (name the false religion). I ask that Your Holy Spirit would help me walk out of all of the practices and sins of this false religion. Lord, I ask that You would forgive me for my sins of idolatry in (name the false religion/cult). Lord Jesus, I ask that You would now separate me from every individual with whom I have an ungodly soul tie/spiritual connection established in and through my involvement with (name the false religion/cult). Please release me from the ungodly ties to (names of those who trained, indoctrinated or led me or shared with me in this false religion).

Prayer partner speaks:

> In the name of Jesus, I speak forgiveness to you for the sins of idolatry that you just confessed. In the name of Jesus, I command every spirit of idolatry from (name the false religion/cult) to leave (name of the brother/sister) now. [Wait a moment for God to drive out the spirits.] In the name of Jesus I command the spirit of (name the god or idol renounced earlier) to leave (name of the brother/sister) now. [Wait a moment for God to drive out the spirit.] [Repeat this last command for each god or idol renounced. Check with the Holy Spirit to be sure that all deliverance that was necessary has taken place.]

> Lord, please separate (name of the brother/sister) from (his/her) ungodly soul tie with (name of person he/she was attached to) in (name the false religion/idolatrous practice). Jesus, please return everything of (name of the brother/sister)'s life to him/her that was wrongly invested in (name of the person with whom you were joined in the sin of idolatry) and release everything of (that person) from (name of the brother/sister). In the name of Jesus, I command every evil spirit that inhabited or influenced that relationship to now leave (name of the brother/sister). [Prayer partner: wait and watch to see what happens, checking with the Holy Spirit to be sure that any deliverance necessary has taken place.]

Everything (books, pamphlets, certificates, objects, images, pieces of jewelry, items of clothing, badges, emblems, trophies, awards, etc.) from the false religion/cult must be removed from your home or property and be destroyed, not sold or given away.

Question sequence five—fleshly idols of life

Now turn to your responses to question sequence five in your Prayer Journal for Chapter 2. This question sequence is meant to sweep a little more broadly through your life to help you discover where you are not trusting God to supply all your needs. These areas of your soul are where something has taken the place of God in bringing peace, comfort, satisfaction, importance, prestige, material goods, safety, relationships, places where you have made flesh your strength (Jeremiah 17:5), etc. When we depend upon something/someone other than God to meet our needs, that substitute may, in effect, have become an idol (see Appendix IV).

The prayer ministry that corresponds to your discovery of idols in your life is as follows.

Your prayer:

> Dear Heavenly Father, I come to You in the name of Jesus and confess the sin of idolatry (through the use of alcohol, narcotics, tobacco, masturbation, comfort eating, materialism, money, etc.). By an act of my free will I renounce this pathway to (comfort, peace, safety, confidence, etc.) that I was receiving from this (process, substance, etc., i.e. substitute for God). Holy Spirit, I ask that You would strengthen me to not fall into this substitute for God and His provision again. I agree that substance abuse and over-eating shortens human life. Therefore, I confess the sin of self-murder (shortening my life) and ask that You would forgive me for this. I claim the shed blood of Jesus between me and this sin. By an act of my free will I choose to forgive myself for this practice.

Where someone has helped you to begin or sustain this habit you will need to forgive him/her for leading you into or helping you carry out this sin. The following prayer would be appropriate.

Your prayer:

> Dear Heavenly Father, by an act of my free will, I now choose to forgive (name of the person(s) who led you into this sin or

assisted you in it) for (his/her/their) part in my sin of (name the sin).

Prayer partner speaks:

> In the name of Jesus, I speak forgiveness to you for the sins of idolatry that you just confessed. In the name of Jesus, I command every spirit of idolatry from (name the idolatrous practice just confessed) to leave (name of the brother/sister) now. [Wait a moment for God to drive out the spirits. Watch to see what happens and check with the Holy Spirit to be sure all deliverance necessary has taken place. Repeat this last command for each idolatrous practice renounced.]

Where there was an expressed partnership in this sin, i.e. someone who helped begin or sustain this sin as named in their prayer above, the prayer partner continues:

> Lord, please separate (name of the brother/sister) from (his/her) ungodly soul tie with (name of person he/she was attached to through substance abuse). Jesus, please return everything of (the person's name for whom you are praying)'s life to him/her that was wrongly invested in (name of the person with whom you were joined in the sin of idolatry) and release everything of (that person) from (person's name for whom you are praying).

Where there has been substance abuse, abuse of food, alcohol, tobacco, illegal use of drugs, etc., that leads to a shortened life and this was confessed by the brother/sister to be self-murder in their prayer above, then the prayer partner continues:

> In the name of Jesus, I speak forgiveness to you for the sin of (self) murder. [Look directly into their eyes and say the following:] I speak life to you in the name of Jesus. Now, in

the name of Jesus, I command the spirits of death that came in through (name the sinful practice of substance abuse from which the person has just renounced and repented) to go. [Wait a moment for God to drive out the spirits. Check with the Holy Spirit to be sure that all necessary deliverance has taken place.]

Chapter 3, "Forgiveness: A Deeper Look"—prayer ministry

Chapter 3 helps us enter into the process of forgiveness by showing us that many people who hurt us actually do so because of their own damage and hurts. It is not necessary for us to see or know why someone hurt us, nor do we need to judge or accept any reason or excuse for someone damaging us as valid. However, knowing that we could have been damaged because of these hurts is helpful in opening us up to forgive others.

The Prayer Journal "Ministry Questions" at the end of Chapter 3 are designed to remind you of those whom you need to forgive in response to God's command to forgive others. It is possible to have multiple issues (spiritual problems) with one person. You will need to pray through each issue separately. It is also possible to have the same type of problem with a number of people or in a number of similar circumstances. It is important to pray into each issue with each person separately. Let's now begin to work our way through your Prayer Journal responses to the ministry issues highlighted by the Ministry Questions at the end of Chapter 3.

Question sequence one—freedom from unforgiveness

In reviewing your answers to the "Preparatory Questions to Deepen Understanding" from Chapter 3 you will discover that God is requiring you to forgive (with a whole heart) those who have hurt you. Let's now begin to pray through our list of those whom we need to forgive. Again, we recommend that you have a prayer partner to witness and minister to you where needed. You can use the following model prayer to forgive each person on your list.

Your prayer:

> Lord Jesus, please forgive me for holding unforgiveness towards (person's name or group's name). I now choose by an act of my own free will to forgive (him/her/them) for (identify or explain what they did to you). I now release to You all my thoughts about this damage, any ungodly decisions I have made because of this hurt and damage I received from them, and all the feelings that I have stored up inside me in regard to what happened to me because of their hurting me. I specifically give You all my hurt, feelings of vengeance, and all my stored-up and unprocessed anger, etc. Lord, I was so (angry, hurt, embarrassed, etc.). I now ask that You would release me from all these things in the name of Jesus and through His precious blood that was shed for my sins. I ask that Your Holy Spirit would now come and cleanse me and empower me to continue in my choice to forgive. [Please note: you need to work through this process for each person on your "Unforgiven List" from your Prayer Journal response to question one from Chapter 3.]

Prayer partner speaks:

> In the name of Jesus, I speak forgiveness to you for your sin of unforgiveness towards (name of the person being forgiven). Lord Jesus, please help my (brother/sister) release (his/her) feelings over this issue to You. In the name of Jesus, I speak healing into your human spirit. Holy Spirit, please come and heal and comfort my (brother/sister) from all the wounds suffered in this issue into which we are now ministering.

Question sequence two—forgiving myself

Perhaps one of the most difficult persons to forgive is yourself. Some of us are good at making excuses for our failings, but many have a great deal of difficulty in releasing ourselves from our own sins. The problem is that this personal condemnation disagrees with God's love for you and His provision of forgiveness through confession, repentance, and the shed blood of Jesus. When we refuse to forgive ourselves, we are then in a position that disagrees with God. This place is not a good one in which to be and it then opens the doorway to failure and visitation of the enemy.

We need to turn from our self-condemnation and personal unforgiveness. The model prayer for this personal unforgiveness is as follows:

Your prayer:

> Dear Heavenly Father, I choose to forgive myself for (name the thing that you did). I renounce my self-criticism and condemnation in Jesus' name. I now choose to look at myself through Your eyes and see myself as forgiven. [Note: You will need to forgive yourself for each place where you are holding things against yourself.]

Prayer partner speaks:

> I speak forgiveness to you through the blood of Jesus for your condemnation and unforgiveness towards yourself. Now, in the name of Jesus, I break every self-curse that has come upon you through this unforgiveness and command every spirit that used this opportunity to bring trouble to leave in the name of Jesus. [Wait a moment for God to drive out the spirits. Watch to see what happens and check with the Holy Spirit to be sure any or all deliverance necessary has taken place.]

Question sequence three—making peace with those you've hurt

It is important to make peace with those that you have hurt. Of course, there may be reasons why these things happened, but, where possible, we need to go to those we've injured and tell them we were wrong and ask their forgiveness. Now is not the time to make excuses or offer up reasons for what you did. It is simply a time for confession of your wrongdoing, an owning of the fact that you hurt the person. The process should begin in personal, private prayer, seeking the Lord's help in bringing the matter to peace. Then, with the Lord's help, you can go to the person, or if they live too far away, you could write them a letter. Before communicating with the person(s) you hurt, you will also need to put your sin under the blood of Jesus. You might pray something like the following:

Your prayer:

> Dear Heavenly Father, I come to You in the precious name of Jesus. I now realize that I have hurt (name the person(s)) by my actions. Lord, I ask that You would forgive me for my sin of (name the sin) in which I hurt (name the person(s)). I choose to not to commit this sin again and ask Your Holy Spirit to help me not behave that way again.

Prayer partner speaks:

> In the name of Jesus I speak forgiveness to you for your sin of (name the confessed sin).

Again, when you communicate with those you hurt, realize that they have reasons for not wanting to talk to you, reasons that you gave to them. There are four key elements that need to be in your communication with those you hurt:

- I was wrong when I did this to you.
- I am sorry I hurt you.
- I have no excuse for what I did.
- Please forgive me; I will try never to do what I did to you again.

Question sequence four—restitution

We may steal something, damage something that belongs to another person, or our sin may cause a financial loss to someone. Our spiritual duty, where it lies within our ability, is to compensate for the loss we have caused. This compensation is the principle of restitution. It applies to things rightfully borrowed but damaged by us, things stolen, and damage we have caused by our sinful behavior.

In your Prayer Journal you responded to this fourth question concerning restitution. You prayed asking God to help you remember any things you did that require compensating someone. For any person(s) to whom the Lord has told you to make restitution, you must obey Him and replace what they lost. It may be that the Lord will tell you to give them more than their original loss as a payment covering their grief and inconvenience from your behavior.

As in your response to question three, you must go to the person(s) you hurt and tell them the same things that were recommended:

- I was wrong when I did this to you.
- I am sorry that I hurt you.
- I have no excuse for what I did.
- Please forgive me; I will try to never do what I did to you again.

In addition, you need to bring to them the financial compensation or replacement item, as well as any extra gift that the Lord would put on your heart.

Chapter 4, "Sins of the Family"—prayer ministry

Chapter 4 introduces the concept that the sins of our ancestors may be causing us present-day personal problems. The questions you answered in your Prayer Journal were designed to help you discover some of the hindrances to your life in Christ whose origins are in your direct bloodline, either through your mother's or father's family tree. Let's now begin to bring these problems before the Lord so that you may receive freedom and healing.

Question sequence one—sins of the family

Looking in your Prayer Journal for Chapter 4, you will discover that there are two separate sections of your responses: "Preparatory Questions" and "Ministry Questions." We are now working through your responses to the Ministry Questions. In the first question sequence, you have written down any sins (excluding idolatry, which will be treated later) that were carried out by those in your direct bloodline, before you were born. The following is a model prayer sequence for you to receive freedom from each of these family sins of which you are aware:

Your prayer:

> Dear Heavenly Father, I come to You in the name of Jesus. I confess the sin of (name the sin) committed by my (name relative, including the bloodline—mother's or father's). I turn away from this sinful practice; I repent and claim the blood of Jesus between my (mother, father or mother's/father's relative) and me. I now choose to forgive my (name the relative) for his/her opening the doorway to trouble coming into my life.

Prayer partner speaks:

> In the name of Jesus and through His precious blood, I separate you from the sins of your (mother/father or maternal/

paternal, name relative). In the name of Jesus I command every generational evil spirit that came down the bloodline to (name of the brother/sister receiving prayer) to leave him/her now. [Wait a moment for God to drive out the spirits. Watch to see what happens and check with the Holy Spirit to be sure any or all deliverance necessary has taken place.]

Question sequence two—besetting personal sins

In this question we are looking for hindrances to your Christian walk, things which seem to be besetting sins: those stumbling blocks which you have tried your best to overcome but could not. One possibility for the strength of these sins is that they have a spiritual force imparted by their permission to be there through the sins of your family. We can make a declaration of our position in regard to a certain sin (sin category) without knowing who, if anyone, in our bloodline committed that sin. If there was a generational root to our continual failings in this area, then its strength and nurture will be cut off.

Your prayer:

> Dear Heavenly Father, I come to You now in Jesus' name. I repent, turning away from the sin of (name the sin—the one which has been a problem for you) for any of my ancestors, in my mother's and father's bloodlines. By an act of my free will, I forgive any of my family who committed this sin, opening a spiritual doorway of trouble into my life. I now claim the blood of Jesus between me and any family members who sinned in this way.

Prayer partner speaks:

> In the name of Jesus and through His precious blood, I separate you from the sin of (name the sin), committed by

anyone in your mother's and father's families. In the name of Jesus, I release you from the power of this sin. In the name of Jesus, I command every evil spirit involved with (name the sin) that came down the generational bloodline to (name of the brother/sister receiving prayer) to leave (him/her) now. [Wait a moment for God to drive out the spirits. Watch to see what happens and check with the Holy Spirit to be sure any or all deliverance necessary has taken place.] Lord Jesus, I ask that You would close and seal every one of these doorways into (brother's/sister's name)'s life. Amen.

Question sequence three—removing illegitimacy

In Chapter 4 we discovered the Law of Illegitimacy (Deuteronomy 23:2), which tells us that the sin of begetting children outside of marriage will bring curse into the family line. The life experience of those under this curse is rejection from God's people and others. It also makes it easier for us to sin sexually. But, more importantly, it also results in a lack of intimacy with God our Father through Jesus Christ. In the natural sense, illegitimate sons and daughters do not have legal claim to earthly inheritance. Our experience in ministry shows that many Christians (with illegitimacy in their family line) also are not receiving the earthly blessings that their sonship and daughtership would otherwise qualify them to receive.

If we were conceived out of wedlock, or if any of those in our direct bloodline were (going back ten generations), then we ourselves are under this curse. If we know we were conceived out of wedlock or we know of others in our direct bloodline who were, then we can pray specifically for release, forgiving those who brought this curse into our life. However, we can also pray, repenting from the sins of any family members of whom we are unaware. The prayers releasing you from this curse will be similar in either case.

Your prayer:

> Dear Heavenly Father, I come to You in the name of Jesus. I choose by an act of my free will to forgive (name your ancestors) [If you don't know who it was, then just say "any and all in my direct bloodlines"] who conceived a child outside of wedlock. I forgive them for bringing curse into my life. I confess that what they did was a sin. In the name of Jesus, I repent from this sin. I now claim the blood of Jesus between their sin and me.

Prayer partner speaks:

> In the name of Jesus and through His precious blood, I separate you from the sexual sin that resulted in (name of the brother/sister receiving prayer) being conceived by your (mother and father, or maternal/paternal (name relatives)). In the name of Jesus I release you from the curse of illegitimacy. In Jesus' name I command every generational evil spirit that came down the bloodline to (name of the brother/sister receiving prayer) to leave him/her now. [Wait a moment for God to drive out the spirits. Watch to see what happens and check with the Holy Spirit to be sure any or all deliverance necessary has taken place.]

> Lord Jesus, I ask You to come and heal the deep wounds of rejection and loneliness and isolation that have been in this (brother's/sister's) life. I now speak your acceptance as a (son/daughter) to you right now. [Don't hurry through this ministry. Watch and wait to see what the Holy Spirit will do. Give Him time to do what He wants.]

Question sequence four—generational idolatry

In the prayer ministry for Chapter 2 you worked through the effects of your own idolatry from any non-Christian religions. The curse effects of idolatry and false religions can travel down the bloodline for three to four generations (Exodus 20:4–5).

There are several key elements involved in removing the influence of these inherited influences from your life:

1. First, go through the prayer ministry for your personal involvement (if there were any, as you did in your response to Chapter 2).
2. Confess and repent—turning away from the false religion(s) and gods (idols) of your ancestors.
3. Forgive your ancestors for opening these spiritual doorways into your life.
4. Command every evil spirit associated with this religion and its gods to leave you (see Appendix VI) in Jesus' name.
5. Remove all materials from the false religion/cult from your life that may be in your home. Again, may we remind the reader that it is important to have a prayer partner during the ministry sessions? This is particularly true when evicting evil spirits.

Let's now pray through to freedom for the generational sins which you named in your Prayer Journal for your family in responding to the fourth question sequence at the end of Chapter 4. You will need to pray through each false religion and idol worshiped by each of your ancestors. If you don't know of any of these religions or idols and your family was unable to help you with this information, then ask the Holy Spirit for help. A model prayer ministry for this follows.

OBTAINING YOUR FREEDOM FROM ANCESTORS' INVOLVEMENT
YOUR PRAYER:

Dear Heavenly Father, I repent, turning away from the idolatrous practices of the false religion/cult of (name it) of those in my direct bloodline, for my father and his family going back through the generations and for my mother and her family going back through the generations.

I renounce all their false gods and deities (name all that you know about). I forgive my family (name any specific direct bloodline relatives as is appropriate) who by their practicing these things have opened spiritual doorways of curse into my life. I claim the blood of Jesus between me and those who sinned in this way.

Prayer partner speaks:

In the name of Jesus, I command every inherited spirit of idolatry from (name the false religion / cult) to leave (name of the brother/sister) now. [Wait a moment for God to drive out the spirits.] In the name of Jesus, I command the spirit of (name the god or idol renounced earlier) to leave (name of the brother/sister) now. [Wait a moment for God to do this, watching and checking with the Holy Spirit that all deliverance necessary was accomplished. Repeat this last command for each god or idol renounced.]

Question sequence five—generational fleshly idols of life

Turn to your responses to question sequence five in your Prayer Journal for Chapter 4. We are now addressing generationally the same issues that you prayed through for yourself in Chapter 2. This question sequence sweeps a little more broadly through the sins of your ancestors to help you discover where, as a result of them not trusting God to supply all their needs, they opened the doorway of sin into your bloodline.

The key areas are soulish reliance on something which replaces God in bringing peace, comfort, satisfaction, importance, prestige, material goods, safety, and relationships. This area is where your ancestors made flesh their strength (Jeremiah 17:5). Dependence upon something or someone other than God to meet our needs ultimately makes that substitute an idol (see Appendix IV).

The prayer ministry that corresponds to the generational idols of the flesh that you listed in your Prayer Journal in response to question sequence five is as follows.

Your prayer:

> Dear Heavenly Father, I come to You in the Name of Jesus and confess the generational sin of idolatry committed through the use of (alcohol, narcotics, tobacco, masturbation, comfort eating, materialism, money, etc.). By an act of my free will I renounce this false pathway to (comfort, peace, safety, confidence, etc.) that members of my family were using from this (process, substance, etc., i.e. substitute for God). I repent from my family's ways. Holy Spirit, I ask that You would strengthen me to resist making this a substitute for God and His provision.
>
> I agree that substance abuse and over-eating shorten human life. Therefore, I confess the familial sin of self-murder (shortening of life) and repent from this sin. I forgive my family members for making me vulnerable to curses of death through their sin. I claim the shed blood of Jesus between this family sin and me.

Prayer partner speaks:

> In the name of Jesus, I claim the blood of Jesus between (name of the brother/sister) and the sinful practice of (name the sin just repented from). I release you from the curses that have come down the family bloodline for this sin through the blood of Jesus. In the name of Jesus, I command every spirit of idolatry from (name the idolatrous practice just confessed) to leave (name of the brother/sister) now. [Wait a moment for God to drive out the spirits. Watch to see what happens and check with

the Holy Spirit to be sure all deliverance necessary has taken place. Repeat this last command for each idolatrous practice renounced.]

Where there has been substance abuse, abuse of food, alcohol, tobacco, illegal use of drugs, etc., that leads to a shortened life and this sin was confessed by the brother/sister to be self-murder in their prayer above, then the prayer partner continues:

In the name of Jesus, I claim the blood of Christ between (name of the brother/sister) and the familial sin of (self-) murder. [Look directly into this brother's or sister's eyes and say the following:] I speak life to you in the name of Jesus. Now, in the name of Jesus, I command the spirits of death that came in through (name the sinful practice of substance abuse which the person has just renounced and repented of) to go. [Wait a moment for God to drive out the spirits. Check with the Holy Spirit to be sure that all deliverance that was necessary deliverance has taken place.]

Chapter 5, "Where Have All the Fathers Gone?"— prayer ministry

Chapter 5 is a gateway both to intimacy with Father God and to our godly character development. God intends to reveal Himself through Scripture and through our earthly father's relationship with us. It is in this chapter that we discover our difficulty in seeing and knowing God as He has revealed Himself in the Bible. He has made us in His image and called us to be like Himself. The problem is that Satan has damaged the most powerful childhood God-model, our earthly father. In that damaging, we have also lost much of our formative imprinting of Daddy God.

As we observed and interacted with our imperfect fathers, we erected barriers between us and God. Two of these barriers are unforgiveness and judgment towards our earthly fathers. But all is not lost; Jesus, through the Holy Spirit, wants to come and reveal the Father, Daddy God, to us personally.

The table "Qualities of God the Father" at the end of Chapter 5, carefully and prayerfully filled out, helps us discover where our image of God is faulty. It points to where we need to forgive our earthly fathers for their poor modeling of our Heavenly Father. The last column of the table reveals where we need to repent of our own ungodly ways. Then, with the help of the Holy Spirit, our character can begin to be God-(trans)formed.

Let's begin our journey towards a God-transformed character. We will now work through your Prayer Journal responses to the Ministry Questions at the end of the chapter. (Please be sure that you have worked through the Preparation Exercise first.)

Question sequence one—looking for God as He really is
The journey towards knowing God, as He has proclaimed Himself to be, starts with telling Him that you want to know Him. In your response to this first question sequence, you have discovered some areas where you have a view of God's character that differs from the biblical claim. It is time to be honest with God and acknowledge each of your wrongful viewpoints. You need to ask Him to make Himself known to you as He really is in each of your problem areas.

Your prayer:

> Dear Heavenly Father, I come to You now in Jesus' name. Thank You for this chance to discover who You really are. I have discovered that I somehow have a wrongful understanding of Your character. I have not been able to see You as (name the character trait) towards me but believed You to be less than that. I renounce this faulty belief. Please forgive me for the things I have thought, spoken, and done that were in accord

with that faulty belief system. I choose to know You as You say You are in the Bible. Please make Yourself known to me experientially as (name the character trait). Amen.

Prayer partner speaks:

I speak forgiveness in Jesus' name to you (name of the brother/sister) for your acting, speaking, and thinking in unbelief about God's character trait of (name the character trait). Lord, I stand in agreement with (name of the brother/sister) in (his/her) request to know You as (name the character trait). Amen.

Repeat the above prayer sequence for each misunderstood character trait of God discovered in this Prayer Journal exercise.

Question sequence two—discovering damaged parental modeling

In our Prayer Journal response to the second question sequence we began to see the possibilities that some of our wrong opinions of God were influenced primarily by the character of our fathers and mothers. Where both your faulty beliefs about God and your parental modeling are similar, there is a probability that there is a connection. There are two levels of forgiveness we need to walk through to begin to know God as He is in this area of His character.

Your prayer:

Dear Heavenly Father, I come to You now in Jesus' name. I am now seeing a correlation between the damaged character of my (father and/or mother) and my faulty belief about You. I renounce any judgments that I had of my (father and/or mother) for the character trait of (name the ungodly character trait) which prevented me from knowing You as (name the character trait). I also choose to forgive my (father and/or mother) for modeling this ungodly character trait to me. Amen.

Prayer partner speaks:

> In the name of Jesus, I forgive you (name of the brother/ sister) for your confessed sin of judging your (father and/ or mother) for (his/her/their) (name the ungodly character trait). Lord Jesus, I ask that You would release any ungodly soul tie between (name of the brother/sister) and (his or her) (father and/or mother) which was established in the outworking of this parental ungodliness in the family.

> In the name of Jesus I speak forgiveness to you (name of the brother/sister) for any unforgiveness that you held in your heart towards your (father and/or mother) for their faulty modeling of God's character.

Question sequence three—stepping out of bad character

In your Prayer Journal response to the third question, you compared your character to those characteristics listed for God in the "Qualities of God the Father" table at the end of Chapter 5. In this comparison you discovered some areas of your life that were not matching God's character very well.

Earlier in the chapter we learned that God can be expected to treat us according to the way we think and behave (Psalm 18:25–26). Therefore, if we are behaving badly, it will make it difficult to see God as He is, since He may mirror our behavior, responding to us as we behave.

Our only hope then is to choose to change our ways according to His Word to be more like Him. For this we will need the help of the Holy Spirit. We will also need to repent from our ungodly ways. The prayer ministry responses to each of your discoveries about yourself are as follows.

Your prayer:

> Dear Heavenly Father, I come to You in the name of Jesus and confess my sinful behavior of (name your personal character trait that does not match God's). I choose to be more like You in this area of my life and ask that You would help me through Your Holy Spirit. I am sorry for behaving the way that I have been behaving and ask that You would forgive me. I also choose to forgive myself for this wrongful behavior. Amen.

Prayer partner speaks:

> In the name of Jesus, I speak forgiveness to you (name of the brother/sister) for your sinful behavior of (name the sinful character trait just confessed). Lord Jesus, I stand in agreement with my (brother/sister, name of the brother/sister) asking that You would help (him/her) be transformed in this area of (his/her) character by Your kind attention in their discipleship walk with You.

Chapter 6, "The Family: God's Building Block for Society"—prayer ministry

In Chapter 6 we were introduced to the concept that neglect within the family brings curse. To be free from this curse, God's law that prescribes punishment for the sin of neglect must be satisfied. Our old friends—confession, repentance, and forgiveness—will help us get out of curse. But the key to freedom is understanding what God wants from us. Neglect is simply not being diligent in carrying out our responsibilities. Let's remind ourselves of these God-specified duties studied in Chapter 4.

God has commanded us to love one another. In the context of Malachi 4:6, the love (hearts) of the children are called to be towards the parents, and the parents' (especially the father's) hearts are called to be towards the children. Neglect of this responsibility given to us by God brings curse. As Chapter 4 opened, we discovered that fathers were to be prophets, priests and kings within the family unit. They are to represent God to the family, to represent the family to God, and, finally, to help instill godly practices both within the home and going out into the community. We are called to love and care for each other, particularly within the family. When a family fails in these responsibilities, it is opened to curse. When this neglect is the cultural norm, then the curse spreads from the family level to villages, cities, and nations.

God's law stated in Malachi 4:6 provides curse for disobedience. Satan knows the spiritual command to have a heart for one another in families and he uses the law against us. In his quest for dominion, his strategy is to entice as many as possible to sin and come under the curses of the spiritual laws. When we go along with this enticement to sin, we enter into Satan's kingdom and become his slaves.

Satan, knowing God's heart and plan for families, has attacked this area of life with worldwide strategies that encompass every aspect of life and culture. In this book, we are looking primarily at the common cultural sins that arose from the influence of Freemasonry. These sins will vary from family to family depending upon circumstances and the condition of the father who was involved with this organization

Now, with understanding, we are ready to walk out from under the curse of Malachi through forgiving those who damaged us and by being covered with the shed blood of Jesus. Confession and repentance must be part of the process. Our repentance must include setting our hearts, so we can be the families that God has called us to be.

Question sequence one—dealing with neglect

In your Prayer Journal response to the first Ministry Question, you listed the activities that turned your mother's and father's hearts away from you and the family. These things resulted in their not being there for you and, in the extreme, making you an orphan either spiritually or literally. With God's help, it is time to begin to set yourself free from this neglect.

Your prayer:

> Dear Heavenly Father, I come to You in the name of Jesus and ask that You would lift off me and my family the curse that comes from parents neglecting their family. I now choose, by an act of my free will, to forgive my (father and/or mother) for the activities of (name the activities) that took them and their hearts away from me and the family. I renounce all judgment that I had of my (father and/or mother) in regard to their neglect of family. I repent from this family sin and ask that You would set me free from any ungodly soul ties between me and my parents that were established in response to the sin of neglect. Amen.

Prayer partner speaks:

> In the name of Jesus I speak forgiveness to you (name of the brother/sister) for your confessed unforgiveness towards your (father and/or mother) in regard to (his/her/their) neglect of you and the family. I release you from your judgment(s) of your (father and/or mother) in Jesus' name. I stand in agreement with my (brother/sister) and ask that you would release any ungodly soul ties that were established with (his/her) parent(s) in this sin of neglect. Lord Jesus, I now ask that You would help my (brother/sister, name of the brother/sister) to be transformed in this area of (his/her) character to be kind and attentive, particularly to their family. Amen.

Question sequence two—release from rejection and abandonment

Curse is one result from fathers (parents) neglecting their children. Another is the wounding, crushing and starvation (lack of nurture) of your human spirit. The degree to which we were deprived or rejected results in corresponding damage, both to the spirit and to the soul. Until this damage is healed, we continue to try to make others into our mother/father, seeking the affirmation, care, and nurture that we missed in our formative years. As we do this, people react negatively towards us, resulting in further rejection in our lives. This issue is a deep one that may take some time to heal, but we can initiate that healing now.

Your prayer:

> Dear Heavenly Father, I come to You in the name of Jesus and ask that You would heal me from the deep wounds of rejection that came to me through neglect, misunderstanding, and abandonment in my childhood. I don't know why I suffered (some level of) abandonment, neglect or misunderstanding by my (father and/or mother). I choose to forgive (him/her/them) for the lack of parental nurture, love and acceptance that I suffered in growing up.

Prayer partner speaks:

> In the name of Jesus I invite You, Holy Spirit, to come as the Comforter and Healer to visit (name of the brother/sister) and begin to heal (his/her) human spirit. In the name of Jesus, I speak healing and nurture into (name of the brother/sister)'s human spirit. Lord, I ask that You would come and heal the crushing rejection. [Wait and watch for the Lord to come and do the healing.]

Now, (name of the brother/sister), begin to speak out and give Jesus the pain of rejection and neglect that came through this damaged parental relationship. [Wait and watch to see what happens here—often there will be tears and other responses. Touching a hand, shoulder, and/or hugging/embracing may be appropriate here. Touching is part of the comfort and healing of "God-with-skin-on," but you need to be of the same gender so there are no mistakes about the relationship. Continue to pray and comfort as long as the Lord is doing so.]

Question sequence three—dealing with parental role deficiencies

In this question sequence we want to focus on the three primary roles for fathers: prophet, priest, and king. To the extent that these roles were missing in our father's parenting of us, we will tend to have weakness where our father had shortcomings. The ministry goals for this sequence are twofold: 1), releasing what we've held against our fathers for their not giving us what we needed, and 2), asking God to release us where we were deficient in our parenting roles of prophet, priest, and king as a father. If you are a wife and mother, guilty of not supporting your husband in these roles, ask God to release you from the sin and guilt of this position.

Your prayer:

Dear Heavenly Father, thank You for this opportunity to get free from the penalty due me for my unforgiveness and judgment towards my father for his weakness in his role as prophet, priest, and king in my family as I was growing up. By an act of my free will, I now choose to forgive my earthly father for his failure to be (specify which functions were deficient: prophet, priest, and/or king). I also now renounce any and all judgments of my father in regard to his failure to

144

be prophet, priest and king for me and our family as I was growing up. I ask that You, Lord, would separate me from any ungodly soul ties that were established between my father and me because of this. Lord Jesus, thank You for the earthly parents that You gave me. I now ask that You would restore all that was lost to me in the parenting process because of the deficiencies and damages that were present in my father and mother. Amen.

Prayer partner speaks:

In the name of Jesus, I speak forgiveness to you, (name of the brother/sister), for your confessed unforgiveness and judgment of your father in his role as your parent. Lord Jesus, I also ask that You would release any ungodly soul ties that were a result of (name of the brother/sister)'s coming under a wrong influence from (his or her) father in areas where he did not act according to God's plan and purpose as prophet, priest, and king in the family.

Now, let's look at these same areas for your personal performance as an adult where you have not, as a parent, practiced fathering in the prophet, priest, and king roles as a man, or where you as a wife have not supported your husband in these roles.

Your prayer:

Dear Heavenly Father, I come to You now in the name of Jesus in regard to my family role (of prophet, priest, and king as a father, or as a wife and mother where I did not support my husband in the roles of prophet, priest, and king). Please forgive me for my neglect and/or disobedience to Your plans for my life in the family. I am sorry for the way I have been and now choose to follow You in these assignments for my life, even at this time, no matter how old my children are. I ask that

You would come and restore to my (child/children) that which they should have received (through me and/or my husband).

Prayer partner speaks:

In the name of Jesus, I speak forgiveness to you for your neglect and/or disobedience to God's wishes that the father of the family fulfill the roles of prophet, priest and king. Lord, I ask that You would release every ungodly soul tie established between (name of the brother/sister) and (his or her) (mother/father) established in this neglect of performing as prophet, priest, and king in the nuclear family unit.

Where there are areas of personal failure to obey God's wishes for these roles to be fulfilled in the family, it would be correct to admit your failings to the affected family members and ask for forgiveness. It is never too late to take on your God given-roles in the family. Ask God to help you to begin where things are right now.

Question sequence four—turning my heart back to my parents
In this question sequence we are ministering into your life where you as a child had your heart turned away from your parents, family, and God by any of the Freemasonry youth groups: DeMolay, Rainbow Girls, and/or Job's Daughters. (For a more complete treatment of this subject, see Part II of this book, "Spiritual Prisoners—Getting Free.") In Malachi 4:6, God speaks not only about the fathers' hearts being turned away from the children, but that the children's hearts were turned away from the fathers (against God's plans and purposes). God holds us accountable for the way we treated our parents (Matthew 15:4).

Your prayer:

Dear Heavenly Father, I come to You now in the name of Jesus in regard to my heart being turned away from my parents as I was growing up. Lord, I now realize that I was affected by the Freemasonry youth groups, with the result that my heart was turned away from my father and mother, God, and my family. I am sorry for my part in this sin and I now choose to turn my heart in a godly, respectful, way towards my parents (living or dead). I forgive the leaders in these groups. Although I was misled, I ask You, Lord Jesus, to forgive me for my part in neglecting my parents and family. Amen.

Prayer partner speaks:

In the name of Jesus, I now speak forgiveness to you, (name of the brother/sister), for dishonoring your parents and your neglect of your family when you were in the Freemasonry-based youth groups. I speak forgiveness to you for any continuing disrespect of your parents through neglect of them as your heart was turned away from them. Lord Jesus, I now ask that You would release every ungodly tie between (name of the brother/sister) established in membership and participation in these Freemasonry youth groups. I particularly ask that where hands were laid on (name of the brother/sister) by leaders in these youth groups that You would set (him or her) free from every ungodly soul tie established. Amen.

PART II
Spiritual Prisoners—
Getting Free

CHAPTER 8

Prisoners

... My people go into exile [social/spiritual imprisonment away from their land of blessings] *for their lack of knowledge ....*

Isaiah 5:13 (also see Hosea 4:6)

Most people have no idea that Freemasonry makes us prisoners in life. I was among those who had it in my generation line, yet I had no idea what it was about. My maternal grandfather was in the Shriners and at the 32nd Degree of membership in Freemasonry. The following story reveals my awakening, to give you a point of departure in your personal voyage of discovery. After that, we will examine how cults and false religions work, in preparation for an objective comparison with Freemasonry.

My First Experience Ministering into Freemasonry

It was a cool spring morning in Lancashire, England. We ushered the person we were going to pray for into the large lounge of the former mayor of Liverpool's 1860s country mansion. He took a seat in one of the overstuffed wing chairs by the window. Although the mayor was long dead, and his mansion now a prayer ministry center, opulence still engulfed the room and stillness lay heavily upon us. Both the inner and outer thick oak doors were now closed, and a small sign hung outside reading, "Do Not Disturb: Counseling In Progress." We were sequestered with God. But none of the three of us were prepared for what would happen next as we sought His help.

After a few formalities and answered questions, we gave an invitation for God to come and accomplish what He wanted to do to help our new friend. We asked this person why he had come for help, and learned that he was a pastor. He was having some difficulties in his personal life, and he attributed these issues of his to having Freemasonry in his family background. In truth, back in 1991, none of us had much of an idea about Freemasonry, but somehow suspected that it might be problematic.

I was full of faith, having personally seen God do amazing, tremendous, miraculous things for people (including myself) when we invited Him to come, bringing understanding and help in time of need for affliction, oppression and sickness of all kinds. One time, when God asked me to, I had laid my hand on a hunchbacked person and merely pronounced the name of Jesus and they were instantly healed and transformed. The huge deformity somehow immediately shrank, like a balloon when you let the air out of it. Having had those kinds of experiences, I was eager to see a prayer victory in this pastor's life. But what happened next was not the miracle hoped for.

As I invited the Holy Spirit to come and help, the pastor's legs pushed out in front of him. His arms went behind him pressing into the seat cushion, and he slid down out of the chair with his knees folding upwards, like a giant articulated crab or spider, in a most undignified manner. My prayer partner and I were speechless as we watched this pastor run around the room on all fours with his bottom skimming the carpet. Every now and then he popped up in a small vertical leap as if each of his four "legs" had built-in pogo sticks. At first it was kind of comical and totally amazing as he traversed the room to and fro in some un-choreographed dance without music.

But as I watched, amusement and awe gave way to an immense wave of anger. This person was a sincere man of God who was somehow being drastically influenced by the powers of darkness to keep God from helping him. "Stop that!" I commanded the unseen spiritual agents of Satan. "You release this man in the name of Jesus!" The now somewhat terrified and totally confused pastor just collapsed in a heap on the floor as the powers of darkness released their invisible hold.

As we helped him back to his chair, questions were running rampant through our heads and we all began to earnestly seek God for answers. While we did get some direction from God that day, and managed to bring a measure of relief to the pastor, we could not completely free him because there remained hidden rights (held by the powers of darkness) to his life which we did not understand. We were thankful for the relief we could bring through the ministry of the Holy Spirit, but we still had many unanswered questions. In the end, I simply asked God to show me how to help people with Freemasonry backgrounds.

It was amazing what happened after asking God for help with Freemasonry. As I traveled to various cities and countries in ministry, without any prompting or knowledge of that amazing prayer ministry appointment, different people would spontaneously come up to me, one even as he was greeting me on arrival in an airport—and each gave me a different book detailing people's experiences with Freemasonry! The books explained something about the rituals of indoctrination into that organization. Each person just said something like this: "Here's a book about Freemasonry and I thought you needed to have it."

As I devoured the material, God began to outline a plan for bringing freedom to individuals who either were formerly Freemasons or who had this as a generational inheritance in their direct family bloodline. In a few short months, with my newly gained understanding, God had given me the outline of a ministry approach. I could now, in new effectiveness, help many that He brought to the healing ministry that I was part of. After being shared with the whole organization, this ministry outline has helped free many from the afflictions of Freemasonry. In addition, other prayer ministers have been trained to set people free.

These precious experiences we have had over the last twenty-three years, in Christian conference settings, Bible school classrooms, and in private prayer ministry over the years, have motivated me to write this book so that many others may be helped. There are so many people whom we will never meet, who need this freedom. They don't even know what it is that holds them back from the fullness of God's blessings. But there is liberation for them—a liberation generously given by God through His Son Jesus Christ.

Often as we obey God, we are surprised at the results. As we ministered, God revealed to me the inner workings of cults, false religions, and some secular fraternal organizations like the Freemasons. Through deception and misrepresentation, they use God's powerful spiritual laws to entrap and ensnare the ignorant, the unsuspecting, the damaged, and the needy. Both Christians and non-Christians alike are enticed to enter into sinful oaths, indoctrinations, and rituals.

Now it's time to take a broader look at cults and false religions in general. It will be helpful to examine, in outline form, how they function. Knowing this will give us a basic understanding of the premise of this section of the book: Freemasonry is false religion. A better understanding of the structure and principles of Freemasonry will undergird your escape from it.

Cults, False Religions, and Idolatry

THE POWER TO HOLD IN BONDAGE

Cults and false religions are web-like deceptions, presented as an organized body of ideas, ideals and concepts to a group of people. The group members, in self-deception, continually hold up before themselves these ideals and their supposed benefits. These benefits are then offered to prospective members, if they will only join the system and practice a certain lifestyle or behavior governed by the group's rules and concepts.

Much like fishing nets, the various forms of propaganda (e.g. interwoven promotional materials, presentations, and public relations materials) for these groups are dragged by Satan's minions through society to catch and hold the ignorant and unsuspecting. These schemes are designed to play upon our needs and desires while taking advantage of our ignorance; they capture and hold us in bondage through sin's power. We need understanding of these devices, as the apostle Paul wrote to the Corinthians:

> ... so that no advantage would be taken of us by Satan, for we are not ignorant of his schemes.

> 2 Corinthians 2:11

For many, the idea that there is an intelligent evil being is a concept never considered at all, or at least not taken seriously. However, the Bible is quite clear that there are schemes designed to entrap us into unintentionally serving Satan. If we are ignorant of God's laws and are not walking in holiness, without realizing it we can easily begin living according to his dictates. In our personal attempts to attain the things that God wants to freely give us, we are deceived into participating in the plans and schemes of the enemy.

The problem is that, in attempting to follow the proclaimed pathway to the promises, rewards and benefits of a cult or false religion, you must commit sin. Of course, their ideals and practices are not presented as sin. But, in following them, we are hooked into unrighteousness.

If we can be induced to sin, we will be held in bondage through the devil's lies to do his will. Amazingly, it is not Satan's power that holds us, but God's spiritual laws regarding sin. Sadly, our ignorance and state of being deceived keeps us from repenting of the sin and being set free. Idolatry, the very core of false religions and cults, has set the hook and we remain captive under the influence of the devil.

... the power of sin is the law ....

1 Corinthians 15:56

Common factors

Cults and false religions have many common characteristics. Understanding some of these characteristics will open our eyes to them in everyday life. This knowledge will facilitate bringing freedom to those in bondage without the prayer minister or counselor having to know the complete depths and details of the doctrine and practices. In Chapter 9 we will apply these concepts to Freemasonry.

Some of the basic elements cults and false religions share are:

- Idolatry, worshiping someone/something other than God (Exodus 20:3–4), brings curse.
- Personalities or principalities or goals (including human and spiritual beings) who are worshiped, referenced, reverenced or respected—gods, even Satan, self, money, security, power, safety, science, intellectualism, acceptance or prestige, world domination or world peace, to name a few.
- At the core, along with idolatry, will be mockery, things opposing God's ways and His Word (Jeremiah 10:15).

- Deception and enticement.
- Systems of support—principles, concepts, rules of behavior, doctrines, practices, rituals.
- Succession of personal agreements, pledges and oaths, ritualistic indoctrination.
- Love and care for one another is often missing or diminished from the biblical ideal, and is replaced with control, domination, and even some level of bondage or slavery to authority.

SCRIPTURAL TRUTHS REGARDING PRACTICES OF CULTS, FALSE RELIGIONS, AND IDOLATRY

- Worship of other gods (and images) brings a curse: Exodus 20:3–4; Psalm 115:4–8; Jeremiah 10:14–15.
- Idolatry-based objects (jewelry, clothing, paraphernalia, books and pamphlets) in your house or possession bring curses (Deuteronomy 7:25–26).
- Oaths, rituals, agreements, and dedications that we (or our family on our behalf) perform can have spiritual power over us, even after we leave a false religion, cult, or idolatrous situation. This curse occurs even if we ourselves were never involved, but an antecedent family member was (Galatians 6:7–8; Isaiah 65:6–7).

WHAT IS IDOLATRY, A CULT, OR FALSE RELIGION?

Idolatry

Definition: worshiping, seeking internal or external peace or favor from spirits, false gods, processes and/or procedures, substances or powers/forces; to receive, wield, or distribute:

- Power
- Health and well-being
- Information

- Prosperity (finances)
- Contact with the dead (dead loved ones).

Cults and false religions

Definition: groups of people who adhere to teachings, beliefs, and practices that have at their root a basis or platform which is idolatrous (i.e. worshiping something/someone other than the God of Abraham, Isaac and Jacob, God the Father, Jesus the Son, and the Holy Spirit, the God of the Bible). They practice some form of religion (either disguised or undisguised) other than biblical Christianity. There are several kinds of these non-Christian groups that may be studied or examined:

- Groups calling themselves Christian or masquerading as such, for example, Mormonism,[18,19,20] Jehovah's Witnesses,[21,22,23] Christian Science;[24,25]
- Groups covertly religious, but claiming something else, perhaps even asserting compatibility with Christianity, for example: Freemasonry,[26] martial arts[27] and yoga,[28] or those against Christianity, like Communism;[29]
- Groups directly opposed to Christianity, who more openly worship other gods, for example, Hinduism[30,31,32] or Islam.[33,34,35,36]

IDOLATROUS SYSTEMS—SOME PERSONAL REASONS FOR INVOLVEMENT

- Persecution and fear in despotic or false religion dominated cultures and governmental states
- Acceptance
- Social needs—friendship
- Spiritual needs
- Emotional needs
- Political or business aspirations
- Family values

- Family/cultural/social inculcation
- Unmet needs
- Search for meaning of life in general, of one's life in particular, or of the origin of life or a search for God
- Desire to better the world
- Rewards, prestige, power, control, protection
- Fear of failure, feelings of helplessness or impotence.

POWER TO HOLD IN BONDAGE

The powers holding people in bondage will be the same or similar for all idolatrous systems, cults, and false religions. They all depend upon spiritual laws, but the power behind each system is the power of sin—our disobedience to God. If these systems ensnare us, we will be induced to sin—usually without realizing it. Then two things happen: we are held captive by God's perfect justice system, and doorways opened into the spiritual realm give demonic access to our lives (see Matthew 18:34–35). The structural elements used by systems that are idolatrous at the core are as follows:

- Oaths, agreements, rituals, pledges, dedications
- Curses, generational vows, deception and enticement
- Indoctrination, inculcation, initiation, discipleship
- Jewelry, statues, images, books and literature, regalia, uniforms/apparel, medals, art objects or souvenirs with occult or idolatrous roots
- Faulty belief systems previously held or indoctrinated by the group, including deception that includes a thread of truth amid lies and/or reversal of truth, redefinition of Christian terms (e.g. in Mormonism, Jesus is Satan's brother) (Deuteronomy 32:31)
- Fear that departing from the dogma, practice, and belief system will lead to projected trouble as proclaimed by the group
- Isolation from the truth, from non-initiates, and often from family intimacy

- Domination and control—ungodly soul ties
- Successive demonization
- Fear of retribution from the group/individuals involved with the group
- Misdirected belief in attaining self-protection, exercise and peace attained through martial arts, yoga (which incorporates an intrinsic allegiance to unclean spirits), etc.[37,38]

KEYS TO FREEDOM FROM IDOLATRY, FALSE RELIGIONS, AND CULTS

Conceptually there are two keys to freedom from idolatry, cults and false religions. Accessing freedom through these keys is a process involving several steps.

The **first key** to freedom is to end the sin. As Christians, once we become aware of God's view of our present and past sinful and idolatrous activities, we can choose to stop them and renounce them (in Jesus' name) for what they are in God's eyes. We must cease from associating with the group and its practices and remove all their materials from our possession.

But there is another aspect to this. The Bible is clear that the sins of our family cannot keep us from heaven, but in many cases they will have an influence on our well-being and propensity to sin in this present life. Without renouncing these familial sins and putting them "under the blood of Jesus," there remains a generationally initiated ungodly influence in our life.

This problem (or hook) was what the pastor had in our first Freemasonry ministry case. We couldn't get him completely free since we were unaware of the systematic details of the "Freemasonry" sins in his bloodline. Of course, God can and does reveal these sins to us during prayer ministry, but with complicated systems of enslavement, there is an advantage to knowing how these things are constructed. That way, you can agree with God and undo the web of the enemy's rights in an accelerated fashion. This is particularly true for Freemasonry.

The **second key** is to get spiritually clean through the blood of Jesus and the power of His name. There will be residual spiritual problems that require prayer, usually with the help of one or more Christian friends. This involves a number of steps. Some of the things that will need to be addressed are curses, spiritual wounding of the soul and spirit, ungodly soul ties (i.e. upward with leaders, horizontally with associates, and downward if you were in a leadership position), influence from spiritual forces of darkness (which have access to your life), and damaged relationships outside of the cult or false religion (i.e. idolatrous practice).

There is no other salvation except that which is achieved by Jesus Christ (Acts 4:12). Therefore, freedom from any cult or false religion is achieved the same way (Isaiah 61:1). Of course, the procedural details of prayer ministry will differ, depending on the particular conditions of a person's or their family's involvement in the enemy's schemes. The process steps, in outline form, are as follows:

1. Belief in Jesus Christ as the only begotten Son of God as personal Savior and Lord;

2. Confession, repentance, renouncing and receiving forgiveness:

   - For all of our parents' and ancestors' participation in sinful rituals, oaths, and agreements
   - For the same things that we ourselves have done, or in which we participated. This participation includes any dedication of our lives willingly or unwillingly to gods, temples, non-Christian ideals, persons (real or imagined) and all spirits or gods aside from or in place of God the Father, Son, and Holy Spirit;

3. Prayer ministry for:

- Release from any kingdom of darkness access to our life as a result of personal or generational involvement
- Forgiving those who brought these sinful practices into our lives (including forgiving ourselves)
- Breaking all ungodly soul ties to those with whom we were involved
- Destruction of all physical materials and objects from the cult or religion
- Breaking of ungodly soul ties to those in the idolatrous group
- It is recommended that those wishing to receive this type of ministry be involved in their own personal prayer life, Bible study, worship, and discipleship through the local church. Those wishing to go forward with God and to keep their freedom would need to continue in these things.

☞ LIFE IMPACT ☜

Let's stop for a moment, catch our breath, and remind ourselves of our purpose in looking so carefully at idolatry. It has been our preparation for objectively examining the form and power of Freemasonry. In the next chapter we will apply our new understanding of idolatry to this examination. Together, these ideas and concepts will point the way to personal freedom from the residual effects of exposure to this form of idolatry.

But before we move on to Chapter 9, let's take some time to clarify the foundational ideas presented in this chapter. They are reviewed in the "Key Concepts" section located in the box at the end of the chapter.

To receive the full benefit of this chapter's study, continue in your Prayer Journal by answering the questions under the title "Key Personal Questions" in the box. These questions are designed to help you begin to use the information that you've gathered in this chapter. Again, write out each question and answer it in your journal before going on to the next.

Key Concepts from Chapter 8

Freemasonry, a form of false religion, is one of many spiritual traps designed to hold people in bondage to Satan.

We can understand more about Freemasonry's power by examining other cults, false religions, and idolatry. These deceptive schemes of the enemy are designed to appear to have some benefit to us, but they require us to sin.

It is the power of God's spiritual law that holds us in bondage; trespassing God's boundaries (commandments) places us outside the territory of blessings and into the land of curse, vulnerability, loss, and death.

Cults and false religions will have many common characteristics: idolatry, doctrine, god(s) or person(s) venerated, deception and enticement, practice and ritual, lack of love, pledges and oaths, ritualistic indoctrination.

Idolatry is worshiping, seeking internal or external peace or favor from something or someone other than God. False religion is a practice or system of idolatry. The only way to be spiritually free from cults, false religions, and idolatry is through knowing Jesus Christ as your Lord and Savior and taking the steps below.

Confession, repentance, and forgiveness of/for the specific sins that we have committed in the idolatry and false religion will begin to set us free, along with:

- Deliverance from any demonization as a result of personal or generational involvement
- Forgiving those who brought this sinful practice into our lives (including forgiving ourselves)
- Breaking all ungodly soul ties to those with whom we were involved
- Destruction of all physical materials and objects from the cult or religion
- Breaking of ungodly soul ties to those in the idolatrous group
- Personal prayer life, Bible study, worship, and discipleship through the local church.

Key Personal Questions from Chapter 8

1. Have you ever renounced Freemasonry?
2. Do you have any materials from Freemasonry in your possession? This includes items that came from your participation in Freemasonry, Job's Daughters, Rainbow Girls, Eastern Star, or DeMolay. What about things from your family's participation—things in the attic, or in a box in the garage or displayed somewhere in your home?

CHAPTER 9

Spiritual Roots of Freemasonry

Introduction

When individuals come to Christ out of a non-Christian religion like Hinduism, Islam, or Buddhism, it is necessary to renounce their false gods (idols). It is also important for them to renounce all of their dedications, indoctrination oaths, practices, and rituals.

After repentance, spiritual cleansing is necessary to remove the influence of the powers of darkness from their lives. The spiritual cleansing process is simply receiving prayer ministry from one or more Holy Spirit-baptized prayer ministers, as will be described in the next three chapters. Neglecting repentance and spiritual cleansing results in great struggles for both the new and seasoned believer alike. Omitting this process also keeps believers from understanding the Word of God and from deepening their intimacy with God Himself and maintains a barrier to being filled with the Holy Spirit. Spiritual cleansing is almost never performed for Christians with direct or inherited influences from Freemasonry.

This omission is one cause of legalism, stunted Christian growth, backsliding, and powerlessness in the church.

Freemasonry, as practiced worldwide in various forms, is more than a men's fraternal organization with auxiliaries for women and children. As we will examine later, it has all the elements of a false religion. Therefore, all who have come under its influence and/or have practiced it, either themselves or who have family members who did, will inherit the curses, and suffer under the judgment of God in their earthly lifetime (Exodus 20:3–6). Furthermore, these curses will affect future generations. But Jesus Christ, who became cursed on our behalf, offers a way to freedom. He came proclaiming liberty to captives and freedom to prisoners (Isaiah 61:1).

We need to understand just what kind of freedom from Freemasonry we can expect Jesus to bring:

- Freedom from spiritual oppression associated with the false gods worshiped
- Freedom from oaths of self-destruction taken in Freemasonry
- Freedom from sicknesses and infirmities associated with Freemasonry
- Freedom from economic failure and loss associated with the curses of Freemasonry
- Freedom from breakdown of the family
- Freedom from the physical and social damages associated with Freemasonry, and many more of the afflictions listed in Chapter 1 under the heading "Some typical symptoms suffered by Masons and their descendants."

Assessment of Freemasonry's Spiritual Impact

As we develop this chapter, we will look more closely at the implications of our and our family's participation (willingly and unwillingly) in the various aspects of Freemasonry to discover:

- The spiritual roots and power of Freemasonry as practiced worldwide;
- Its impact on our culture, our community, our country, and us (see Psalm 135:15–18).

With this understanding we will be in a position to receive:

- Release and healing from the after-effects of our experience through the name, love and power of Jesus;
- Training to help others get free just as we have been set free (see 2 Corinthians 1:4).

Repentance: The Doorway to Freedom

If Freemasonry is a false religion, our doorway to freedom is repentance. But what is the spiritual truth about Freemasonry? We cannot repent of something when we do not have a biblical understanding of its true sinful nature.

Jesus told the children of Israel that the truth would set them free, but in their ignorance they denied being enslaved or in bondage (John 8:33). Not only were the Israelites ignorant of their sin, but their sin induced dullness. It completely blocked their minds to the truth. Because of their sin, the Roman army occupied the nation; effectively, they were all slaves to Caesar. But Jesus wasn't referring to political conditions; He meant they were enslaved to sin. So it is today for many of us. We do not understand how God's Word applies to our lives. If we are to be set free, we need to truly see our present and past behavior, as well as that of our ancestors, in relation to the Scriptures.

Knowing/understanding God's Word is necessary, but we cannot get free without:
- Knowing Jesus
- Seeing our life through His eyes
- Applying the provisions of Scripture to our life

167

- Submitting our lives to Jesus and the provision of His shed blood because true freedom is only available to believers.

My people [perish] for lack of knowledge ....

Hosea 4:6

We can be "good Christians," and be zealous for God without knowledge of our slavery. We can be led into legalistic mixtures that miss God's love and righteousness in our Christian life (Romans 10:2–3; 1 Corinthians 13:3). God deals similarly with individuals, people groups, and nations.

Concepts That Lead to Freedom

Before looking deeper into the specifics of Freemasonry, let's pause for a moment of review and trim our lamps before journeying along this dark path. We need to understand our current spiritual position, resulting from our life's activities, to determine the way out of our captivity. Let's consider the following:

- Disobedience (sin) leads to trouble (Deuteronomy 28:15–68; Leviticus 26:14–39).
- We are responsible for all our words and deeds (Matthew 12:36–37; 2 Corinthians 5:10), both before and after salvation.
- The way to freedom and restoration is through confession and repentance: for personal sin, national sin, and the sin of our past generations (see Leviticus 26:40–42; 2 Chronicles 7:14; Acts 3:19; James 5:16).

Freemasonry's Spiritual Content

In this final section of Chapter 9, we are examining Freemasonry in the light of Chapter 8 to see what it establishes and propagates spiritually, and how it indoctrinates its subjects. As we look more carefully, past Masonry's publicly proclaimed good works like children's hospitals, burn centers, etc., it becomes clear that an underlying ideology exists which incorporates an idolatrous core. Although the indoctrination rituals, pledges and purposes of Freemasonry are "secret," not published publically, and the members are sworn not to divulge these secrets, many Masons who have turned away from the "Craft" have made these materials available to everyone. Surprisingly, Freemasons make vows to the false gods of ancient Egypt and other idolatrous cultures. Let's take a closer look at the core issues of Freemasonry using the terms of Chapter 8. To aid us in our evaluation, we will use Freemasonry's not-so-secret tenets, oaths, rituals, beliefs, and dogma. If Freemasonry is found to have doctrine, gods, priests, temples, worship songs, indoctrination ceremonies, and more, then it is a religion. And if it is not a Christ-centered religion, then it is a false religion incorporating idolatry.

FREEMASONRY AS A RELIGION: IDOLATRY

Doctrine

- "Every Masonic Lodge is a temple of religion; and its teachings are instruction in religion."[39] (Teachings of the 13th Degree, Holy Royal Arch)
- "Masonry ... is the universal, eternal immutable religion, such as God planted it in the heart of universal humanity. No creed has ever been long-lived that was not built on this foundation ... The ministers of this religion are all Masons who comprehend it and are devoted to it; its sacrifices to God are good works, the sacrifices of the base and disorderly passions, the offering up of self-interest on the altar of humanity, and perpetual efforts to attain to all the moral perfection of which man is capable."[40] (Teachings of the 14th Degree, Grand Elect, Perfect, and Sublime Mason)

- "Perfect truth is not attainable anywhere ... thus Masonry is a continual struggle toward the light .... Religion, to obtain currency and influence with the great mass of mankind, must needs be alloyed with such an amount of error as to place it far below the standard attainable by the higher human capacities .... The religion of the many must necessarily be more incorrect than that of the refined and reflective few ...."[41] (Teachings of the 14th Degree, Grand Elect, Perfect, and Sublime Mason)

- Masonry's Truth (light)—"We do not undervalue the importance of any Truth. We utter no word that can be deemed irreverent by any one of any faith. We do not tell the Moslem that it is only important for him to believe that there is but one God, and wholly unessential whether Mahomet was His prophet. We do not tell the Hebrew that the Messiah whom he expects was born in Bethlehem nearly two thousand years ago; and that he is a heretic because he will not so believe. And as little do we tell the sincere Christian that Jesus of Nazareth was but a man like us, or His history but the unreal revival of an older legend. To do either is beyond our jurisdiction. Masonry, of no one age, belongs to all time; of no religion, it finds its great truths in all."[42] (Teachings of the 26th Degree, Prince of Mercy or Scottish Trinitarian)

- Self-initiated good works—"The ministers of this religion are all Masons who comprehend it and are devoted to it; its sacrifices to God are **good works**, the sacrifices of the base and disorderly passions, the offering up of self-interest on the altar of humanity, and perpetual efforts to attain to all the **moral perfection** of which man is capable.[43]" (Teachings of the 14th Degree, Grand Elect, Perfect, and Sublime Mason)

- Identical to the ancient Mysteries[44] (Teachings of the 28th Degree, Knight of the Sun, or Prince Adept)

- Salvation—In Freemasonry, salvation is seen to be attained through good works and by progressing through the various degree levels. In the Royal Arch Degree, the inductee receives a "triple tau"

170

mark on the forhead indicating salvation. In this degree there is also participation in a (false) communion (which, in Chrisitianity, indicates salvation), drinking wine from a human skull. Further, the Mason is told that the way to heaven is via a ladder with the three principle rounds (rungs) being Faith, Hope and Charity; by these he may enter heaven.[45] In the 17th Degree, salvation is also viewed as an accomplishment through the shedding of your own blood.

Gods

- The Great Architect of the Universe (T.G.A.O.T.U.)—In Degrees 1–3 each Mason is encouraged to believe that this is just another name for the god that they or their family may worship.[46]
- Jah-Bul-On—"a revelation of the 'real' name of the True and Living God Most High." This name is made up of three parts: Jah, who is disclosed to be the god of the Israelites (YHWH); Bul, a god of the Syrians (an abbreviation of Baal, a Babylonian, Canaanite, and Syrian idol); and On, one of the gods of Egypt, generally believed to be an abbreviation for Osiris, god of the underworld. (In the "Royal Arch" Degree, following the 3rd Degree or given as the 13th Degree)[47]
- Ahura Mazda—a spirit of light (a nature god of Zoroastrianism, worshiped in ancient Persia with fire).
- AUM—his name is also revealed "in the sacred and mystic symbol AUM of the Hindoos."[48] "This Trilateral name for god is composed of three Sanskrit letters. The first letter A stands for the creator [Brahma]; the second letter U stands for [Vishnu] the preserver; the third letter M for [Shiva] the destroyer." This is revealed in the initiation of the Mason reaching the 32nd Degree of Freemasonry, the "Prince of the Royal Secret."[49]
- Allah—the demonic spirit worshiped by Muhammad and his father, whose name was Son of Allah. Invoked in the initiation into

the Shriners' "Ancient Arabic Order, Nobles of the Mystic Shrine," as "Allah, the god of Arab, Moslem and Mohammedan, the god of our fathers ..."[50]

- "Lucifer, the Light-bearer! Lucifer, the Son of the Morning! Strange and mysterious name to give to the Spirit of Darkness! Is it he who bears the Light, and with its splendors intolerable blinds feeble, sensual, or selfish Souls? Doubt it not!"[51] Albert Pike, Grand Commander, Sovereign Pontiff of Universal Freemasonry on July 14, 1889, reportedly, made this god of Freemasonry more clear in his "Instructions to the 23 Supreme Councils of the World." As recorded by A.C. De La Rive, *La Femme et l'Enfant dans la Franc-Maconnerie Universalle*, page 588: "Yes Lucifer is God and unfortunately Adonay is also god." Earlier in the text Pike instructed, "To you, Sovereign Grand Inspectors General, we say this, that you may repeat it to the Brethren of the 32nd, 31st, and 30th Degrees—the Masonic Religion should be by all of us initiates of the high Degrees maintained in the purity of the Luciferan Doctrine."[52,53] This direct allegiance to Satan (Lucifer, the light-bearer) is more obliquely revealed in the text of the "Royal Arch" Degree where, in "The Address of the Third Chair—the Historical Lecture," the dates before Christ are not indicated by "BC" but by "Anno Lucis," the years of light (i.e. a reversal of truth, since the world was in darkness under Satan before Christ). There are references to bogus "Lodges" that were opened in biblical times with the dates being given in years, Anno Lucis.

Priests

- Worshipful Master who spiritually presides over the local Freemasonry temple;
- Each Mason a priest—"Masonry ... is the universal, eternal immutable religion, such as God planted it in the heart of universal

humanity. No creed has ever been long-lived that was not built on this foundation .... The **ministers of this religion are all Masons** who comprehend it and are devoted to it; its sacrifices to God are good works, the sacrifices of the base and disorderly passions, the offering up of self-interest on the altar of humanity, and perpetual efforts to attain to all the moral perfection of which man is capable."[54] (Teachings of the 14th Degree, Grand Elect, Perfect, and Sublime Mason)

Temples

- The Freemasonry Grand Lodges and local temples (lodges) around the world[55]

Hymns and worship songs

- *The Magic Flute* by Mozart
- Many Freemasonry songs, largely acknowledging brotherhood, bringing homage to their gods, ambiguously sounding like acknowledgments of the God of Abraham, Isaac and Jacob.

OATHS AND RITUALS OF INDOCTRINATION[56,57,58]

1st Degree of Indoctrination: Entered Apprentice

- Oath: "To protect secrets of the Lodge—binding myself under no less penalty than that of having my throat cut from ear to ear, my tongue torn out by its roots, and buried in the sands of the sea a cable's length from shore, where the tide ebbs and flows twice in twenty-four hours; if I should ever willingly knowingly or unlawfully violate this my Entered Apprentice oath. So help me God and keep me steadfast."
- Ritual: Candidate may dress in his clothes or special Lodge-provided pajamas. The left breast is naked, the right sleeve is

rolled up, the left trouser leg rolled up and a slipper is on the left foot. He is "hoodwinked" (blindfolded) and a blue "cable tow" (rope noose) is put around the neck. The initiate is led into the Lodge, his left breast is jabbed (often painfully) with a large ceremonial compass (point) and he is moved around the room answering various preset questions. He finally kneels at a Freemasonry altar, in an occult pose, and takes the oath with his hand on a Masonic Bible, finally sealing that by kissing the Bible. He is given a secret handshake and password "BOAZ" to identify himself to other Masons. He also receives a Mason's lambskin apron.

2nd Degree of Indoctrination: Fellow Craft

- Oath: "binding myself under no less a penalty than that of having my left breast torn open, my heart plucked out and given to the beasts of the field and fowls of the air as a prey" rather than knowingly or willingly violate the tenets of the complete oath.
- Ritual: The inductee will be attired similarly to the 1st Degree with the exception (varies from country to country) that the right breast may be uncovered and the opposite arm and leg may be exposed with the slipper on the other foot as compared to the 1st Degree. The rope may be put around the bare arm. In some countries, at entrance to the Lodge, a metal mason's square may be used to press (with its corner) into the right breast. As in the 1st Degree the candidate is led around blind and makes various responses to set questions. He also makes various special steps and kneels at the Freemasonry altar to make his pledges and oaths, sealing them by kissing the Masonic Bible. He receives another secret handshake procedure and is given a secret identification word, "JACHIN" as well as a Lodge password for entry, "SHIBBOLETH," and a Fellow Craft apron.

3rd Degree of Indoctrination: Master Mason[59]

- Oath: "that of having my body severed in twain, my bowels taken out and burned to ashes, the ashes scattered to the four winds of heaven that there should be no more remembrance among men and Masons forever of so vile a wretch as I should be, should I ever knowingly or wittingly violate or transgress this my solemn and binding Master Mason's obligation. So help me God and keep me steadfast."

- Ritual: In this ritual, both arms, both breasts, and both knees are made bare and both feet are either bare or shod in slippers (slipshod). In some locations the cable tow is wound around the initiate's body several times. He is blindfolded and, again, entered into the Lodge by the points of the compass being pressed into his breasts simultaneously. He is then led around the Lodge with various set questions, answers, and ritual steps, including kneeling at appropriate places in the ritual before the altar, and this time taking oaths with both hands on the Masonic Bible. In an indoctrination drama, there is also a mock murder of the candidate in which he is struck on the head and buried, in some lodges only symbolically, however; some use a special grave pit and even a coffin. He is raised from the dead by the Lodge's Worshipful Master. The candidate receives the Master Mason apron (or has the Fellow Craft apron fitted out), and also receives a new identifying "grip," a password, "TUBAL-CAIN," and an identification phrase variously reported as "MACHABEN" (or "MACHBINNA") and, in the USA, as "MAH-HAH-BONE."

13th Degree of Indoctrination usually given following the 3rd Degree: The Holy Royal Arch of Enoch, Jerusalem or Solomon[60]

- Oath: "[under no less penalty, on the violation of any of them, than that of suffering loss of life by having my head struck off].

So help me the True and Living God Most High, and keep me steadfast in this ...."

- Ritual: The candidate enters the Lodge blindfolded and clothed in the regalia of the Master Mason. He enters into an acted-out play using Masonic tools, receives instruction and kneels to receive the "benefit of Masonic prayer." He kneels and bows before the altar and sacred shrine. He is given a new pass word, "AMMI RUHAMAH," and receives special distinguishing badges on his white ceremonial robe in the play.

POSSIBLE SYMPTOMS FROM MASONIC INVOLVEMENT (see Chapter 1 for more symptoms)

In life:

- Sickness, illness, infirmity: headaches (migraine) or tight bands around head and particularly at the forehead, throat problems, bowel problems, heart problems, head or neck problems, allergies
- Accident
- Deaths
- Poverty and financial difficulties
- Spiritual blockages to growth in Christianity.

In prayer ministry:

- Head falls to one side as if person hung by neck (1st Degree symptom)
- Pain at left and/or right breast (1st, 2nd, 3rd Degree symptoms)
- Pain in heart (2nd Degree symptom)
- Frozen body and countenance—spirit of idolatry (Psalm 115:4–8)
- Laughing and derision; spirit of mockery (Jeremiah 10:14–15)
- Mental confusion
- All-seeing "third eye" in forehead
- Doubt and unbelief (skepticism).

CONTROL OF MIND, WILL, AND EMOTIONS

- Mind: rewarded for thinking about issues that are permissible and Lodge-related, and rebuked for new thoughts or ideas outside of the official Freemasonry ideology and dogma; for example, no prayers to Jesus, no worship to Jesus;
- Will: rewarded when bent to the will, plans, and purposes of Freemasonry;
- Emotions: rewarded for controlling them in indoctrination rituals.

FREEMASONRY MATERIALS

Jewelry, clothing/uniforms/regalia, books and literature, certificates, badges, emblems, aprons, hats, shoes, sashes, scarves, swords, photographs, Masonic artifacts and remembrances of our or a relative's participation in Freemasonry, i.e. all physical materials belonging to Freemasonry that may be in our possession.

In Deuteronomy 7:25–26 we are informed that these things in our possession or household will bring a curse on the whole house/family dwelling therein.

The Promise of Freedom

In the next chapter we will outline the way to freedom through confession and repentance of the sins of Freemasonry in which we or our family participated. Model prayers are provided, but before we pray through to freedom, it is important for us to have an understanding of our spiritual inheritance and personal condition.

❧ LIFE IMPACT ❧

This marks the end of the instructional material specific to those who have a history of exposure to Freemasonry, either personally or generationally. In the next chapter, we will begin our prayerful walk out of the spiritual effects of Freemasonry.

Before we move on to Chapter 10, let's take some time to clarify the core ideas presented in this chapter. They are reviewed in the "Key Concepts" section located in the box at the end of the chapter.

To receive the full benefit of this chapter's study, continue in your Prayer Journal by answering the questions under the title "Key Personal Questions" in the box. These questions are designed to prepare you for the prayer ministry in Chapter 10. Again, take some time to ask the Lord to help you and then write out each question and answer it in your journal before going on to the next.

Key Concepts from Chapter 9

Freemasonry incorporates idolatry that has the form and function of a false religion, including:

- Doctrine, gods, priests, temples, hymns and worship songs, oaths and rituals
- Spiritual control of the mind, will, and emotions
- Participation (willingly or unwillingly) in a false religion incorporates systematic idolatry, which always brings curses upon the individuals and people groups who practice these things. (See "Spiritual Laws—the Keys to Freedom and Happiness" in Chapter 2, and Appendix IV, "Idolatry"). The spiritual law concerning idolatry is incorporated into the first two of the Ten Commandments.
- The oaths, rituals, and indoctrinations in which you and/or your family participated have spiritual power over your earthly life until you confess, renounce, and repent of these sinful practices.

- The oaths of DeMolay, Rainbow Girls, and Job's Daughters endorse and bind you into the sins of Freemasonry (e.g. murder, terror).
- You are also under spiritual influence from the sins in which your ancestors participated in Freemasonry.

Note: The practice of Freemasonry varies from Lodge to Lodge and between the various states, provinces, and countries. Therefore, some practices and degrees may be unfamiliar or slightly different than those to which you have been exposed.

Key Personal Questions from Chapter 9

1. To what degree of indoctrination in Freemasonry did you participate?
2. To what degree of indoctrination in Freemasonry did your antecedents belong?
3. What certificates, membership books and identity cards, or idolatrous (and antichrist) Freemasonry materials do you have in your possession (e.g. lambskin aprons, badges, jewelry, etc.)? Burn them!

CHAPTER 10

Stepping into Prayer Ministry for Removing the Residual Effects of Freemasonry

Introduction

In this chapter we are making a transition from information gathering to stepping into the freedom that the Holy Spirit longs for you to have. It has been quite a journey. We're moving into payoff land, so hang in there. If there had been a simpler path to freedom, we would have taken it. But, while straightforward in concept, the details are a bit more complicated than we would wish: Jesus said, "You will know the truth and the truth will set you free." The problem is we need to apply God's truth to a detailed problem, one piece at a time. In Chapters 11 and 12 you will be thankful for the ministry guidelines that are like a spiritual map or GPS to keep you on track.

Albert Pike, the author of *Morals and Dogma*, the Freemason's fundamental guidebook, was first and foremost an occultist. Through his standardized indoctrination rituals for masonry, founded in his text, Pike is personally responsible for opening countless lives around the planet to the influence of dark spiritual powers. To do this he required Freemasonry's initiates, for each Degree of acceptance, to swear allegiance to various false gods, pronounce self-curses for any default on their promises of allegiance to the brotherhood, wear clothing, jewelry, and regalia dedicated to these practices, and pay money for the privilege of these spiritual defilements. Why did he cause all this trouble? No one knows for sure and we all make choices, but on the surface, it seems like somehow his mama and papa didn't raise him right.

In the light of the last two chapters, what Albert did wasn't really all that clever: induce someone to sin and they are open to trouble in their life. It's like a kid learning how to make a knot and then covertly tying someone's shoelaces together. Albert tied our shoelaces together with knots for each Freemasonry Degree. Then, when we try to walk with God, we fall on our faces rather than receive His blessings. In growing up, when some kid tied our laces together, we learned to untie the knots and go on with life. In the next three chapters, we are going to untie Albert's Freemasonry knots to set you free. What he did was intentional, but Jesus is bigger than that, and in Him so are we. But first a little preparation.

For those of you who have read and gone through all the exercises and prayers in Chapters 1–7, please feel free to skip the next section, "First Ministry Preparation Steps," and go to the following section, "Closing the Door to Sin and Receiving Cleansing." If you have not completed the first half of this book, please know that release from Freemasonry is only attainable by Christians and will be facilitated by water baptism, baptism in the Holy Spirit, and a verbal, heartfelt allegiance to Jesus in all areas of your life (see the Lordship Prayer). To that end, we have repeated some of the material from Chapter 7 for those who may need one or more of these steps before proceeding into the prayer ministry to remove Freemasonry from your life. Please feel free to skip those areas in which you are already prepared.

For some, the presence of Freemasonry in your life may have prevented your baptism in the Holy Spirit, but don't worry; God will help you anyway. For some Christians, the denominational beliefs of your stream of Christianity may not support water baptism and/or baptism in the Holy Spirit, but these beliefs should not prevent you from obtaining the release from Freemasonry that you are seeking. (Please see Appendix I for a further discussion of baptism in water and the Holy Spirit.)

First Ministry Preparation Steps

There are five major steps that we need to take in order to escape from the effects of sin and enter into the blessings of God:

- Receive Jesus and His atoning death for our sins (Appendix I, Sections 1 and 2).
- Make Jesus Lord over every area of our lives (Appendix I, Section 3).
- Be baptized in water and the Holy Spirit (Appendix I, Section 4).
- Bring our individual past sins before the Lord in confession and repentance, and receive forgiveness in the name of Jesus (Appendix II, Sections 6 and 7).
- Remove all demonic influences and bondages that used our sin and our family's sin as a right to trouble our lives (Appendix VI, Sections 3.4, 3.5, 5.1, and 5.2).

These steps were presented in Chapters 1–7, but are addressed again below.

STEPPING INTO GOD'S BLESSINGS

Power in the process

The process of stepping into God's blessings begins with drawing near to Him and joining His family through Jesus' sacrifice on the cross. Many of you who are reading this may already know Jesus as Savior and be advanced in your walk with God; for others this may not be the case. In prayer, let's now begin our journey towards God and His freedom. (If the Lord leads you to skip over some of the first steps because you've done them already, that's fine.)

Prayer is talking to God and involving ourselves with Him in the process. Without directing ourselves to God in this chapter, all these steps will be without His power to rescue us. They would be a meaningless exercise!

Foundational steps

Salvation

If you wish to know God and walk in His goodness, please pray the Salvation Prayer provided in the box on the next page (from Appendix I). It is important that you speak out this prayer declaration with your mouth (or if you can't speak, to write it out). If at all possible, you should have a person witness your declaration to God. In this and the next two chapters, your witness and prayer helper, whom we are calling a "prayer partner," will be an invaluable aid. See Appendix I, Sections 1 and 2, for a more detailed explanation of salvation.

Lordship

If we are to walk out of the effects of our past sins and continue on to enter the behavioral land of God's blessings, we will need help. We need God to be Commander and Chief over all that we think and do. We do not know the way, nor do we know how to walk. We need someone to guide, direct, protect, and lead us. We need Jesus in the position of Lord (*Adonai* or Master) over our life. Of course, when we receive Jesus as our Savior, God becomes our Father, but we need to acknowledge His total Lordship. To be successful in our Christian walk, we need to bring our whole soul and body (Appendix I,

Salvation Prayer

If you have come to a belief in Jesus Christ as Lord and Savior, the next step is to use these salvation keys to acknowledge your belief in audible testimony and prayer. Enter the doorway to salvation by praying the following model prayer aloud:

Dear Heavenly Father, I come to You now in the name of Your only begotten Son, Jesus.

- I acknowledge that I have not known You and have not lived my life according to Your righteous ways. Therefore, I have been headed on a course away from You and towards hell.
- I ask that You would forgive me for my sinful ways.
- I choose to change my ways and live my life according to Your ways.
- I confess today that Jesus is God and choose to make Him my Lord.
- I gratefully accept the work Jesus did in suffering the penalty of my sins in His body and dying on the cross, that I might live.
- I believe that You, Heavenly Father, raised Jesus from the dead.
- I ask that You would receive me now as Your child, through the precious blood that Jesus shed for me.
- I ask that You would reveal Yourself to me further, and that you would strengthen me to be able to walk in Your ways, Amen.

Sections 3 and 8) under His direction. See Appendix I sections for further explanation.

The model prayer provided in the box on the next page will help you enter into submission to the Lordship of Jesus. If at all possible,

Lordship Prayer

Lord Jesus, I acknowledge my need of You and I accept You as my Savior, my Redeemer, my Lord, and my Deliverer.

I invite You to be Lord of my whole life:

- Over my spirit—my prayers, my worship, my spiritual understanding, my creativity, and my conscience
- Over my mind—my thoughts, my memories, my dreams
- Over my emotions—my feelings and emotional expressions and responses
- Over my will—all my decisions and purposing.

I invite You to be Lord over my body:

- Over my eyes: all that I look at and over every look that I give outward
- Over my ears and all that I listen to
- Over my nose and all that comes into it
- Over my mouth and all that goes into it and every word that comes out of it
- Over my sexuality
- Over all my physical activities.

I invite You to be Lord over all my relationships: past, present, and future.

I invite You to be Lord over my resources: time, energy, finance, property, and all that I have.

I invite You to be Lord over the time and manner of my death.

Come, Lord Jesus, and take Your rightful place in all the areas of my life.

Thank You that Your blood was shed that I might be set free from the influence of selfishness and Satan.

Amen.

when you pray this prayer to God have a person witness your declaration. You need to give audible assent to God. If for some reason you cannot physically speak, a written declaration in your own handwriting will also work.

Baptism

The Kingdom of God overcomes the kingdom of darkness. Our personal troubles originate in the kingdom of darkness. If we are to overcome our earthly troubles, we ourselves need to enter the Kingdom of God, i.e. enter into God's light.

In John 3:5 Jesus tells us to be baptized in both water and the Spirit for entry into the Kingdom of God. The Bible does not say that we need baptism to know God or receive a healing or deliverance from bondage. Nor does it say we must be baptized in order to go to heaven. However, to enjoy a continuing experience of God's presence (His Kingdom manifestation here on earth), being baptized in water and Spirit increases our availability to Him. If we are going to operate in His spiritual gifts, the baptisms are God-recommended (see Appendix I, Section 4). In Matthew 28:19, Jesus commands us to baptize all of our disciples (the converts whom we are training). This means every Christian is to be baptized.

Water Baptism

Our progress in and towards God is aided by being water-baptized in the name of the Father, the Son, and the Holy Spirit. This procedure is to be done by immersion (see Appendix I for a discussion of the original Greek word, *baptizo*), wherein we are put completely under the water. We do not baptize ourselves; another baptized Christian must baptize us.

Frequently the local church will be present and a pastor or elder will administer this sacrament to us. The biblical record shows that baptism was performed by those who had given their lives completely to God and were operating as His representatives (see Ephesians 4:11–12; Romans 12:6–8; 1 Corinthians 12:4–11). Those helping Jesus equip new converts are recognized as qualified to baptize others. If you have not yet been baptized in water, and you are in or near a local church, please ask them to perform this sacrament for you. In an area where there is no church, then a qualified servant of God, e.g., evangelist, local believer who led you to the Lord, etc., should be asked.

Baptism in the Holy Spirit

The next step following water baptism is baptism in the Holy Spirit. Sometimes God does this baptism for us where and when He wishes, all by Himself. (One of our friends was baptized in the Holy Spirit while riding public transportation going to work. I was baptized in the Holy Spirit while sitting in church during my first visit to a charismatic service.) Sometimes it happens immediately following water baptism, even as the person arises from the water. Another way is for someone already baptized in the Holy Spirit to "lay hands" upon us and invite Jesus to baptize us in the Holy Spirit. Often, we will begin to speak with the gift of tongues as the Holy Spirit comes upon us in power, but this is only one of the gifts listed in 1 Corinthians 12 that God may be bestowing on us through this baptism.

Baptism in the Holy Spirit is often a strong experience. It is not something that will go unnoticed, where we will need to exercise our faith to believe, or "claim it" after someone has ministered to us. If we did not have a notable, supernatural experience with God, we are not yet baptized in the Holy Spirit. In much the same way, if your body did not go under the waters of baptism (all at once, becoming submerged and wet) you were not baptized in water—you may have been christened or dedicated to Jesus, but not yet have had the full sacrament that Jesus commanded in Matthew 28.

Closing the Door to Sin and Receiving Cleansing

In the next section we will begin our first Freemasonry-specific prayer ministry, where we begin to close the doors that Albert Pike assisted us and our families to open. The process of closing the door to sin is addressed in Appendix II, Sections 6 and 7. God has provided the way out of our sins through confession of our sins, one to another. We repent from each of these sins individually and on behalf of our family. We then receive forgiveness through the shed blood of Jesus. This procedure removes the rights of the enemy to bring punishment upon us. We may also need to command the tormenting enemy and his influences to leave our life, once we have prayed through this process (see Appendix VI, Sections 3, 4, and 5).

Before we go into the next section, we need to conceptually understand how we, as a human being, function:

- We all have a physical body, but we also have two, non-physical parts to our life: a human soul and a human spirit.
- For the purposes of this chapter we are giving attention to the soul, which influences our outward expression and what we do in and with our earthly body.
- The soul has several functions operating together which operate the human body.

The three main influence areas in the soul are:

- The **mind** (not the brain) which thinks, remembers, and volitionally controls what the body does
- The **will,** where we decide and purpose what the body will do
- The **emotions**, where we process and initiate expression of our feelings.

These three areas of the soul inseparably influence everything we do. Both our past experiences and choices, and the influences of the spiritual realm on our soul, affect how we function in life. Godly influence comes through our human spirit. Ungodly influence comes into our soul through the doorways of our own past and through the ungodly behavior of our ancestors. With this understanding, we can begin cleansing each area of influence in our soul from the effects of Freemasonry.

GENERAL PRAYER MINISTRY FOR THE RESIDUAL EFFECTS OF FREEMASONRY

Prayer sequence—clearing the soul

In Chapter 9 we learned that we and/or our family members willingly or unwillingly submitted our soul (mind, will and emotions) to the purposes of Freemasonry. This territory is the battleground that we must take back. We and/or our family have subjected ourselves (bowed down) to the organization in matters that are ultimately spiritual, as we saw in the last chapter. Some amount of slavery results.

A slave to sin, no matter how slight the bondage, will have trouble following the Lord's plan for his or her life. Here is how we became slaves in our souls:

1. If we did not train our minds to respond to the "truths" of Freemasonry, we could not succeed as members. Therefore, we had to reason and parrot back the dogma and doctrine we were fed. We were taught what kinds of thoughts were acceptable within the Freemasonry framework.
2. If we did not bend our will to obey the organization, we faced personal loss of privileges.
3. In order not to lose status or approval, we dared not display our negative emotions, particularly in the highly stressful indoctrination rituals.

Our minds, in particular, need to be released from the grip of the organization since our mind is the primary pathway of Freemasonry into our life. Let's now begin to stop these influences on our soul.

Your prayer for removal of mind control:

> Dear Heavenly Father, I come to You in the name of Jesus. I repent for (my and/or my father's and mother's family) submitting (my/our) mind(s) to the lies, curses, and thinking processes of the Freemasonry organization. I forgive my family for opening this spiritual doorway into my life. I now renounce Freemasonry, its false light, morals and dogma and confess it was sin to train the mind to come under control of this organization. We should have been using the reasoning power that you planted in us at conception. I now choose to use my mind as You intended. Please forgive me. I repent for this same sinful practice in my father's and mother's family. I claim the shed blood of Jesus between me and the generational effects of mind control.

Prayer partner speaks:

> In the name of Jesus, I speak forgiveness for any of your sins of submitting your mind and thought processes to the idolatrous, deceptive, Freemasonry practices. Lord, I stand in agreement with (name of the brother/sister), and claim the blood of Jesus between (him/her) and any of these same sinful practices in (his/her) mother's and father's family. In the name of Jesus, I bind up the generational spirits of mind control that came down (name of the brother/sister)'s bloodlines. I also bind up all the spirits of mind control that came in with any of (name of the brother/sister)'s

practice of submitting (his/her) mind to the purposes of Freemasonry.

Now, in the name of Jesus, I command the generational witchcraft spirits of mind control and confusion to release and leave (name of the brother/sister)'s mind. [Wait a moment for God to do this. Check with the Holy Spirit to be sure that all deliverance that was necessary has taken place.]

Your prayer for freedom of the will:

Dear Heavenly Father, I come to You in the name of Jesus. I repent for my and/or my father's and mother's family submitting our will and choices to the intimidation and control of the Freemasonry local lodge, (state/provincial) Grand Lodge and international organization. I now renounce this practice and confess it as sin, training my will to come under the control of Freemasonry instead of submitting it to the conscience that you planted in me at conception. I now choose to use my will as You intended and to submit my future choices to Your will. Please forgive me. I repent for this same sinful practice for any of my father's and mother's family. I forgive any of my family members who opened these spiritual doorways of domination and control into my life. I claim the shed blood of Jesus between me and the generational effects of domination and control over my will.

Prayer partner speaks:

In the name of Jesus, I speak forgiveness for any of your sins of submitting your will and choices to the idolatrous, deceptive, controlling Freemasonry system. I stand in agreement with you, (name of the brother/sister), in claiming the blood of Jesus between you and these same sinful practices of any of your mother's and father's family. In the name of Jesus, I bind up the generational witchcraft spirits of domination and control that came down (name of the brother/sister)'s bloodlines. I also bind up all the witchcraft spirits of domination and control that came in with any of (name of the brother/sister)'s practice of submitting (his/her) choices and decisions to the will of the Freemasonry organization.

Now, in the name of Jesus, I command the generational witchcraft spirits of domination and control, indecision and fear of making decisions, to leave (name of the brother/sister)'s will. [Wait a moment for God to cause them to go. Check with the Holy Spirit to be sure that all spiritual release that was necessary has taken place.]

Now, in the name of Jesus, I command the witchcraft spirits of domination and control to which he/she submitted and the spirits of indecision and fear of making decisions, to release and leave (name of the brother/sister)'s will. [Wait a moment for God to cause them to go. Check with the Holy Spirit to be sure that all spiritual release that was necessary has taken place.]

Your prayer for freedom of the emotions:

Dear Heavenly Father, I come to You in the name of Jesus. I repent for (my and/or my father's and mother's family) suppressing the emotions that You gave (me and/or us). I confess that (I and/or we) substituted learned, false, emotional responses for (my/our) true feelings, particularly during the indoctrination ceremonies. To be accepted and gain what they offered, (I and/or we) submitted (my/our) emotional expression to the will, intimidation and control of the Freemasonry lodge/organization. I now renounce this practice and confess it as sin to deceptively suppress or display/express false emotions under the control of Freemasonry.

I now choose to express my true feelings as You intended, to develop, build, and strengthen godly relationships. I submit my future emotional expression to Your will and ways. Please forgive me. I repent for this same sinful practice in any of my father's and mother's family. I forgive my family members who opened the spiritual doorways of emotional control into my life. I claim the shed blood of Jesus between me and the generational effects of both suppressing emotions and expressing false emotions.

Prayer partner speaks:

In the name of Jesus, I speak forgiveness for any of your sins of submitting your emotions and their expression to the idolatrous, deceptive, controlling Freemasonry system. I stand in agreement with you, (name of the brother/sister), in claiming the blood of Jesus between you and these same sinful practices in any of your mother's and father's family. In the name of Jesus, I bind up the generational witchcraft spirits of domination and control that came down (name of the brother/sister)'s bloodlines. I also bind up all the witchcraft spirits of domination and control that came in with any of (name of the brother/sister)'s practice of suppressing and/ or denying (his/her) emotions and expressing false emotions, as required for acceptance in the Lodge and Freemasonry organization.

Now, in the name of Jesus, I command the generational witchcraft spirits of domination and control and emotional confusion to release and leave (name of the brother/sister)'s emotions. [Wait a moment for God to cause them to go. Check with the Holy Spirit to be sure that all deliverance that was necessary has taken place.]

Finally, I ask the Holy Spirit to come; clean, fill, and seal (name of the brother/sister) from the effect of the sins committed in submitting (his/ her) mind, will, and emotions to the Freemasonry organization and from the spirits that were involved.

CHAPTER 11

Release from Freemasonry for the First Four Degrees

Residual Spiritual Oppression

INTRODUCTION

In this chapter we will begin to step out from the specific bondages of Freemasonry that we examined in Chapters 8 and 9. In those chapters, we discovered that Freemasonry involves idolatry and that it incorporates many other sinful practices and ideologies. If we, or our family, participated in these practices and ideologies, then these sins are also our sins—they are still affecting us. Just as we discovered in Chapter 7, "Praying Our Way to Freedom," the process involves getting things right with God through confession, repentance and forgiveness. If we want to be free from the results of our past activities, we must consider how these activities put us in conflict with God and His ways. They separate us from God. Now let's see how we may get things right with God in order to enter the land of blessings.

In this chapter we will be only addressing the first four levels of indoctrination into Freemasonry, as most Masons never progress into the higher Degrees. For those whose personal involvement or that of their antecedents goes further, you will find prayers of release in Chapter 12, "Release from Freemasonry for Degrees beyond Master Mason."

As you read on, you will first learn how to set Christians free from the dark spiritual oppression of Freemasonry. Then you will be led through a series of specific prayer sequences to begin receiving your own freedom. Although some of the practices, oaths, rituals and indoctrinations vary across the nations, the bondages induced are similar. As in all prayer ministries, it is important to invite the Holy Spirit into the process. Listen to the Holy Spirit and let Him guide you into all truth and freedom.

Before we begin prayer ministry, let's examine a list of spiritual strongholds we have encountered over the years when helping individuals be released from Freemasonry. These strongholds are ones which typically are present as a result of personal and generational involvement with Freemasonry:

- Domination and control (witchcraft)
- Deceptions/Lies
- Fear
- Betrayal/Distrust
- Idolatry
- Murder
- Rebellion
- Accident and injury
- Division
- Anti-Christ
- Mockery
- Suspicion
- Death—emotional
- Death—initiative (will)
- Death—thinking (mind)
- Physical death and infirmity

CONCEPTUAL SUMMARY OF MINISTRY PROCEDURE

The personal prayer ministry in this chapter is not recommended without having first worked through the ministry elements of

Chapter 7. This is a ministry only for Christians. There must be a previous prayerful, serious commitment of your whole life to Jesus, including specific, willing, and in-depth prayer dedication of your mind, will, emotions, body, sexuality etc. (see Appendix I).

Let's now review the general prayer ministry form we will use to remove the residual bondages of Freemasonry. Notice that we advise you to have at least one (two or more would be better) Holy Spirit-baptized Christian prayer partners to assist you in the ministry. Please see Appendix I, Sections 4.4–4.5, for their recommended qualifications. First you will pray. Then your prayer partner will respond to help you get free, healed and cleansed.

The Prayer Ministry

OUR ROLE

- Confessing the sins of self, family, and making verbal assent: owning what we and/or our family did and participated in, with our hearts, mouths, and bodies;
- Agreeing with what God's Word says about what we and/or our family did and what that made us (e.g. murderer, liar, thief, adulterer, idolater);
- Repenting, by deciding in our hearts and declaring verbally that we will turn from the confessed areas of sin; telling God we are sorry for our own behavior and that of our family;
- Forgiveness—releasing from guilt, condemnation, judgment etc:
  - Forgiving those who led us into these sins
  - Forgiving our family members who opened these spiritual doorways into our lives
  - Forgiving ourselves for making these mistakes
  - Asking God to forgive us for the personal wrongdoings we've confessed.

OUR PRAYER PARTNER'S ROLE

- Speaking forgiveness in Jesus' name for the sins confessed and repented of;

- Commanding the various spirits, one group or kind/type at a time, to leave you;

- Asking the Lord to fill you with His Holy Spirit and to seal the work and doorways that were opened by the sins;

- Leading in thanks, praise, and worship of Jesus who came to set the captives free!

Detailed Prayer Ministry for the Residual Effects of Freemasonry

PRAYER SEQUENCE—THE IDOLATRY OF FREEMASONRY

Your prayer:

> Dear Heavenly Father, I come to You in the name of Jesus and ask You to lift the curses off me and my family that came from our participation in the Freemasonry system. I now choose, by an act of my free will, to renounce Freemasonry as an idolatrous system, having the form of a false religion. I confess it as sin and turn from its practices. I repent for my participation and that of any of my father's and mother's family participation and I forgive them for opening my life up to the consequences of their sins.

> I claim the shed blood of Jesus between me and those sins of idolatry in Freemasonry that have come down my family line. Heavenly Father, I claim the shed blood of Jesus over my sin of idolatry in Freemasonry and ask that You forgive me for these sins.

Prayer partner speaks:

In the name of Jesus, I speak forgiveness for any of your sins of idolatry in Freemasonry and I stand in agreement with you, (name of the brother/sister), in claiming the blood of Jesus between you and Freemasonry's idolatry in any of your mother's and father's family. In the name of Jesus, I bind up the generational spirits of idolatry that came down (name of the brother/sister)'s bloodline. I also bind up all the spirits of idolatry that came in with (name of the brother/sister)'s practice of Freemasonry.

Your prayer:

In the name of Jesus, I now renounce all the gods of Freemasonry. Heavenly Father, please forgive me and/or my family for putting these idols above You. I forgive my family members who opened me up to the influence of these false gods. I claim the blood of Jesus between me and these idols and I command every spirit behind them to leave me in the name of Jesus. I specifically renounce:

- The Great Architect of the Universe (T.G.A.O.T.U.)
- Jah-Bul-On the trilateral god—the false Jehovah, Baal, and Osiris
- Ahura-Mazda
- AUM, of the Hindus—A, the false creator god, Brahma; U, the false preserver god, Vishnu; M, the false destroyer god, Shiva
- Allah—the spirit worshiped by Muhammad.

Prayer partner speaks:

In the name of Jesus, I speak forgiveness to you for your and your family's sin of idolatry, for putting these idols of Freemasonry above or in place of God, and I stand in agreement with you, (name of the brother/sister), in claiming the blood of Jesus between yourself and the false gods of Freemasonry. In the name of Jesus, I bind up idolatry and mockery and the spirits behind these false gods and command them to release and leave (name of the brother/sister). T.G.A.T.O.U., leave; Jah-Bul-On, leave; Ahura Mazda, leave; AUM—Brahma, Vishnu, and Shiva—leave; Allah, leave. [Wait a moment after commanding each of these spirits for God to cause them to leave. Check with the Holy Spirit to be sure that all deliverance that was necessary at this stage has taken place.]

[The Holy Spirit may have you order these spirits out specifically by name, for each Degree where they were first named (see Appendix VI, "Deliverance Ministry"). For example, "In the name of Jesus, I command the spirit of 'The Great Architect of the Universe' to leave (name of the brother/sister)." Again, wait a moment for God to cause them to go. Check with the Holy Spirit to be sure that all deliverance that was necessary has taken place.]

[Finally speak] I ask You, Holy Spirit, to come; clean, fill, and seal (name of the brother/sister) from the effect of these sins and from the spirits behind them.

Please remember to thank Jesus for His release and healing in these matters.

PRAYER SEQUENCE—THE DOCTRINES OF FREEMASONRY'S BLUE LODGE (Degrees 1–3)

Your prayer:

In the name of Jesus, I renounce and repent of the ungodly false doctrines of Freemasonry. I claim the shed blood of Jesus between (me and my sins and/or my family's sins) of agreement with these doctrines. I forgive my family members who opened me up to these influences. Please forgive me, Father, and set me free from these things.

Prayer partner speaks:

In the name of Jesus, I speak forgiveness to you for your and your family's sins of agreement with these false and sinful doctrines and I stand in agreement with you (name of the brother/sister) in claiming the blood of Jesus between (himself/herself) and the false and sinful doctrines of Freemasonry. Through the power of His precious shed blood, I command each spirit behind these doctrines to release and go from (name of the brother/sister) in the name of Jesus. [Wait a moment for God to cause them to go. Check with the Holy Spirit to be sure that all deliverance that was necessary has taken place.]

[Note: Name any of the spirits that the Holy Spirit is highlighting to you. Some may leave in the general command, and others may wait for specific command.]

Finally, I ask the Holy Spirit to come; clean, fill, and seal (name of the brother/sister) from the effect of these sins and from the spirits behind them.

Please remember to thank Jesus for His release and healing in these matters.

Prayer sequence—the songs, creeds, and slogans of Freemasonry.

Your prayer:

Dear Heavenly Father, I come before You now and, in the name of Jesus, I renounce the Freemasonry songs that I and/

or my family sang and the creeds and slogans that I and/or my family spoke and recited publically and in private. Please forgive me, Lord, for the blasphemy of these things and the lies that they propagated and for which they stood. I forgive any of my family who entered into these and opened me up to the curses that follow these practices. I claim the shed blood of Jesus between me and these sins and the sins of my family.

Prayer partner speaks:

In the name of Jesus, I forgive you for your belief, and/or your family's belief in and recitation of the Freemasonry songs and creeds that were part of your previous life, as you have just confessed and repented. I command first the generational blasphemy, lies, deception, mockery, idolatry and every evil spirit that accessed or influenced (name of the brother/sister)'s life through these creeds and songs to go now in Jesus' name. [Wait a moment for God to cause them to go. Check with the Holy Spirit to be sure that all deliverance that was necessary has taken place.]

Now, secondly, I command the same type of spirits that came in with any of (name of the brother/sister)'s (and/or family's) same practices to leave (name of the brother/sister) now. [As indicated by the Holy Spirit, continue to command the spirit(s) to leave and include in this command the name(s) of any spirit(s) the Holy Spirit indicates.]

Finally, I ask the Holy Spirit to come; cleanse, fill, and seal (name of the brother/sister) from the effect of these sins and from the spirits behind them.

Please remember to thank Jesus for His release and healing in these matters.

PRAYER SEQUENCE—RELEASE FROM THE 1ST DEGREE: ENTERED APPRENTICE

Your prayer:

I confess and repent of (my and/or any of my father's and forefathers') involvement with the sinful oaths, curses, rituals and regalia of the 1st Degree—that of Entered Apprentice. I also forgive my family for opening me up to the curses and afflictions of this Degree. I renounce off my life, and off my family's life, the ungodly inheritance of agreeing that the Masonic temple is an acceptable place to worship. I renounce the Freemasonry Lodge: a temple where Your Word is not accepted by all as the whole truth, a temple where Jesus Christ is not acknowledged as Lord of all, a temple where the very Name of Jesus Christ is forbidden to be mentioned. It is a temple where the black and white floor proclaims the lie that Jesus Christ and Satan are both equals in power and authority, a temple where Egypt—the biblical model of the ungodly world—is revered and exalted. I stand in full agreement with You, Lord, that the Masonic temple is a temple of Satan—a complete abomination and an accursed place with an accursed altar and an accursed doctrine of devils.

I renounce off my life the ungodly inheritance of accepting the Masonic penny and acknowledging the Masonic poor box.

I renounce off my life the ungodly inheritance of the pauper's clothing, the hoodwink over the eyes, the cable tow rope around the neck, and the dagger or compass point pressed against the heart or nose or chin.

I renounce off my life, the ungodly inheritance of the curse "of having my throat cut across from ear to ear, my tongue torn out by the root and being buried in the sand of the sea at low water or a cable's length from the shore where the tide regularly ebbs and flows twice in twenty-four hours."

I renounce all legal rights given to Satan through the oaths and rituals of the Entered Apprentice Degree upon my tongue and throat that could lead to throat disorders, cancer of the throat or mouth, speech disorders, cleft palate and the inability to communicate. I confess and repent of any sexual violations of the mouth or throat personally and in my family. I forgive (anyone) who violated me or my family members in these ways.

I renounce off my life the ungodly inheritance of the secret handshake, the due guard, the penal sign, and the secret password "BOAZ" (the left pillar of Solomon's temple).

I renounce off my life the ungodly inheritance of accepting the Masonic covering provided by the 1st Degree apron.

I renounce off my life the ungodly inheritance of the kissing of the Bible through a square and compass and the sealing of this Degree ritual with the witchcraft oath of "so mote it be."

I renounce off my life the ungodly inheritance of being "born again" into Freemasonry under the deacon's wands held overhead to form the female generative parts.

I renounce off my life the ungodly inheritance of the lie that "light is darkness visible."

I renounce all surrender and submission to an antichrist spirit.

I renounce off my life the ungodly inheritance of accepting the working tools of this Degree—the 24-inch gauge, chisel, square, level, plumb line, tracing board, ashlars, and skirret.

I renounce off my life the ungodly inheritance of being yoked together with unbelievers in an ungodly brotherhood of false unity.

As one, Lord, I and my family repent of our generational line willingly entering into this blasphemous covenant with Satan.

None of this, Lord, now belongs to me and my family. It was spoken onto our generational line. And now, Father, in the name of the Lord Jesus Christ, I speak it off my generational line.

In the name of the Lord Jesus Christ and by the power of His blood, I break the curse of a "cut throat" over all areas affecting my and my family's lives, financial dealings, business, character, personality, relationships and physical body. I command all these spirits to leave me.

Prayer partner speaks:

I speak forgiveness to you for all your sins of the 1st Degree of Freemasonry, in Jesus' name, and I stand in agreement with you, (name of the brother/sister), in claiming the blood of Jesus between yourself and the generational sins of the 1st Degree of Freemasonry. I separate you from the generational curses by the blood of Jesus.

In Jesus' name, I break off any violence in the mouth area through accidental injury, unnecessary surgery or dental procedures.

I speak forgiveness to you in the name of Jesus for these sins and now speak health to your throat, tongue, respiratory passages, sinuses, vocal cords, dental structures, and all your vocal communication. In Jesus' name I break the curse of speechlessness, inability to speak the oracles of God, loss of speech, and inability to move in the vocal gifts of the Holy Spirit. I pray for a release to flow in the gifts of speaking: teaching, exhortation, and wisdom and that you may know when to speak. In Jesus' name I release you from the curse of the false unity of Freemasonry. Spirits of curse, your rights are gone; now leave. [Wait a moment for God to cause the curses to leave. Check with the Holy Spirit to be sure that all deliverance that was necessary has taken place. If necessary, continue to command the spirit(s) to leave and include in this command the name(s) of any spirit(s) the Holy Spirit indicates.] In Jesus' name I release you to flow in unity with the Holy Spirit.

Please remember to thank Jesus for His release and healing in these matters.

PRAYER SEQUENCE—RELEASE FROM THE 2ND DEGREE: FELLOW CRAFT

Your prayer:

I confess and repent of my and any of my father's and forefathers' sins through involvement with the oaths, curses, rituals and regalia of the 2nd Degree—that of "Fellow Craft." I also forgive my family for opening me up to the curses and afflictions of this Degree.

I renounce off my life the ungodly inheritance of the pauper's clothing, the hoodwink over the eyes, the cable tow rope wound twice around the right arm, and the claw-like hand drawn across the chest.

I renounce any curse of weakness over the organs within my chest, of heart attack, of breast cancer, and of death through heart or lung disease through this blood oath of Freemasonry.

I renounce off my life the ungodly inheritance of the curse of "having my left breast laid open, my heart torn out and given to ravenous birds of the air or devouring beasts of the field as prey."

I renounce all fear of death through heart attack or other ailments of organs within the chest.

I renounce any emotional hardness, hardness of heart to spiritual things, apathy, indifference, unbelief, deep-seated anger stemming from the oaths and rituals of the 2nd Degree.

I renounce off my life the ungodly inheritance of the secret handshake, the due guard, the penal sign, the fidelity sign, the hailing sign, the secret step, and the secret passwords "JACHIN" and "SHIBBOLETH."

I renounce all improper obsession with gaining knowledge especially through the paths of "Heavenly Science" to the "Throne of God."

I renounce off my life the ungodly inheritance of kissing the Bible through a square and compass and the sealing of this Degree ritual with the witchcraft oath of "so mote it be."

I renounce off my life the ungodly inheritance of accepting the Masonic covering provided by the 2nd Degree apron.

I renounce off my life the ungodly inheritance of accepting the working tools of this Degree—the plumb line, square, level, compass, trowel, and the acknowledgment of the Degree tracing board.

As one, Lord, I, and my family, repent of our generational line willingly entering into this blasphemous covenant with Satan.

None of this, Lord, now belongs to me or my family. It was spoken onto our generational line, and now Father, in the Name that is above all other names, the Name of the Lord Jesus Christ, we speak it off our generational line.

Prayer partner speaks:

I witness and stand in agreement with your confessions, repentance and renunciations. Now, in Jesus' name and by the power of His blood, I forgive you for all of these sins and separate you from these sins of (yours and) your family. I command all the curses of the 2nd Degree to come off (name of brother/sister), including all the curses of heart attack, breast cancer, and lung disease and lung cancer through this blood oath of Freemasonry. I command every spirit of infirmity associated with this Degree to leave (name of brother/sister) now in Jesus' name. All these curses, go now! [Wait a moment for God to cause these curses to go. Check with the Holy Spirit to be sure that all necessary deliverance has taken place. If you need to, continue to command the spirit(s) to leave and include in this command the name(s) of any spirit(s) the Holy Spirit indicates.]

In Jesus' name I break every curse of being shot or stabbed through the heart, heart failure, heart transplant and the pressing of the compass points into the heart through these murderous blood oaths of the 2nd Degree. Spirits of heart trouble, lift off (name of brother/sister) now. In Jesus' name I speak healing of the heart to (name of brother/sister). I command all these curses to go now! [Wait a moment for God to cause these curses to go. Check with the Holy Spirit to be sure that all necessary deliverance has taken place. If you need to, continue to command the spirit(s) to leave and include in this command the name(s) of any spirit(s) the Holy Spirit indicates.]

In Jesus' name, I break the curse of premature death or death before reaching a mature age stemming from these blood oaths of the 2nd Degree. I declare a breakthrough to full maturity in God for you and your household. Spirit of curse or infirmity, leave (name of brother/sister); God has ordained every one of his/her days. I command all these curses to go now! [Wait a moment for God to cause these curses to go. Check with the Holy Spirit to be sure that all necessary deliverance has taken place. If you need to, continue to command the spirit(s) to leave and include in this command the name(s) of any spirit(s) the Holy Spirit indicates.]

In Jesus' name I break the curse of false Masonic justice and righteousness as represented by the Masonic plumb line. There is only one plumb line: that of the Holy Scriptures. Spirit of heresy, leave (name of brother/sister) now. I command all the associated curses to go now! [Wait a moment for God to cause these curses to go. Check with the Holy Spirit to be sure that all necessary deliverance has taken place. If you need to, continue to command the spirit(s) to leave and include in this command the name(s) of any spirit(s) the Holy Spirit indicates.] I now speak a filling up of (name of brother/ sister) with true righteousness and justice. Holy Spirit, please come and bring healing and restore godly order.

Please remember to thank Jesus for His release and healing in these matters.

PRAYER SEQUENCE—RELEASE FROM THE 3RD DEGREE: MASTER MASON

Your prayer:

I confess and repent of (my and/or) any of my family, father's and forefathers' sins through involvement with the oaths, curses, rituals and regalia of the 3rd Degree—that of the Master Mason. I also forgive my family for opening me up to the curses and afflictions of this Degree.

I renounce off my life the ungodly inheritance of the pauper's clothing, the hoodwink over the eyes, the cable tow rope wound three times around the waist, and the dagger or compass point pressed against the heart or the nose or chin, and the hand drawn across the stomach.

I renounce off my life the ungodly inheritance of the curse "of being severed in two, my bowels burned to ashes and those ashes scattered over the face of the earth and wafted by the four winds of heaven so that no trace of so vile a wretch as me may be found among men."

I renounce the false humility, the false valley of the shadow of death, the false resurrection, the penal sign, the robe and hood, and all surrender of the will to Satan.

I renounce the blasphemy of referring to Satan as the "Most High" and the re-enactment of the legend of Hiram Abiff as the death and resurrection of Jesus Christ. I renounce the false gospel it represents.

I renounce off my life the ungodly inheritance of the secret handshake known as the "lion's paw grip", the due guard, the secret signs of "horror," "sympathy," "grief and distress," "joy and exultation," and the secret passwords "MACHABEN" (or "MAH-HAH-BONE," literally meaning "brought down" to be "brought under") and "TUBAL CAIN."

I renounce off my life the ungodly inheritance of the two swords placed in a "V" against the kidneys or waist.

I renounce off my life the ungodly inheritance of agreeing to identify with the person of Hiram Abiff in the Master Mason ritual. I renounce the ritual attack by the three ruffians and violent blows to the throat, chest and head. I renounce the falling into the (image of death) open stretcher, the gazing upon the death symbols and being buried, first under the temple rubbish, and then under the acacia tree.

I renounce off my life the ungodly inheritance of "welcoming the grim tyrant of death sent by the Masonic 'Supreme Grand Master,'" and I reject the false heaven known as the Masonic "celestial lodge above."

I renounce the fear of rape, fear of attack, fear of assault, and fear of death stemming from the violent blood oaths of the 3rd Degree.

I renounce headaches, migraine headaches, vision impairment, loss of sight, blindness, concussion, and brain damage stemming from the oaths and rituals of the 3rd Degree.

I renounce the skull and crossbones, and any music, movies, or video games that are obsessed with death or the flirting with death.

I renounce the seduction to death through suicide, anorexia, excessive risk-taking, death by hanging, etc., stemming from the power of the Freemasonry coffin.

I renounce all that has to do with death over my body, my marriage, my children, my employment, and my relationships stemming from Freemasonry oaths, rituals, and regalia.

I declare that I shall not die through the symbolic blows to the throat, chest and head, or of stroke, a brain hemorrhage or aneurysm, or the effects of Alzheimer's disease.

I renounce the false light of Freemasonry, the Angel of Light, and the false "Sons of Light."

I declare that "God is Light, and in Him there is no darkness at all" (1 John 1:5).

I renounce the five points of fellowship of the 3rd Degree ritual, "foot to foot, knee to knee, breast to breast, hand to mouth, and mouth to ear" and the sealing with the sign of the cross as well as all counterfeit suffering, pain, and false martyrdom stemming from the oaths of Freemasonry.

I renounce the Master Mason as a "great reflector of light," as the "spokesman of the Most High," the "power of the Hydra, the great snake from whose mouth pours the light of god," and the curse of relating to Father God as a "stern judge and task master."

Prayer partner speaks:

I witness and stand in agreement with your confessions, repentance, and renunciations. Now, in Jesus' name and by the power of His blood, I forgive you for all of these sins and separate you from these sins of (yours and) your family. I now command all the curses of the 3rd Degree to come off (name of brother/sister), including all the curses of death by accidents stemming from the oaths and rituals of the 3rd Degree on (name of brother/sister). I release you from the curses of accidents leading to injury, maiming, scarring and death. I command these curses to go now! [Wait a moment for God to cause these curses to go. Check with the Holy Spirit to be sure that all necessary deliverance has taken place.

If you need to, continue to command the spirit(s) to leave and include in this command the name(s) of any spirit(s) the Holy Spirit indicates.]

In Jesus' name, I release you from the curse of violent death through accidents stemming from violent blood oaths. Curses, go now! [Wait a moment for God to cause them to go. Check with the Holy Spirit to be sure that all necessary deliverance has taken place. If you need to, continue to command the spirit(s) to leave and include in this command the name(s) of any spirit(s) the Holy Spirit indicates.]

In Jesus' name, I release you from the curse of being brought down or brought under, stemming from the secret passwords "MAH-HAH-BONE" or "MACHABEN." Curses, go now! [Wait a moment for God to cause them to go. Check with the Holy Spirit to be sure that all necessary deliverance has taken place. If you need to, continue to command the spirit(s) to leave and include in this command the name(s) of any spirit(s) the Holy Spirit indicates]

In Jesus' name, I release you from the curse of stroke, blood hemorrhage, or aneurysm stemming from the oaths of Freemasonry. I take authority over every spirit of stroke, etc., and command them to leave. [Wait a moment for God to cause them to go. Check with the Holy Spirit to be sure that all necessary deliverance has taken place. If you need to, continue to command the spirit(s) to leave and include in this command the name(s) of any spirit(s) the Holy Spirit indicates]. Please come and bring Your healing, Lord.

In Jesus' name, spirit of death, leave (name of brother/sister) now. Spirits assigned to death of the physical body, marriage, children, employment, and relationships, leave (name of brother/sister) now in Jesus' name. Every spirit assigned to bring death to relationships, come off. In the name of the Lord Jesus Christ I break the curse of disease on abdominal organs, including mouth, esophagus, stomach, intestines (small and large), appendix, liver, pancreas, kidneys, gall bladder. [Wait a moment for God to remove these curses. Check with the Holy Spirit to be sure that all necessary deliverance has taken place. If you need to, continue to command the spirit(s) to leave and include in this command the name(s) of any spirit(s) the Holy Spirit indicates.] Holy Spirit, please come and cleanse (name of brother/sister) and fill him/her where the enemy previously had rights. Lord Jesus, I ask You to now come and heal (name of brother/sister) and fill him/her by Your Holy Spirit. I ask You to undo all the enemy has done. In Your name, Lord Jesus, we cancel all work of the enemy.

Please remember to thank Jesus for His release and healing in these matters.

PRAYER SEQUENCE—RELEASE FROM THE 13TH DEGREE: HOLY ROYAL ARCH MASTER OR KNIGHT OF THE NINTH OR ROYAL ARCH OF SOLOMON
(May be given out of order to follow the 3rd Degree to complete a Master Mason)

Your prayer:

I confess, repent and renounce (my and/or) the sins of my family in the rituals, oaths taken, and the curses of the Master or Knight of the Ninth or Royal Arch of Solomon or 13th Degree, its blasphemous use of the secret password

"JEHOVAH" (in some places) and/or (traditionally) "JAH-BUL-ON," and its penalties. I also forgive my family for opening me up to the curses and afflictions of this Degree.

I renounce the vow, "I consent to suffer all the pains of the former obligations (Degrees 1–3)," and the binding to the Order forever, at the peril of my own life, including the oath regarding the removal of the head from the body and exposing the brains to the hot sun.

I renounce off my life the ungodly inheritance of the hoodwink over the eyes, the cable tow, and Master Mason's apron/regalia worn in this indoctrination.

I renounce off my life the ungodly inheritance of being lowered into a dark vault under the temple and removing the cornerstone in order to allow in more light. I affirm it to be blasphemy, Lord, as Your Word makes it clear that the Lord Jesus Christ is the cornerstone of Your Temple. He is the Light, and Jesus Christ is the Word, and I deeply renounce my and any of my forefathers' participating in this ritual under the name Zerubbabel and agreeing to "rise, wrench forth the Keystone, and prepare to receive the light of the Holy Word." This ritual is but Satan's way to get men to renounce and remove Jesus Christ under an accursed oath of death.

I renounce off my life the ungodly inheritance of agreeing that the name Jah-Bul-On is the secret and "Sacred and Mysterious Name of the True and Living God Most High." Lord, I affirm this to be a blasphemy, a demonic trinity composed of Your Name, the name of Baal, and the name of Osiris, and I deeply renounce (my and/or) any of my forefathers' accepting this lie.

I renounce the false communion taken in this Degree and all the mockery, skepticism, and unbelief about the redemptive work of Jesus Christ on the cross.

I renounce off my life the ungodly inheritance of the penal sign, hailing sign, penitential sign, monitorial sign, fiducial sign, and the secret passwords "KEB RAIOTH," "MAHER-SHALAL-HASH-BAZ," and "AMMI RUHAMAH," and all that they mean.

I renounce off my life the ungodly inheritance of kissing the Bible four times through a square and compass and the sealing of this Degree ritual with the witchcraft oath of "so mote it be."

I renounce off my life the ungodly inheritance of accepting the working tools of this Degree.

I renounce off my life the ungodly inheritance of being clothed in "robes of innocence" and receiving the jewel, badge, and ribbon.

I renounce off my life the ungodly inheritance of receiving the mark of the mysterious triple tau on the forehead as a mark of salvation.

Prayer partner speaks:

I witness and stand in agreement with (name of brother/ sister)'s confessions, repentance and renunciations. In Jesus' name, I forgive you for all of these sins and separate you from these sins of (yours and/or) your family and I command all the curses of the Holy Royal Arch Degree to come off (name of brother/sister), including all blasphemy, death, witchcraft, unbelief, violence and dismemberment; these must leave (name of brother/sister) now. [Wait a moment for God to remove these curses. Check with the Holy Spirit to be sure that all necessary deliverance has taken place. If you need to, continue to command the spirit(s) to leave and include in this command the name(s) of any spirit(s) the Holy Spirit indicates.] Holy Spirit, please come and cleanse (name of brother/sister) and fill him/her where the enemy previously had rights. Please bring Your healing now to (name of brother/sister) where he/she was affected by these curses.

Please remember to thank Jesus for His release and healing in these matters.

Prayer Sequence—General Closing Prayer for Freemasonry Ministry

Your prayer:

I renounce (my and/or) my antecedents' willingly entering into these blasphemous agreements with Satan. None of this covenant, Lord, now belongs to me or my family. It was spoken onto our generational line. And now Father, in the Name that is above all other names, the Name of Jesus Christ, I speak it *off* me and my family. I continue to forgive my family for opening me up to the curses and afflictions of Freemasonry.

Jesus Christ is my Lord, and I proclaim that I come under the New Covenant of the precious blood of the Lord Jesus Christ and that covenant negates and totally obliterates every other contract, covenant, agreement, choice, decision, allegiance, or oath given to Satan.

I renounce every evil spirit associated with Freemasonry and witchcraft and all other sins. I now claim my legal freedom and command the spirits of darkness, in the name of Jesus Christ, to remove from me every right and claim and hold you have had upon me through Freemasonry.

I command in the name of Jesus Christ that every evil spirit given rights to my life through the Blue Lodge Freemasonry Degrees 1–3 and the Scottish Rite Degree 13 is to leave me now, touching or harming no one; go to the place appointed for you by the Lord Jesus Christ, never to return to me or my family members. I call on the Lord Jesus Christ to be delivered of these spirits, in accordance with the many promises of the Bible.

I ask to be delivered of every sickness, infirmity, curse, affliction, disease, or allergy associated with these sins I have confessed and renounced. I surrender to God the Father, Jesus the Son, and the Holy Spirit, and to no other spirit all the places in my life where these sins have been.

Every evil spirit, principality, and demonic being given rights through these four Degrees, I address you, saying that your rights through these Degrees are canceled. Therefore, I command you to be gone from me and my generation line forever in the Name of Jesus Christ. Jesus Christ is my Lord. Amen.

Key Concepts from Chapter 11

The core idea from this chapter is that personal and familial generational participation in the false religion of Freemasonry leaves a deposit of spiritual bondages within us. While these bondages cannot keep us from going to heaven, this nest of spiritual refuse will continue to plague our earthly life in our relationships with God and mankind. It will pressure us to walk away from godly behavior and values, undermining our discipleship and obedience to God in general. The only way to freedom is through confession of sins linked to Freemasonry, both ours and those of our ancestors, repentance from those sins, and receiving forgiveness through the blood of Jesus. Deliverance from the influence of the spirits that inhabit these sins is necessary. Typically, our prayers for freedom from the spiritual bondage of this ungodly system include the following elements:*

- Confessing the sins of self and family, making verbal assent: owning what we did and participated in, with our hearts, mouths, and bodies;
- Agreeing with what God's Word says about what we and/ or our family did, and what that made us (e.g. murderer, liar, thief, adulterer, idolater);
- Repentance—deciding in our hearts and declaring verbally to turn from the confessed areas of sin; telling God we are sorry for our own behavior and that of our family;
- Forgiveness—releasing from guilt, condemnation, judgment, etc;

  - Forgiving those who led us into these sins
  - Forgiving our family who opened these spiritual doorways into our lives

- Forgiving ourselves for making these mistakes

- Asking God to forgive us for the personal wrongdoings we've confessed.

In addition to prayer ministry, we must also destroy (not sell or give away) all idolatrous, antichrist, ungodly materials associated with our personal and our family's involvement with Freemasonry, including jewelry, medals, pins, certificates, membership cards, uniforms/clothing, scarves, flags, literature, books, papers—all that are actually in our personal residence, our possession, or our control.

It should be noted that there may be other issues and practices under Freemasonry as experienced by you and your family which were not treated in this book. Please pray through them using the model that we've presented in this chapter.

* We would need a prayer partner to assist us in releasing forgiveness into our life and to help us break away from any spiritual bondages that were present. (Observe how this is modeled in the ministry of this chapter).

CHAPTER 12

Release from Freemasonry for Degrees beyond Master Mason[61,62,63,64,65]

In this chapter we will include the numbered Degrees up to the 33rd Degree (of the Scottish Rite, i.e. the Degrees above 3rd) and then address some of the other orders that a Mason might enter at a qualifying level (e.g. the Shriners, which may be elected at 32nd Degree level). We will also address the York Rite, which parallels the Scottish Rite. Please feel free to skip the ministry sections that do not apply to you or your family.

In Europe, particularly, it has become more widely known that there are additional Degrees, beyond the published 33rd, that are not available in printed literature. Information on them is not as common. To receive freedom from these higher and/or un-numbered levels, you will need increased assistance from the Holy Spirit to guide you into the appropriate ministry.

Let us now turn our attention to each of the Scottish Rite Degrees. Although presented here individually, during indoctrination these levels are usually entered into in groupings of several at once.

Prayer Ministry for the Scottish Rite

PRAYER SEQUENCE—RELEASE FROM THE 4ᵀᴴ DEGREE: SECRET MASTER

Your prayer:

> I renounce (my and/or) the sins of my family in the blasphemy, uncleanness, oaths taken, and the curses and penalties included in the Secret Master or 4th Degree; its secret password, "ADONAI," used blasphemously, and its penalties. I forgive my family for opening me up to the curses and afflictions of this Degree.

> I renounce the seven-branched candlestick of light, the Masonic symbol of a serpent with its tail in its mouth and its sexual symbolism, and the worship of the phallus.

Prayer partner speaks:

> I witness and stand in agreement with these renunciations of (name of brother/sister). In Jesus' name, I forgive you for all of these sins and separate you from these sins of (yours and/or) your family and I command the curses of the 4th Degree to come off (name of brother/sister). All blasphemy, uncleanness, death, witchcraft, unbelief, violence, and dismemberment, leave (name of brother/sister) now. [Wait a moment for God to cause them to leave. Check with the Holy Spirit to be sure that all necessary deliverance has taken place. If you need to, continue to command the spirit(s) to leave. Include in this command the name(s) of any spirit(s) the Holy Spirit indicates.] Holy Spirit, please come and cleanse (name of brother/sister) and fill him/her where the enemy previously had rights. Please bring Your healing now to (name of brother/sister) where he/she was affected by these curses.

Please remember to thank Jesus for His release and healing in these matters.

PRAYER SEQUENCE—RELEASE FROM THE 5TH DEGREE: PERFECT MASTER

Your prayer:

> I renounce (my and/or) the sins of my family from the oaths taken, and the curses of the Perfect Master or 5th Degree, its secret password "MAH-HAH-BONE," and its penalty of being smitten to the earth with a setting maul. I forgive my family for opening me up to the curses and afflictions of this Degree.

Prayer partner speaks:

> I witness and stand in agreement with these renunciations of (name of brother/sister).

> In Jesus' name, I forgive you for all of these sins and separate you from these sins of (yours and/or) your family and I command the curses of the 5th Degree to come off (name of brother/sister). All blasphemy, death, witchcraft, unbelief, violence, and dismemberment, leave (name of brother/sister) now. [Wait a moment for God to cause them to leave. Check with the Holy Spirit to be sure that all necessary deliverance has taken place. If you need to, continue to command the spirit(s) to leave and include in this command the name(s) of any spirit(s) the Holy Spirit indicates.] Holy Spirit, please come and cleanse (name of brother/sister) and fill him/her where the enemy previously had rights. Please bring Your healing now to (name of brother/sister) where he/she was affected by these curses.

Please remember to thank Jesus for His release and healing in these matters.

PRAYER SEQUENCE—RELEASE FROM THE 6TH DEGREE: INTIMATE SECRETARY

Your prayer:

> I renounce (my and/or) the sins of my family; in the oaths taken, and the curses of the Intimate Secretary or 6th Degree, its secret password, "JEHOVAH," used blasphemously, and its penalties "of having my body dissected, and of having my vital organs cut into pieces and thrown to the beasts of the field." I forgive my family for opening me up to the curses and afflictions of this Degree.

Prayer partner speaks:

> I witness and stand in agreement with these renunciations of (name of brother/sister). In Jesus' name, I forgive you for all of these sins and separate you from these sins of (yours and/or) your family and I command the curses of the 6th Degree, Intimate Secretary, to come off (name of brother/sister). All blasphemy, death, witchcraft, unbelief, violence, and dismemberment, leave (name of brother/sister) now. [Wait a moment for God to do this. Check with the Holy Spirit to be sure that all necessary deliverance has taken place. If you need to, continue to command the spirit(s) to leave and include in this command the name(s) of any spirit(s) the Holy Spirit indicates.] Holy Spirit, please come and cleanse (name of brother/sister) and fill him/her where the enemy previously had rights. Please bring Your healing now to (name of brother/sister) where he/she was affected by these curses.

Please remember to thank Jesus for His release and healing in these matters.

PRAYER SEQUENCE—RELEASE FROM THE 7TH DEGREE: PROVOST AND JUDGE

Your prayer:

> I renounce (my and/or) the sins of my family; in the oaths taken, and the curses of the Provost and Judge or 7th Degree, its secret password "HIRUM-TITO-CIVI-KY," and the penalty of having my nose cut off. I forgive my family for opening me up to the curses and afflictions of this Degree.

> I renounce the Tribunal of Freemasonry, the court case of Freemasonry, and losing the Masonic court case because of injustice.

> I renounce the oath, "I will be dishonored and my life forfeited with pain and torture."

> I renounce all pain and torture in every area of my life— emotionally, psychologically, physically, vocationally, relationally, spiritually, and financially.

> I renounce the oath, "to inflict vengeance on traitors."

Prayer partner speaks:

> I witness and stand in agreement with these renunciations of (name of brother/sister). In Jesus' name, I forgive you for all of these sins and separate you from these sins of (yours and/or) your family in the 7th Degree, Provost and Judge. In the name of the Lord Jesus Christ, I:

> 1. Break the curse of dishonor with pain in your workplace, over your Christian faith, over your reputation, over your employment and every other area of your life.
> 2. Break the curse of being "disgracefully expelled with public marks of ignominy that can never be erased."

3. Break the curse of dishonor and of being dishonored by your children.
4. Break the curse of exile and pull you out from under these curses.

In Jesus' name, I command all curses of the 7th Degree to come off (name of brother/sister). All blasphemy, death, witchcraft, unbelief, violence, shame, and dishonor and dismemberment, leave (name of brother/sister) now. [Wait a moment for God to cause them to leave. Check with the Holy Spirit to be sure that all necessary deliverance has taken place. If you need to, continue to command the spirit(s) to leave. Include in this command the name(s) of any spirit(s) the Holy Spirit indicates.] Holy Spirit, please come and cleanse (name of brother/sister) and fill him/her where the enemy previously had rights. Please bring Your healing now to (name of brother/sister) where he/she was affected by these curses.

Please remember to thank Jesus for His release and healing in these matters.

PRAYER SEQUENCE—RELEASE FROM THE 8ᵀᴴ DEGREE: INTENDENT OF THE BUILDING

Your prayer:

I renounce (my and/or) the sins of my family; in the oaths taken, and the curses of the Intendant of the Building or 8th Degree, its secret password "AKAR-JAI-JAH," and the penalties of all my former obligations, "besides having my eyes put out, my body cut in two and exposing my bowels." I forgive my family for opening me up to the curses and afflictions of this Degree.

I renounce the false doctrine of perfectionism.

In Jesus Christ's name, every spirit of perfectionism is to leave me now!

Prayer partner speaks:

> I witness and stand in agreement with these renunciations of (name of brother/sister). In Jesus' name, I forgive you for all of these sins and separate you from these sins of (yours and/or) your family in the 8th Degree, Intendent of the Building. I command all the curses of the 8th Degree to come off (name of brother/sister), including all blasphemy, death, witchcraft, unbelief, violence, perfectionism, eye damage, and dismemberment; these must leave (name of brother/sister) now. [Wait a moment for God to cause them to leave. Check with the Holy Spirit to be sure that all necessary deliverance has taken place. If you need to, continue to command the spirit(s) to leave. Include in this command the name(s) of any spirit(s) the Holy Spirit indicates.] Holy Spirit, please come and cleanse (name of brother/sister) and fill him/her where the enemy previously had rights. Please bring Your healing now to (name of brother/sister) where he/she was affected by these curses.

Please remember to thank Jesus for His release and healing in these matters.

PRAYER SEQUENCE—RELEASE FROM THE 9TH DEGREE: MASTER OF ELECTED KNIGHTS OF THE NINE

Your prayer:

> I renounce (my and/or) the sins of my family; in the oaths taken, and the curses of the Master or Elected Knights

of the Nine or 9th Degree, its secret password, "NEKAM NAKAH," and its penalty of 'having my head cut off and stuck on the highest pole in the east." I forgive my family for opening me up to the curses and afflictions of this Degree.

I renounce any Masonic retaliation in my family line, and murder in the retaliation (i.e. being stabbed to death and/or death to my emotions as a result of retaliation).

Prayer partner speaks:

I witness and stand in agreement with these renunciations of (name of brother/sister). In Jesus' name, I forgive you for all of these sins and separate you from these sins of (yours and/or) your family in the 9th Degree, Master of Elected Knights of the Nine. In Jesus' name, I command the curses of the 9th Degree to come off (name of brother/sister). All blasphemy, death, death to emotions, murder witchcraft, unbelief, vengeance, violence, and dismemberment, leave (name of brother/sister) now. [Wait a moment for God to cause them to leave. Check with the Holy Spirit to be sure that all necessary deliverance has taken place. If you need to, continue to command the spirit(s) to leave. Include in this command the name(s) of any spirit(s) the Holy Spirit indicates.] Holy Spirit, please come and cleanse (name of brother/sister) and fill him/ her where the enemy previously had rights. Please bring Your healing now to (name of brother/sister) where he/ she was affected by these curses.

Please remember to thank Jesus for His release and healing in these matters.

PRAYER SEQUENCE—RELEASE FROM THE 10TH DEGREE: ILLUSTRIOUS ELECT OF FIFTEEN

Your prayer:

I renounce (my and/or) the sins of my family; in the oaths taken, and the curses of the Illustrious Elect of Fifteen or 10th Degree with its secret password "ELIGNAM," and its penalties of "having my body opened perpendicularly and horizontally, the entrails exposed to the air for eight hours so that flies may prey on them, and for my head to be cut off and placed on a high pinnacle, and that I will always be ready to inflict the same punishment on those who shall disclose this Degree, breaking this obligation." I forgive my family for opening me up to the curses and afflictions of this Degree.

I renounce this oath of violence and death off my body.

I renounce the curse of taking Masonic vengeance upon those who betray the secrets of Freemasonry.

Prayer partner speaks:

I witness and stand in agreement with these renunciations of (name of brother/sister). In Jesus' name, I forgive you for all of these sins and separate you from these sins of (yours and/or) your family in the 10th Degree, Illustrious Elect of Fifteen. In Jesus' name, I command the curses of the 10th Degree to come off (name of brother/sister). All blasphemy, death, witchcraft, unbelief, violence, and dismemberment, leave (name of brother/sister) now. [Wait a moment for God to cause them to leave. Check with the Holy Spirit to be sure that all necessary deliverance has taken place. If you need to, continue to command the spirit(s) to leave. Include in this command the name(s) of any spirit(s) the Holy Spirit indicates.] Holy Spirit, please come and cleanse (name of brother/sister) and fill him/her where the enemy previously had rights. Please bring Your healing now to (name of brother/sister) where he/she was affected by these curses.

Please remember to thank Jesus for His release and healing in these matters.

PRAYER SEQUENCE—RELEASE FROM THE 11TH DEGREE: SUBLIME MASTER ELECT OR SUBLIME KNIGHTS

Your prayer:

I renounce (my and/or) the sins of my family in the oaths taken, and the curses of the Sublime Master Elect or Sublime Knights or 11th Degree, its secret blasphemous password "STOLKIN-ADONAI," and its penalty of "having my hand cut in twain." I forgive my family for opening me up to the curses and afflictions of this Degree.

Prayer partner speaks:

I witness and stand in agreement with these renunciations of (name of brother/sister). In Jesus' name, I forgive you for all of these sins and separate you from these sins of (yours and/or) your family in the 11th Degree, Sublime Master Elect or Sublime Knights. In Jesus' name, I command the curses of the 11th Degree to come off (name of brother/ sister). All blasphemy, death, witchcraft, unbelief, violence, and dismemberment, leave (name of brother/sister) now. [Wait a moment for God to cause them to leave. Check with the Holy Spirit to be sure that all necessary deliverance has taken place. If you need to, continue to command the spirit(s) to leave. Include in this command the name(s) of any spirit(s) the Holy Spirit indicates.] Holy Spirit, please come and cleanse (name of brother/sister) and fill him/her where the enemy previously had rights. Please bring Your healing now to (name of brother/sister) where he/she was affected by these curses.

Please remember to thank Jesus for His release and healing in these matters.

PRAYER SEQUENCE—RELEASE FROM THE 12TH DEGREE: GRAND MASTER INTENDENT OR ARCHITECT

Your prayer:

I renounce (my and/or) the sins of my family in the oaths taken, and the curses of the Grand Master Intendent or Architect or 12th Degree, its secret password, "RAB-BANAIM," and its penalty of "having my body severed in two and my memory lost, and looked upon as infamous and foresworn." I command every spirit of murder, Alzheimer's disease, dementia, and memory loss to lift off me now in Jesus Christ's name. I renounce the Masonic building pattern upon my life. I declare my life shall be built upon the foundation of Jesus Christ and no other. I forgive my family for opening me up to the curses and afflictions of this Degree.

Prayer partner speaks:

I witness and stand in agreement with these renunciations of (name of brother/sister). In Jesus' name, I forgive you for all of these sins and separate you from these sins of (yours and/or) your family in the 12th Degree, Grand

Master Intendent or Architect. In Jesus' name, I command the curses of the 12th Degree to come off (name of brother/sister). All blasphemy, death, witchcraft, unbelief, mental degradation, shame, condemnation, violence, and dismemberment, leave (name of brother/sister) now. [Wait a moment for God to cause them to leave. Check with the Holy Spirit to be sure that all necessary deliverance has taken place. If you need to, continue to command the spirit(s) to leave. Include in this command the name(s) of any spirit(s) the Holy Spirit indicates.] Holy Spirit, please come and cleanse (name of brother/sister) and fill him/her where the enemy previously had rights. Please bring Your healing now to (name of brother/sister) where he/she was affected by these curses.

Please remember to thank Jesus for His release and healing in these matters.

PRAYER SEQUENCE—RELEASE FROM THE 13TH DEGREE: HOLY ROYAL ARCH: MASTER OR KNIGHT OF THE NINTH OR ROYAL ARCH OF SOLOMON
(May be given out of order to follow the 3rd Degree to complete a Master Mason)

In the last chapter we went through the prayer ministry to release you from the most common Freemasonry indoctrinations. While completion of the 3rd Degree would seemingly qualify the individual for being a Master Mason (in the lower level, pre-Scottish Rite, Blue Lodge), in practice, many do not consider this title is complete until the 13th Degree is attained.

Higher-level Masons who have completed the 13th Degree all know that in this initiation, it is disclosed, "You perhaps conceive that you have this day received a 4th Degree of Freemasonry; but such, strictly speaking, is not the case; it is only the Master Mason's

Degree completed." The 3rd Degree initiates are deceived, thinking they are Master Masons. But if you have favor in the lodge, you will be encouraged to go further, into the Scottish Rite, and take the 13th Degree to complete the Master Mason status. This can happen as early as four weeks after the 3rd Degree is attained.

Your prayer:

> I renounce (my and/or) the sins of my family in the rituals, oaths taken, and the curses of the Master or Knight of the Ninth or Holy Royal Arch of Solomon or 13th Degree, its blasphemous use of the secret password "JEHOVAH" (in some places) and/or (traditionally) "JAH-BUL-ON," and its penalties. I forgive my family for opening me up to the curses and afflictions of this Degree.

> I renounce the vow, "I consent to suffer all the pains of the former obligations (Degrees 1–3) and the binding to the Order forever, at the peril of my own life," including the oath regarding the "removal of the head from the body and exposing the brains to the hot sun."

> I renounce off my life the ungodly inheritance of the "hoodwink over the eyes," the cable tow and Master Mason's apron/regalia worn in this indoctrination.

> I renounce off my life the ungodly inheritance of being lowered into a dark vault under the temple and removing the cornerstone in order to allow in more light. I affirm it to be blasphemy, Lord, as Your Word makes it clear that the Lord Jesus Christ is the cornerstone of Your Temple, and that Jesus Christ is the Light, and that Jesus Christ is the Word. Furthermore, I deeply renounce my and any of my forefathers' participating in this ritual under the name Zerubbabel and agreeing to "rise, wrench forth the Keystone,

and prepare to receive the light of the Holy Word." This ritual is but Satan's way to get men to renounce and remove Jesus Christ under an accursed oath of death.

I renounce off my life the ungodly inheritance of agreeing that the name Jah-Bul-On is the secret and "Sacred and Mysterious Name of the True and Living God Most High." I affirm this to be a blasphemy, a demonic trinity composed of Your Name, Lord, the name of Baal, and the name of Osiris. I deeply renounce my and any of my forefathers' accepting this lie.

I renounce the false communion taken in this Degree and all the mockery, skepticism and unbelief about the redemptive work of Jesus Christ on the cross.

I renounce off my life the ungodly inheritance of the penal sign, hailing sign, penitential sign, monitorial sign, fiducial sign, and the secret passwords "KEB RAIOTH,", "MAHER-SHALAL-HASH-BAZ," and "AMMI RUHAMAH," and all that they mean.

I renounce off my life the ungodly inheritance of kissing the Bible four times through a square and compass and the sealing of this Degree ritual with the witchcraft oath of "so mote it be."

I renounce off my life the ungodly inheritance of accepting the working tools of this Degree.

I renounce off my life the ungodly inheritance of being clothed in "robes of innocence" and receiving the jewel, badge, and ribbon.

I renounce off my life the ungodly inheritance of receiving the mark of the mysterious triple tau on the forehead as a mark of salvation.

Prayer partner speaks:

> I witness and stand in agreement with these renunciations of
> (name of brother/sister). In Jesus' name, I forgive you for all
> of these sins and separate you from these sins of (yours and/
> or) your family in the 13th Degree, Holy Royal Arch or Master
> or Knight of the Ninth or Royal Arch of Solomon (or Enoch).
> In Jesus' name, I command the curses of the Holy Royal Arch
> Degree to come off (name of brother/sister). All blasphemy,
> death, witchcraft, unbelief, violence, and dismemberment,
> leave (name of brother/sister) now. [Wait a moment for God
> to cause them to leave. Check with the Holy Spirit to be sure
> that all necessary deliverance has taken place. If you need to,
> continue to command the spirit(s) to leave. Include in this
> command the name(s) of any spirit(s) the Holy Spirit indicates.]
> Holy Spirit, please come and cleanse (name of brother/sister)
> and fill him/her where the enemy previously had rights. Please
> bring Your healing now to (name of brother/sister) where he/
> she was affected by these curses.

Please remember to thank Jesus for His release and healing in these
matters.

PRAYER SEQUENCE—RELEASE FROM THE 14TH DEGREE: GRAND ELECT MASON, PERFECT AND SUBLIME

Your prayer:

> I renounce (my and/or) the sins of my family in the rituals,
> oaths taken, and the curses of the Grand Elect Mason, Perfect
> and Sublime or 14th Degree, its secret passwords 'MARAH-
> MAUR-ABREK' and 'IHUH' and their penalties. I forgive my
> family for opening me up to the curses and afflictions of this
> Degree.

I renounce the seal of the Great Architect of the Universe.

I renounce and break the seal of the antichrist in the Name of Jesus Christ.

I renounce the oath, "I consent to my belly being opened, my bowels torn out and given to the hungry vultures, and to inflict vengeance on traitors."

I renounce the cursing of disease and death off my stomach and bowels.

I renounce the oath of inflicting vengeance upon those who renounce Freemasonry.

Prayer partner speaks:

I witness and stand in agreement with these renunciations of (name of brother/sister). In Jesus' name, I forgive you for all of these sins and separate you from these sins of (yours and/ or) your family in the 14th Degree, Grand Elect, Perfect and Sublime. In Jesus' name, I command the curses of the 14th Degree to come off (name of brother/sister). All blasphemy, death, witchcraft, unbelief, violence and dismemberment, leave (name of brother/sister) now.

- I break the seal of the antichrist in the Name of Jesus Christ off (name of brother/sister).
- I release all spirits of disease and death off (name of brother/ sister)'s stomach and bowels.
- Every spirit of infirmity of the stomach and bowels, come off now.

[Wait a moment for God to cause them to leave. Check with the Holy Spirit to be sure that all necessary deliverance has taken place. If you need to, continue to command the spirit(s) to leave. Include in this command the name(s) of any spirit(s) the Holy Spirit indicates.]

Lord Jesus, I ask You to bring healing into (name of brother/ sister) where he/she was affected by these curses. Holy Spirit, please come and cleanse (name of brother/sister) and fill him/her where the enemy previously had rights.

Please remember to thank Jesus for His release and healing in these matters.

PRAYER SEQUENCE—RELEASE FROM THE 15TH DEGREE: KNIGHTS OF THE EAST OR SWORD

Your prayer:

I renounce (my and/or) the sins of my family in the rituals, oaths taken, and the curses of the Knights of the East or Sword or 15th Degree, its secret password, "RAPH-O-DOM," and its penalties. I forgive my family for opening me up to the curses and afflictions of this Degree.

Prayer partner speaks:

I witness and stand in agreement with these renunciations of (name of brother/sister). In Jesus' name, I forgive you for all of these sins and separate you from these sins of (yours and/or) your family in the 15th Degree, Knights of the East or Sword. In Jesus' name, I command the curses of the 15th Degree to come off (name of brother/sister). All blasphemy, death, witchcraft, unbelief, violence and dismemberment, leave (name of brother/sister) now. [Wait a moment for God to cause them to leave. Check with the Holy Spirit to be sure that all necessary deliverance has taken place. If you need to, continue to command the spirit(s) to leave. Include in this command the name(s) of any spirit(s) the Holy Spirit indicates.] Holy Spirit, please come and cleanse (name of brother/sister) and fill him/her where the enemy previously had rights. Please bring Your healing now to (name of brother/sister) where he/she was affected by these curses.

Please remember to thank Jesus for His release and healing in these matters.

PRAYER SEQUENCE—RELEASE FROM THE 16ᵀᴴ DEGREE: PRINCE OF JERUSALEM

Your prayer:

I renounce (my and/or) the sins of my family in the rituals, oaths taken, and the curses of the Prince of Jerusalem or 16th Degree, its secret password, "TEBET-ADAR," and its penalty of "being stripped naked and having my heart pierced with a poniard." I forgive my family for opening me up to the curses and afflictions of this Degree.

In Jesus' name I renounce the false warrior mantle of Freemasonry, the false warrior's sword of retribution, alliance with the Prince of Persia, allegiance with the law of the Medes and Persians, and the pledge of defending the Masonic temple at all costs, including my life and that of my family.

In the Name of the Lord Jesus Christ, I tell the curse of intimidation that comes with fear and threats of violence, spirits of fear, fear of violence, intimidation and panic to leave me now. I renounce the curses of defamation and a lack of godly revelation and vision.

240

Prayer partner speaks:

> I witness and stand in agreement with these renunciations
> of (name of brother/sister). In Jesus' name, I forgive you
> for all of these sins and separate you from these sins of
> (yours and/or) your family in the 16th Degree, Prince of
> Jerusalem. In Jesus' name, I command all the curses of the
> 16th Degree to come off (name of brother/sister), including
> all blasphemy, death, witchcraft, unbelief, violence,
> intimidation, fear, panic, defamation, spiritual blindness,
> and dismemberment, leave (name of brother/sister) now.
> [Wait a moment for God to cause them to leave. Check
> with the Holy Spirit to be sure that all necessary deliverance
> has taken place. If you need to, continue to command the
> spirit(s) to leave. Include in this command the name(s) of
> any spirit(s) the Holy Spirit indicates.] Holy Spirit, please
> come and cleanse (name of brother/sister) and fill him/her
> where the enemy previously had rights. Please bring Your
> healing now to (name of brother/sister) where he/she was
> affected by these curses.

Please remember to thank Jesus for His release and healing in these
matters.

PRAYER SEQUENCE—RELEASE FROM
THE 17TH DEGREE: KNIGHTS OF THE EAST
AND WEST

Your prayer:

> I renounce (my and/or) the sins of my family in the rituals,
> oaths taken, and the curses of the Knights of the East and West
> or 17th Degree, and its secret password "ABADDON." I also
> renounce its penalties of being dishonored, considering my
> life an immediate forfeiture to be taken from me with torture

and pains to be inflicted in the manner I have consented to in the preceding Degrees, and "incurring the severe wrath of the Almighty Creator of Heaven and Earth." I forgive my family for opening me up to the curses and afflictions of this Degree.

I renounce off my life the name and the spirit of Abaddon, king of death and hell, and the lordship of Abaddon.

I renounce, in Jesus' name, every spirit or power of death and infirmity and command them to leave my life and that of my family. Heavenly Father, I want the life of Christ Jesus to reign supreme in our lives.

I renounce the washing of my robe in my own blood and declare it to be a false cleansing and I renounce the ritual blood sacrifice it represents.

I renounce the shedding of my blood for the atonement of sin, being a Masonic blood sacrifice, and being sacrificed upon the altar of atonement. I declare the blood of Jesus Christ, the Lamb of God, to be my only atonement for sin.

I renounce the curse of Masonic martyrdom and the curse of untimely death.

I renounce the blasphemy that the candidate in the 17th Degree is worthy to open the seven seals of the book of Revelation.

I renounce the false explanation of the seals, the mockery of the Lamb of God, the curses of the seven seals, and pledge my life into the life in Christ Jesus!

In the name of Jesus Christ, I renounce the doctrine and belief in the Masonic false atonement.

Prayer partner speaks:

> I witness and stand in agreement with these renunciations of (name of brother/sister). In Jesus' name, I forgive you for all of these sins and separate you from these sins of (yours and/or) your family in the 17th Degree, Knights of the East and West. In the name of Jesus, I command all the curses of the 17th Degree to come off (name of brother/sister). In Jesus' name I break the curse of being sacrificed upon the false altar of atonement and loose (him/her) from the false altar of sacrifice and the curse of Masonic martyrdom. Every spirit of death and infirmity, false worship, martyrdom, self-pity, come off on the breath, as well as all blasphemy, death, witchcraft, unbelief, violence and dismemberment; these must leave (name of brother/sister) now. [Wait a moment for God to cause them to leave. Check with the Holy Spirit to be sure that all necessary deliverance has taken place. If you need to, continue to command the spirit(s) to leave. Include in this command the name(s) of any spirit(s) the Holy Spirit indicates.] Holy Spirit, please come and cleanse (name of brother/sister) and fill him/her where the enemy previously had rights. Please bring Your healing now to (name of brother/sister) where he/she was affected by these curses.

Please remember to thank Jesus for His release and healing in these matters.

PRAYER SEQUENCE—RELEASE FROM THE 18ᵀᴴ DEGREE: KNIGHT OF THE PELICAN AND EAGLE

Your prayer:

> I renounce (my and/or) the sins of my family in the rituals, oaths taken, and the curses of the Knight of the Pelican

and Eagle or 18th Degree (the so-called Christian Degree). I forgive my family for opening me up to the curses and afflictions of this Degree.

I renounce this Degree as being counterfeit Christianity.

I renounce the declaration that Jesus was an apostle of mankind and was neither inspired (by God), nor divine (in nature).

I renounce the oath, "to be perpetually in darkness, my blood continually running from my body, to suffer without intermission the cruel remorse of soul, the bitterest gall mixed with vinegar be my constant drink, the sharpest thorns for my pillow, and death on a cross to complete my punishment."

I renounce the positive answers to the six questions asked of the candidate in this Degree, and the "Gospel of Love" as taught in the Scottish Rite.

I renounce and reject the Pelican witchcraft spirit, as well as the occult influence of the Rosicrucians and the Kabbalah (occult knowledge from the Jewish culture) in this Degree.

I renounce the claim that the death of Jesus Christ was a "dire calamity," the deliberate mockery and twisting of the Christian doctrine of atonement, and the veil of mourning.

I renounce the blasphemy and rejection of the deity of Jesus Christ and the secret words "IGNE NATURA RENOVATUR" and the flaming sacrifice of these words in written form.

I renounce the mockery of the false communion taken in this Degree, including the biscuit, salt, and white wine.

244

I renounce the occult refining fire of Rose-Croix and all ungodly suffering that comes from this occult source. I renounce the blasphemy of the preciousness of the Rose of Sharon.

I renounce the lie of perfection, the titles of perfection, the seal of perfection, and the lie of self-righteousness.

I renounce the spirit guide of Freemasonry, the false angel (Raphael), and declare that I am totally released from the Red Room and Chamber of Death.

I renounce the spiritual yoke and curse of submission to the oath, "I do furthermore swear ... to observe and obey all the decrees which may be transmitted to me by the Grand Inspectors General in Supreme Council of the 33rd Degree."

I now command spirits causing disorder to blood flow and menstruation to go from me. Every spirit of perfectionism and wrong thinking, and every spirit guide, leave me now. Witchcraft and Pelican spirit, spirits of Kabbalah and Rosicrucianism, I command you to leave me right now in the name of Jesus Christ.

Prayer partner speaks:

I witness and stand in agreement with these renunciations of (name of brother / sister). In Jesus' name, I forgive you for all of these sins and separate you from these sins of (yours and / or) your family in the 18th Degree, Knight of the Pelican and the Eagle. In Jesus' name, I command all the curses of the 18th Degree, named and unnamed, to come off (name of brother / sister). All blasphemy, death, witchcraft, unbelief, violence, torture, and dismemberment, leave (name of brother / sister) now. [Wait a moment for God to cause them to leave. Check with the Holy Spirit to be sure that all necessary deliverance has taken place. If you need to, continue to command the spirit(s) to leave. Include in this command the name(s) of any spirit(s) the Holy Spirit indicates.] Holy Spirit, please come and cleanse (name of brother/sister) and fill him/her where the enemy previously had rights. Please bring Your healing now to (name of brother/sister) where he/she was affected by these curses, particularly in his/her blood and circulatory health.

Please remember to thank Jesus for His release and healing in these matters.

PRAYER SEQUENCE—RELEASE FROM THE 19TH DEGREE: GRAND PONTIFF

Your prayer:

I renounce (my and/or) the sins of my family in the rituals, oaths taken, and the curses of the Grand Pontiff or 19th Degree, the blasphemous use of the secret password "EMMANUEL" and its penalties. I forgive my family for opening me up to the curses and afflictions of this Degree.

I renounce the Masonic "Thrice Puissant" impersonating of Christ who has all power.

I renounce the taking of the Priesthood of Jesus Christ on one's own breast. I renounce the divination herein used to hide the priesthood of Satan. I renounce the anointing oil used here and the pronouncement that the candidate becomes "a priest forever after the order of Melchizedek."

I renounce the stars of the zodiac and the powers of darkness behind astrology, divination, and the false fruit that comes with the spirit of Freemasonry.

I renounce the perversion of "the prophecy of the 144,000" in the book of Revelation.

In the Name of Jesus, I break the curse of the Masonic "Thrice Puissant" off my life and the curse of the false Masonic throne and scepter. Every spirit of divination, leave me now in Jesus' name.

I declare that Jesus Christ is the only one who is "a priest forever after the order of Melchizedek."

Prayer partner speaks:

I witness and stand in agreement with these renunciations of (name of brother/sister). In Jesus' name, I forgive you for all of these sins and separate you from these sins of (yours and/ or) your family in the 19th Degree, Grand Pontiff. In Jesus' name, I command the curses of the 19th Degree to come off (name of brother/sister). All blasphemy, false doctrine, astrology, divination, death, witchcraft, unbelief, violence, and dismemberment, leave (name of brother/sister) now. [Wait a moment for God to cause them to leave. Check with the Holy Spirit to be sure that all necessary deliverance has taken place. If you need to, continue to command the spirit(s) to leave. Include in this command the name(s) of any spirit(s) the Holy Spirit indicates.] Holy Spirit, please come and cleanse (name of brother/sister) and fill him/her where the enemy previously had rights. Please bring Your healing now to (name of brother/sister) where he/she was affected by these curses.

Please remember to thank Jesus for His release and healing in these matters.

PRAYER SEQUENCE—RELEASE FROM THE 20TH DEGREE: GRAND MASTER OF ALL SYMBOLIC LODGES OR MASTER AD VITAM

Your prayer:

> I renounce (my and/or) the sins of my family in the rituals, oaths taken, and the curses of the Grand Master of All Symbolic Lodges or Master Ad Vitam or 20th Degree, its secret password "JEKSON/STOLKIN" and its penalties. I forgive my family for opening me up to the curses and afflictions of this Degree.
>
> I renounce the false truth and light of Freemasonry, the light of Lucifer, and the quest for occult knowledge.

Prayer partner speaks:

> I witness and stand in agreement with these renunciations of (name of brother/sister). In Jesus' name, I forgive you for all of these sins and separate you from these sins of (yours and/or) your family in the 20th Degree, Grand Master of All Symbolic Lodges or Master Ad Vitam. In Jesus' name, I command the curses of the 20th Degree to come off (name of brother/sister). All blasphemy, death, witchcraft, unbelief, violence and dismemberment, leave (name of brother/sister) now. [Wait a moment for God to cause them to leave. Check with the Holy Spirit to be sure that all necessary deliverance has taken place. If you need to, continue to command the spirit(s) to leave. Include in this command the name(s) of any spirit(s) the Holy Spirit indicates.] Holy Spirit, please come and cleanse (name of brother/sister) and fill him/her where the enemy previously had rights. Please bring Your healing now to (name of brother/sister) where he/she was affected by these curses.

Please remember to thank Jesus for His release and healing in these matters.

PRAYER SEQUENCE—RELEASE FROM THE 21ST DEGREE: PRUSSIAN KNIGHT OR NOACHITE

Your prayer:

> I renounce (my and/or) the sins of my family in the rituals, oaths taken, and the curses of the Prussian Knight or Noachite or 21st Degree, its secret password, "PELEG," and its penalties. I forgive my family for opening me up to the curses and afflictions of this Degree.
>
> I renounce the blasphemous Masonic sash of this order, mixing truth and lies with its twelve stars representing the twelve stars of the zodiac, the twelve apostles, the twelve fruits of the tree of life, the twelve tribes of Israel, and the twelve gates of the New Jerusalem.

Prayer partner speaks:

> I witness and stand in agreement with these renunciations of (name of brother/sister). In Jesus' name, I forgive you for all of these sins and separate you from these sins of (yours and/or) your family in the 21st Degree, the Prussian Knight or Noachite. I command the curses of the 21st Degree to come off (name of brother/sister). All blasphemy, death, witchcraft, unbelief, violence, and dismemberment, leave (name of brother/sister) now. [Wait a moment for God to cause them to leave. Check with the Holy Spirit to be sure that all necessary deliverance has taken place. If you need to, continue to command the spirit(s) to leave. Include in this command the name(s) of any spirit(s) the Holy Spirit indicates.] Holy Spirit, please come and cleanse (name of brother/sister) and fill him/her where the enemy previously had rights.

Please bring Your healing now to (name of brother/sister) where he/she was affected by these curses.

Please remember to thank Jesus for His release and healing in these matters.

PRAYER SEQUENCE—RELEASE FROM THE 22ND DEGREE: KNIGHT OF THE ROYAL AXE OR PRINCE OF LIBANUS

Your prayer:

> I renounce (my and/or) the sins of my family in the rituals, oaths taken, and the curses of the Knight of the Royal Axe or Prince of Libanus in the 22nd Degree, its secret password "NOAH-BEZALEEI-SODONIAS," and its penalties. I forgive my family for opening me up to the curses and afflictions of this Degree.

> I renounce the power of the Masonic axe to cut down the people of God who are the true Cedars of Lebanon, the axe of Freemasonry that totally opposes the building of God's Tabernacle, and the Prince of Lebanus or Lebanon.

Prayer partner speaks:

> I witness and stand in agreement with these renunciations of (name of brother/sister). In Jesus' name, I forgive you for all of these sins and separate you from these sins of (yours and/or) your family in the 22nd Degree, Knight of the Royal Axe or Prince of Libanus. In Jesus' name, I command the curses of the 22nd Degree to come off (name of brother/sister). All blasphemy, lies, death, witchcraft, unbelief, violence, and dismemberment, leave

(name of brother/sister) now. [Wait a moment for God to cause them to leave. Check with the Holy Spirit to be sure that all necessary deliverance has taken place. If you need to, continue to command the spirit(s) to leave. Include in this command the name(s) of any spirit(s) the Holy Spirit indicates.] Holy Spirit, please come and cleanse (name of brother/sister) and fill him/her where the enemy previously had rights. Please bring Your healing now to (name of brother/sister) where he/she was affected by these curses.

Please remember to thank Jesus for His release and healing in these matters.

PRAYER SEQUENCE—RELEASE FROM THE 23RD DEGREE: CHIEF OF THE TABERNACLE

Your prayer:

I renounce (my and/or) the sins of my family in the rituals, oaths taken, and the curses of the Chief of the Tabernacle or 23rd Degree, the blasphemous use and mixture in the secret password "URIEL-JEHOVAH," and its penalty, the oath of agreement that "the Earth should open up and engulf me up to my neck so I perish." I forgive my family for opening me up to the curses and afflictions of this Degree.

I renounce the false mantle of priesthood, the false fruit of the spirit of Freemasonry.

I renounce the false seven-branched candlestick of astrology.

I renounce the blasphemous lie that the name "Elohim" means the Seven Archangels of God.

I renounce the investiture of this order, the white robe, the scarlet sash with its symbol of a black rosette from which hangs a golden censer, and the Masonic apron with its seven-branched candlestick.

Prayer partner speaks:

I witness and stand in agreement with these renunciations of (name of brother/sister). In Jesus' name, I forgive you for all of these sins and separate you from these sins of (yours and/ or) your family in the 23rd Degree, Chief of the Tabernacle. In Jesus' name, I command the curses of the 23rd Degree to come off (name of brother/sister). All blasphemy, death, witchcraft, unbelief, and violence, leave (name of brother/ sister) now. [Wait a moment for God to cause them to leave. Check with the Holy Spirit to be sure that all necessary deliverance has taken place. If you need to, continue to command the spirit(s) to leave. Include in this command the name(s) of any spirit(s) the Holy Spirit indicates.] Holy Spirit, please come and cleanse (name of brother/sister) and fill him/her where the enemy previously had rights. Please bring Your healing now to (name of brother/sister) where he/she was affected by these curses.

Please remember to thank Jesus for His release and healing in these matters.

PRAYER SEQUENCE—RELEASE FROM THE 24TH DEGREE: PRINCE OF THE TABERNACLE

Your prayer:

I renounce (my and/or) the sins of my family in the rituals, oaths taken, and the curses of the Prince of the Tabernacle or 24th Degree, and its penalty that I should be "stoned to death and my body be left above ground to rot." I forgive my family for opening me up to the curses and afflictions of this Degree.

I renounce the Gnostic view of the soul.

I renounce the Masonic lamp of reason, the Masonic cloak of false liberty, the false staff of Freemasonry, and the spirit of the warlock.

In the name of Christ Jesus, I command the spirits behind the lamp of reason, the Masonic cloak of false liberty, the false staff, and the spirit of the warlock to leave me. Holy Spirit, please come and fill me where these spirits have had influence in my life.

Prayer partner speaks:

I witness and stand in agreement with these renunciations of (name of brother/sister). In Jesus' name, I forgive you for all of these sins and separate you from these sins of (yours and/or) your family in the 24th Degree, Prince of the Tabernacle. In Jesus' name, I command the curses of the 24th Degree to come off (name of brother/sister). All blasphemy, death, witchcraft, unbelief, false doctrine, violence, and dishonor, leave (name of brother/sister) now. [Wait a moment for God to cause them to leave. Check with the Holy Spirit to be sure that all necessary deliverance has taken place. If you need to, continue to command the spirit(s) to leave. Include in this command the name(s) of any spirit(s) the Holy Spirit indicates.] Holy Spirit, please come and cleanse (name of brother/sister) and fill him/her where the enemy previously had rights. Please bring Your healing now to (name of brother/sister) where he/she was affected by these curses.

Please remember to thank Jesus for His release and healing in these matters.

PRAYER SEQUENCE—RELEASE FROM THE 25TH DEGREE: KNIGHTS OF THE BRAZEN SERPENT

Your prayer:

> I renounce (my and/or) the sins of my family in the rituals, oaths taken, and the curses of the Knights of the Brazen Serpent or 25th Degree, the blasphemous mixture in its secret password "MOSES-JOHANNES," and its penalty of having "my heart eaten by the most venomous of serpents" and thus "be left to perish most miserably." I forgive my family for opening me up to the curses and afflictions of this Degree.

> I renounce the worship of the occult brazen serpent, all false healing, the false savior Osiris, and the blockage it brings to being healed completely by God.

> In the Name of the Lord Jesus Christ, I command the curse of a broken heart and all emotional breakdown to leave me and that of the curses of death by any venomous serpent, literal or spiritual.

Prayer partner speaks:

> I witness and stand in agreement with these renunciations of (name of brother/sister). In Jesus' name, I forgive you for all of these sins and separate you from these sins of (yours and/ or) your family in the 25th Degree, Knights of the Brazen Serpent. In Jesus' name, I command all the curses of the 25th Degree to come off (name of brother/sister), including blasphemy, death, idolatry, witchcraft, unbelief, violence, and dismemberment; these must leave (name of brother/sister)

now. [Wait a moment for God to cause them to leave. Check with the Holy Spirit to be sure that all necessary deliverance has taken place. If you need to, continue to command the spirit(s) to leave. Include in this command the name(s) of any spirit(s) the Holy Spirit indicates.] Holy Spirit, please come and cleanse (name of brother/sister) and fill him/her where the enemy previously had rights. Please bring Your healing now to (name of brother/sister) where he/she was affected by these curses.

Please remember to thank Jesus for His release and healing in these matters.

PRAYER SEQUENCE—RELEASE FROM THE 26TH DEGREE: SCOTTISH TRINITARIAN OR PRINCE OF MERCY

Your prayer:

I renounce (my and/or) the sins of my family in the rituals, oaths taken, and the curses of the Scottish Trinitarian or Prince of Mercy, the 26th Degree, the blasphemous mixture of its secret password "GOMEL, JEHOVAH-JACHIN," and its penalty of condemnation and spite by the entire universe. I forgive my family for opening me up to the curses and afflictions of this Degree.

I renounce the triple covenant made with the false god, the Great Architect of the Universe.

I renounce the blasphemy of embracing a gospel of Jesus Christ mixed with the teachings of false religions.

I renounce the Egyptian trinity of Isis, Horeb, and Seb (the mother, child, and father of the gods) and command these to leave me and my family.

Prayer partner speaks:

> I witness and stand in agreement with these renunciations of (name of brother/sister). In Jesus' name, I forgive you for all of these sins and separate you from these sins of (yours and/or) your family in the 26th Degree, Scottish Trinitarian or Prince of Mercy. In Jesus' name, I command all the curses of the 26th Degree to come off (name of brother/sister), including all blasphemy, death, witchcraft, unbelief, rejection, hatred, violence, and false doctrine; they must leave (name of brother/sister) now. [Wait a moment for God to cause them to leave. Check with the Holy Spirit to be sure that all necessary deliverance has taken place. If you need to, continue to command the spirit(s) to leave. Include in this command the name(s) of any spirit(s) the Holy Spirit indicates.] Holy Spirit, please come and cleanse (name of brother/sister) and fill him/her where the enemy previously had rights. Please bring Your healing now to (name of brother/sister) where he/she was affected by these curses.

PRAYER SEQUENCE—RELEASE FROM THE 27TH DEGREE: KNIGHT COMMANDER OF THE TEMPLE

Your prayer:

> I renounce (my and/or) the sins of my family in the rituals, oaths taken, and the curses of the Knight Commander of the Temple or 27th Degree, and the blasphemous use of the secret password "SOLOMON," and its penalty of receiving the "severest wrath of Almighty God inflicted upon me." I forgive my family for opening me up to the curses and afflictions of this Degree.

I renounce the false warrior mantle of the Teutonic Knight and the black two-headed eagle of false prophetic deliverance.

Prayer partner speaks:

> I witness and stand in agreement with these renunciations of (name of brother/sister). In Jesus' name, I forgive you for all of these sins and separate you from these sins of (yours and/or) your family in the 27th Degree, Knight Commander of the Temple. In Jesus' name, I command the curses of the 27th Degree to come off (name of brother/sister). All blasphemy, death, witchcraft, unbelief, false doctrine, curse, and violence, leave (name of brother/sister) now. [Wait a moment for God to cause them to leave. Check with the Holy Spirit to be sure that all necessary deliverance has taken place. If you need to, continue to command the spirit(s) to leave. Include in this command the name(s) of any spirit(s) the Holy Spirit indicates.] Holy Spirit, please come and cleanse (name of brother/sister) and fill him/her where the enemy previously had rights. Please bring Your healing now to (name of brother/sister) where he/she was affected by these curses.

Please remember to thank Jesus for His release and healing in these matters.

PRAYER SEQUENCE—RELEASE FROM THE 28TH DEGREE: KNIGHTS OF THE SUN OR PRINCE ADEPT

Your prayer:

> I renounce (my and/or) the sins of my family in the rituals, oaths taken, and the curses of the Knights of the Sun or Prince Adept, the 28th Degree, its secret password "STIBIUM," and its penalties of "having my tongue thrust through with a red-

hot iron," of "my eyes being plucked out," of "my senses of smelling and hearing being removed," of "having my hands cut off and in that condition to be left for voracious animals to devour me," or "be executed by lightning from heaven." I renounce all eye injury, loss of vision, loss of smell, loss of hearing, loss of hands or fingers, death by animal attack, or death by lightning stemming from the oaths and curses of the 28th Degree. I forgive my family for opening me up to the curses and afflictions of this Degree.

I renounce the lie of being unable to "rightly divide" the Word of God. I proclaim that through Christ Jesus I can do all things that He wishes for me.

I declare that the seven "angels" stationed in the lodge are demonic spirit guides and renounce them.

Prayer partner speaks:

I witness and stand in agreement with these renunciations of (name of brother/sister). In Jesus' name, I forgive you for all of these sins and separate you from these sins of (yours and/or) your family in the 28th Degree, Knights of the Sun or Prince Adept. In Jesus' name, I command the curses of the 28th Degree to come off (name of brother/sister). All blasphemy, death, witchcraft, unbelief, violence, and dismemberment, leave (name of brother/sister) now. [Wait a moment for God to cause them to leave. Check with the Holy Spirit to be sure that all necessary deliverance has taken place. If you need to, continue to command the spirit(s) to leave. Include in this command the name(s) of any spirit(s) the Holy Spirit indicates.] Holy Spirit, please come and cleanse (name of brother/sister) and fill him/her where the enemy previously had rights. Please bring Your healing now to (name of brother/sister) where he/she was affected by these curses.

Please remember to thank Jesus for His release and healing in these matters.

PRAYER SEQUENCE—RELEASE FROM THE 29TH DEGREE: GRAND SCOTTISH KNIGHT OF SAINT ANDREW

Your prayer:

> I renounce (my and/or) the sins of my family in the rituals, oaths taken, and the curses of the Grand Scottish Knight of Saint Andrew, the 29th Degree, its secret password "NEKAMAH-FURLAC," and its penalties. I forgive my family for opening me up to the curses and afflictions of this Degree.

> I renounce the Masonic baptism into knighthood.

> I renounce the antichrist words, "Salah-eddin must die," and the loss of victory in my Christian walk.

Prayer partner speaks:

> I witness and stand in agreement with these renunciations of (name of brother/sister). In Jesus' name, I forgive you for all of these sins and separate you from these sins of (yours and/or) your family in the 29th Degree, Grand Scottish Knight of Saint Andrew. In Jesus' name, I command the curses of the 29th Degree to come off (name of brother/sister). All blasphemy, death, witchcraft, unbelief, violence, and dismemberment, leave (name of brother/sister) now. [Wait a moment for God to cause them to leave. Check with the Holy Spirit to be sure that all necessary deliverance has taken place. If you need to, continue to command the spirit(s) to leave. Include in this command the name(s) of any spirit(s) the Holy Spirit indicates.] Holy Spirit, please come

and cleanse (name of brother/sister) and fill him/her where the enemy previously had rights. Please bring Your healing now to (name of brother/sister) where he/she was affected by these curses.

Please remember to thank Jesus for His release and healing in these matters.

PRAYER SEQUENCE—RELEASE FROM THE 30TH DEGREE: GRAND ELECT KNIGHT KADOSH AND KNIGHT OF THE BLACK AND WHITE EAGLE

Your prayer:

I renounce (my and/or) the sins of my family in the rituals, oaths taken, and the curses of the Grand Elect Knight Kadosh and Knight of the Black and White Eagle, the 30th Degree, its secret passwords "STIBIUM ALKABAR," "PHARASH-KOH," and all they mean. I forgive my family for opening me up to the curses and afflictions of this Degree.

I renounce the pledge, "to devote and consign myself to disgrace and contempt, to execration and punishment of the Grand Elect Knights Kadosh" and the pronouncement to "forget not that the slightest indiscretion will cost you your life" and "one step more and you are bound to us forever and at the peril of your life." I command the death penalty curses to leave me.

I renounce the oath "May the spirit that inhabited this skull rise and testify against me if ever I violate my obligation."

I renounce the secret word "GOLGOTHA" and the familiar spirit of death, and all infirmities associated with the person whose skull the candidate holds.

I renounce the blasphemous, evil use of the word "EMMANUEL," because the god of Freemasonry is Lucifer.

I renounce the "knight's curse" and the "death wish of Judas" and the curse of having my head cut off and placed on top of a church spire.

Every familiar spirit of death, I command you to leave me and my family now in Jesus Christ's name.

Prayer partner speaks:

I witness and stand in agreement with these renunciations of (name of brother/sister). In Jesus' name, I forgive you for all of these sins and separate you from these sins of (yours and/or) your family in the 30th Degree, Grand Elect Knight Kadosh and Knight of the Black and White Eagle. In Jesus' name, I command all the curses of the 30th Degree to come off (name of brother/sister), including blasphemy, death and death wishes, suicide, witchcraft, unbelief, spiritual slavery, perfection, violence, and dismemberment; these must leave (name of brother/sister) now. [Wait a moment for God to cause them to leave. Check with the Holy Spirit to be sure that all necessary deliverance has taken place. If you need to, continue to command the spirit(s) to leave. Include in this command the name(s) of any spirit(s) the Holy Spirit indicates.] Holy Spirit, please come and cleanse (name of brother/sister) and fill him/her where the enemy previously had rights. Please bring Your healing now to (name of brother/sister) where he/she was affected by these curses.

Please remember to thank Jesus for His release and healing in these matters.

PRAYER SEQUENCE—RELEASE FROM THE 31ST DEGREE: GRAND INSPECTOR INQUISITOR COMMANDER

Your prayer:

> I renounce (my and/or) the sins of my family in the rituals, oaths taken, and the curses of the Grand Inspector Inquisitor Commander, the 31st Degree. I forgive my family for opening me up to the curses and afflictions of this Degree.

> I renounce all the gods and goddesses of Egypt which are honored in this Degree, including Anubis with the jackal's head, Osiris the sun god, Isis the sister and wife of Osiris, and the moon goddess.

> I renounce the Soul of Cheres, the false symbol of immortality, the Chamber of the Dead, and the false teaching of reincarnation.

> I renounce the pledge of "consigning of myself to the contempt of my brethren and to their just and terrible anger, to be visited upon my unprotected head ...."

> I renounce the lie that "all religions are but a shadow of the one primitive religion preserved throughout history by the Adepts."

> I renounce the Masonic trial, Masonic legalism, false repentance, the Masonic Tribunal, and being judged by the ungodly.

Prayer partner speaks:

> I witness and stand in agreement with these renunciations of (name of brother/sister). In Jesus' name, I forgive you for all of these sins and separate you from these sins of

(yours and/or) your family in the 31st Degree, Grand Inspector Inquisitor Commander. All blasphemy, death, witchcraft, unbelief, violence, hatred, rejection, false accusation, condemnation, idolatry, and dismemberment, leave (name of brother/sister) now. [Wait a moment for God to cause them to leave. Check with the Holy Spirit to be sure that all necessary deliverance has taken place. If you need to, continue to command the spirit(s) to leave. Include in this command the name(s) of any spirit(s) the Holy Spirit indicates.] Holy Spirit, please come and cleanse (name of brother/sister) and fill him/her where the enemy previously had rights. Please bring Your healing now to (name of brother/sister) where he/she was affected by these curses.

Please remember to thank Jesus for His release and healing in these matters.

PRAYER SEQUENCE—RELEASE FROM THE 32ND DEGREE: SUBLIME PRINCE OF THE ROYAL SECRET

Your prayer:

I renounce (my and/or) the sins of my family in the rituals, oaths taken, and the curses of the Sublime Prince of the Royal Secret, the 32nd Degree, the secret password "PHAAL/ PHARASH-KOL," and all that it means. I forgive my family for opening me up to the curses and afflictions of this Degree.

I renounce Freemasonry's false trinitarian deity AUM, and its parts: Brahma the creator, Vishnu the preserver, and Shiva the destroyer.

I renounce the deity of Ahura Mazda, the claimed spirit or source of all light, including its worship with fire, which is an abomination to God, and the drinking from a human skull in many Rites.

I renounce the "Secret Doctrine," the "Royal Secret," and the "Luciferian Doctrine."

I renounce the words, "a skeleton wraps cold arms of death around its victim," proclaimed as communion out of a human skeleton is served. I renounce this curse of a Masonic covenant with death.

I renounce the oath taken saying, "the wine will turn to poison." I command this death wish and self-curse to leave me, in Jesus' name.

I renounce being "poisoned" in my physical life, my reputation and my relationships. I renounce death through drug overdose, accidental or deliberate. I renounce all poisonous drug use and addiction off my life and the lives of my children.

I renounce death through anesthetic overdose or drug overdose whether intended, authorized or "by mistake."

Prayer partner speaks:

I witness and stand in agreement with these renunciations of (name of brother/sister). In Jesus' name, I forgive you for all of these sins and separate you from these sins of (yours and/or) your family in the 32nd Degree, Sublime Prince of the Royal Secret. In Jesus' name, I command all the curses of the 32nd Degree to come off (name of brother/sister), including idolatry, blasphemy, death, witchcraft, unbelief, violence, and dismemberment; these must leave (name of brother/sister) now. [Wait a moment for God to cause them to leave. Check with the Holy Spirit to be sure that all necessary deliverance has taken place. If you need to, continue to command the spirit(s) to leave. Include in this command the name(s) of any spirit(s) the Holy Spirit indicates.] Holy Spirit, please come and cleanse (name of brother/sister) and fill him/her where the enemy previously had rights. Please bring Your healing now to (name of brother/sister) where he/she was affected by these curses.

Please remember to thank Jesus for His release and healing in these matters.

PRAYER SEQUENCE—RELEASE FROM THE 33RD DEGREE: GRAND SOVEREIGN INSPECTOR GENERAL

Your prayer:

I renounce (my and/or) the sins of my family in the rituals, oaths taken, and the curses of the Grand Sovereign Inspector General, the 33rd Degree, its blasphemous mixture, secret passwords "DEMOLAY-HIRUM ABIFF," "FREDERICK OF PRUSSIA," "MICHA, MACHA, BEALIM and ADONAI," and all that they mean. I forgive my family for opening me up to the curses and afflictions of this Degree.

I renounce all of the invocation of all the former obligations of Freemasonry, including having my tongue torn out by its roots, and all other penalties.

I renounce and forsake the blasphemous, idolatrous, heretical declaration that Lucifer is God.

I renounce the cable tow around the neck and the 33rd Degree Masonic ring.

I renounce the death wish that the wine drunk from a human skull should turn to poison, and the skeleton whose cold arms are invited if the oath of this Degree is violated.

I renounce the investiture of the robes of witchcraft, the three infamous assassins of the Grand Master—law, property and religion—and the greed, witchcraft, and attempt to manipulate and control that they represent.

I renounce the words, "a three-edged blade pierce the eyeball." I break the curse of eye accidents, blindness, cataracts, eye diseases, pain to the eyes, and unnatural deterioration of sight in any way linked to this blood oath.

I cut off and remove the cable tow from around my neck and remove the Masonic ring from my finger, and their symbolic meanings of death penalties and slavery to the spirits behind Freemasonry.

Prayer partner speaks:

I witness and stand in agreement with these renunciations of (name of brother/sister). In Jesus' name, I forgive you for all of these sins and separate you from these sins of (yours and/or) your family in the 33rd Degree, Grand Sovereign Inspector General. In Jesus' name, I command all the curses of the 33rd Degree to come off (name of brother/sister). All allegiance to Satan, blasphemy, death, witchcraft, unbelief, violence, and dismemberment, leave (name of brother/sister) now. [Wait a moment for God to cause them to leave. Check with the Holy Spirit to be sure that all necessary deliverance has taken place. If you need to, continue to command the spirit(s) to leave. Include in this command the name(s) of any spirit(s) the Holy Spirit indicates.] Holy Spirit, please come and cleanse (name of brother/sister) and fill him/her where the enemy previously had rights. Please bring Your healing now to (name of brother/sister) where he/she was affected by these curses, particularly in the area of physical and spiritual sight.

Please remember to thank Jesus for His release and healing in these matters.

PRAYER SEQUENCE—RELEASE FROM THE SHRINERS (AT DEGREES 32 AND ABOVE): ANCIENT ARABIC ORDER OF THE NOBLES OF THE MYSTIC SHRINE

Your prayer:

I renounce (my and/or) the sins of my family in the rituals, oaths taken, and the curses and penalties involved in the Ancient Arabic Order of the Nobles of the Mystic Shrine. I forgive my family for opening me up to the curses and afflictions of this Degree.

I renounce the elements in the Shriners' logo symbol: the Arabic curved sword, the upside-down horns, the five-pointed satanic star, the phallus symbol, and the image of the ancient goddess of Egypt.

I renounce the Red Fez cap with its gold trim and tassel and its murderous bondage, being the symbol of the bloody massacre of Christians by the Moslem hordes.

I renounce the piercing of the eyeballs with a three-edged blade, the flaying of the feet, the madness, and the worship of the false god Allah as the god of our fathers.

I renounce the hoodwink, the mock hanging, the mock beheading, the mock drinking of the blood of the victim, the mock dog urinating on the initiate, and the offering of urine as a commemoration.

I renounce the emitting of electric shock to the body to simulate the walking on the hot sands of the desert, and the nervous disorders resulting from the ritual oath.

I renounce all the spiritualism or necromancy in the workings of the Order.

Prayer partner speaks:

I witness and stand in agreement with these renunciations of (name of brother/sister). In Jesus' name, I forgive you for all of these sins and separate you from these sins of (yours and/or) your family in the Shriners, Ancient Arabic Order of the Nobles of the Mystic Shrine. In Jesus' name, I command the curses of the order of the Shriners to come off (name of brother/sister). All blasphemy, death, witchcraft, unbelief, degradation, filthiness, violence, dismemberment, and murder, leave (name of brother/sister) now. [Wait a moment for God to cause them to leave. Check with the Holy Spirit to be sure that all necessary deliverance has taken place. If you need to, continue to command the spirit(s) to leave. Include in this command the name(s) of any spirit(s) the Holy Spirit indicates.]

In the name of Jesus, I command all idolatry, mockery, uncleanness, blindness, the spirit of Allah, and every other spirit associated with this Degree to leave (name of brother/sister). [Wait a moment for God to do this. Check with the Holy Spirit to be sure that all deliverance that was necessary has taken place. If necessary, continue to command the spirit(s) to leave and include in this command the name(s) of any spirit(s) the Holy Spirit indicates.]

Holy Spirit, please come and cleanse (name of brother/sister) and fill him/her where the enemy previously had rights. Please bring Your healing now to (name of brother/sister) where he/she was affected by these curses, particularly in his/her eyesight, neck and feet, mental stability, and health.

Please remember to thank Jesus for His release and healing in these matters.

Prayer Ministry for the York Rite

(a fraternal structure that parallels the Scottish Rite Freemasonry)

PRAYER SEQUENCE—RELEASE FROM THE MARK MASTER DEGREE, YORK RITE

Your prayer:

I renounce (my and/or) the sins of my family in the rituals, oaths taken, the curses, and penalties involved in the Mark Master Degree in the York Rite of Freemasonry. I forgive my family for opening me up to the curses and afflictions of this Degree.

I renounce the false cornerstone of the temple and declare there is only one cornerstone, the Lord Jesus Christ. I renounce the defiling of the cornerstone by an astrological seal.

I renounce being rejected from "the real Temple of the Lord," the false trinity of Freemasonry, the fourfold cable tow and all that it means, and being immobilized in all areas of my life, physically, in my soul, and spirit.

I renounce the cutting off of the hand, the cutting off of fair pay and financial blessings, the cutting off of the fruit of labor, and the cutting off of favor by fellow employees.

Prayer partner speaks:

> I witness and stand in agreement with these renunciations of (name of brother/sister). In Jesus' name, I forgive you for all of these sins and separate you from these sins of (yours and/or) your family in the Mark Master Degree of the York Rite. In Jesus' name, I command the curses of this Degree to come off (name of brother/sister). All blasphemy, heresy, dismemberment, rejection, poverty, strife, persecution, and conspiracy, leave (name of brother/sister) now. [Wait a moment for God to cause them to leave. Check with the Holy Spirit to be sure that all necessary deliverance has taken place. If you need to, continue to command the spirit(s) to leave. Include in this command the name(s) of any spirit(s) the Holy Spirit indicates.] Holy Spirit, please come and cleanse (name of brother/sister) and fill him/her where the enemy previously had rights. Please bring Your healing now to (name of brother/sister) where he/she was affected by these curses.

Please remember to thank Jesus for His release and healing in these matters.

PRAYER SEQUENCE—RELEASE FROM THE PAST MASTER DEGREE, YORK RITE

Your prayer:

> I renounce (my and/or) the sins of my family in the rituals, oaths taken, the curses and penalties involved in the Past Master Degree in the York Rite of Freemasonry. I forgive my family for opening me up to the curses and afflictions of this Degree.

> I renounce the violent self-curse of having my "tongue split from tip to root" for divulging any of the secrets or stepping away from the oaths of this Degree.

I renounce having leadership without authority, abdication, and ungodly takeover.

Prayer partner speaks:

I witness and stand in agreement with these renunciations of (name of brother/sister). In Jesus' name, I forgive you for all of these sins and separate you from these sins of (yours and/or) your family in the Past Master Degree of the York Rite. In Jesus' name, I command the curses of this Degree to come off (name of brother/sister). All shame, embarrassment, conspiracy, victimization, recrimination, abdication, favoritism, promotion beyond ability, usurping, and curses on speech, the tongue, and communication, leave (name of brother/sister) now. [Wait a moment for God to cause them to leave. Check with the Holy Spirit to be sure that all necessary deliverance has taken place. If you need to, continue to command the spirit(s) to leave. Include in this command the name(s) of any spirit(s) the Holy Spirit indicates.] Holy Spirit, please come and cleanse (name of brother/sister) and fill him/her where the enemy previously had rights. Please bring Your healing now to (name of brother/sister) where he/she was affected by these curses.

Please remember to thank Jesus for His release and healing in these matters.

PRAYER SEQUENCE—RELEASE FROM THE MOST EXCELLENT MASTER DEGREE, YORK RITE

Your prayer:

I renounce (my and/or) the sins of my family in the rituals, oaths taken, the curses and penalties involved in the Most Excellent Master Degree in the York Rite of Freemasonry.

I forgive my family for opening me up to the curses and afflictions of this Degree.

I renounce the indoctrination ritual of yielding to temptation and falling into sin.

Prayer partner speaks:

I witness and stand in agreement with these renunciations of (name of brother/sister). In Jesus' name, I forgive you for all of these sins and separate you from these sins of (yours and/or) your family in the Most Excellent Master Degree of the York Rite. In Jesus' name, I command the curses of this Degree to come off (name of brother/sister). All evil spirits sent to bring weakness of spirit, will and conscience, lack of conviction, covetousness, envy, and unbelief (that God is the supplier of your needs), leave (name of brother/sister) now. [Wait a moment for God to cause them to leave. Check with the Holy Spirit to be sure that all necessary deliverance has taken place. If you need to, continue to command the spirit(s) to leave. Include in this command the name(s) of any spirit(s) the Holy Spirit indicates.] Holy Spirit, please come and cleanse (name of brother/sister) and fill him/her where the enemy previously had rights. Please bring Your healing now to (name of brother/sister) where he/she was affected by these curses.

Please remember to thank Jesus for His release and healing in these matters.

PRAYER SEQUENCE—RELEASE FROM THE ROYAL ARCH DEGREE, YORK RITE

Your prayer:

I renounce (my and/or) the sins of my family in the rituals, oaths taken, curses, and penalties involved in the Royal

Arch Degree in the York Rite of Freemasonry. I forgive my family for opening me up to the curses and afflictions of this Degree.

I renounce the self-destructive oaths of:

- "having my right ear smote off that I may forever be unable to hear the word and my right hand struck off as the penalty of an imposter"
- "having my bowels torn asunder, and that the earth may open and swallow me up as it did Korah, Dathan and Abiram for their rebellion"
- "having the crown of my head struck off, and my brains taken out and burnt to ashes"
- "having the skull struck off and the brain exposed to the scorching rays of the noonday sun."

I renounce the triple crown, proclaiming self-godhood as king over heaven, earth, and hell, and the blasphemy of that claim.

I renounce the four veils and the rod of divination used in this indoctrination, as well as the proclamation, "I AM, I AM," declaring equality with God.

I renounce the mimicking of Moses' "putting his hand inside his clothing and withdrawing it" (as leprous and again withdrawing it as whole) and the passwords "HAGGAI," "JOSHUA," "ZERUBBABEL," and "RABBONI."

I renounce the false sonship declared in the lodge meeting of blasphemy, counterfeit miracles, and usurping God's position—a place where Satan reigns.

I renounce off my life and refute the mark of the "mysterious triple tau," representing salvation by good works.

I renounce off my life the altar inscription, mixing the name of God, Jehovah, with the false trinity, Jah-Bul-On, a demonic trinity composed of Your Name, Lord, the name of Baal, and the name of Osiris. I deeply renounce (my and/or) any of my forefathers' accepting this lie.

I renounce the curses from opening the counterfeit Ark of the Covenant and the Masonic "law of sin and death."

I renounce the irreverent comparison of God to the Hindu trinity, creator, preserver, and destroyer: Brahma, Vishnu, and Shiva (sometimes, Brahman, Krishna, and Kali [death]).

I renounce the false love and unity of Freemasonry.

Prayer partner speaks:

I witness and stand in agreement with these renunciations of (name of brother/sister). In Jesus' name, I forgive you for all of these sins and separate you from these sins of (yours and/or) your family in the Royal Arch Degree of the York Rite. In Jesus' name, I command all the curses of this Degree to come off (name of brother/sister), including blasphemy, death and death wishes, suicide, witchcraft, unbelief, spiritual slavery, false perfection, violence, and dismemberment; these must leave (name of brother/sister) now. In the name of Jesus, I command every Hindu spirit, the spirit of Osiris, Baal, and the spirits of confusion, mind and memory problems, decapitation, brain cancer, burial alive, and murder to leave (name of brother/sister). Yes, everything that came in through this Degree must go now in Jesus' name! [Wait a moment for God to cause them to leave. Check with the Holy Spirit to be sure that all necessary deliverance has taken place. If you need to, continue to command the spirit(s) to leave.

Include in this command the name(s) of any spirit(s) the Holy Spirit indicates.] Holy Spirit, please come and cleanse (name of brother/sister) and fill him/her where the enemy previously had rights. Please bring Your healing now to (name of brother/sister) where he/she was affected by these curses.

Please remember to thank Jesus for His release and healing in these matters.

PRAYER SEQUENCE—RELEASE FROM THE SUPER EXCELLENT MASTER DEGREE, YORK RITE

Your prayer:

I renounce (my and/or) the sins of my family in the rituals, oaths taken, the curses, and penalties involved in the Super Excellent Master Degree in the York Rite of Freemasonry. I forgive my family for opening me up to the curses and afflictions of this Degree.

I renounce the indoctrination ritual of having the thumbs cut off, being bound in bronze shackles, the rebellion and irresponsibility found in King Zedekiah, the binding of the will, physical and/or spiritual blindness, and the control of witchcraft.

Prayer partner speaks:

I witness and stand in agreement with these renunciations of (name of brother/sister). In Jesus' name, I forgive you for all of these sins and separate you from these sins of (yours and/or) your family in the Super Excellent Master Degree of the York Rite. In Jesus' name, I command the curses of this Degree to come off (name of brother/sister). All evil spirits sent to bring weakness of will, rebellion, irresponsibility, dismemberment, physical and spiritual blindness, captivity, and witchcraft; all these leave (name of brother/sister) now. [Wait a moment for God to cause them to leave. Check with the Holy Spirit to be sure that all necessary deliverance has taken place. If you need to, continue to command the spirit(s) to leave. Include in this command the name(s) of any spirit(s) the Holy Spirit indicates.] Holy Spirit, please come and cleanse (name of brother/sister) and fill him/her where the enemy previously had rights. Please bring Your healing now to (name of brother/sister) where he/she was affected by these curses.

Please remember to thank Jesus for His release and healing in these matters.

PRAYER SEQUENCE—RELEASE FROM THE ORDER OF THE RED CROSS DEGREE, YORK RITE

Your prayer:

I renounce (my and/or) the sins of my family in the rituals, oaths taken, the curses and penalties involved in the Order of the Red Cross Degree in the York Rite of Freemasonry. I forgive my family for opening me up to the curses and afflictions of this Degree.

I renounce the indoctrination ritual of being nearly stabbed before speaking the password "TRUTH." I renounce this password and the false light and truth of Freemasonry.

I renounce the further passwords "JUDAH" and "BENJAMIN," instated to give the initiate the character of a lion and a wolf.

I declare that there is one Lion of Judah, Jesus Christ, whom I worship. I renounce all other affiliations and claims of this Degree, including that of a wolf.

276

Prayer partner speaks:

> I witness and stand in agreement with these renunciations
> of (name of brother/sister). In Jesus' name, I forgive you
> for all of these sins and separate you from these sins of
> (yours and/or) your family in the Order of the Red Cross
> Degree of the York Rite. In Jesus' name, I command the
> curses of this Degree to come off (name of brother/sister).
> All evil spirits sent to bring attempted murder, to bring an
> animal spirit or idolatry, and the false light and false truth
> of Freemasonry must leave (name of brother/sister) now.
> [Wait a moment for God to cause them to leave. Check
> with the Holy Spirit to be sure that all necessary deliverance
> has taken place. If you need to, continue to command the
> spirit(s) to leave. Include in this command the name(s) of
> any spirit(s) the Holy Spirit indicates.] Holy Spirit, please
> come and cleanse (name of brother/sister) and fill him/her
> where the enemy previously had rights. Please bring Your
> healing now to (name of brother/sister) where he/she was
> affected by these curses.

Please remember to thank Jesus for His release and healing in these
matters.

PRAYER SEQUENCE—RELEASE FROM THE ORDER OF
THE KNIGHTS OF MALTA DEGREE, YORK RITE

Your prayer:

> I renounce (my and/or) the sins of my family in the rituals,
> oaths taken, the curses and penalties involved in the Order of
> the Knights of Malta Degree in the York Rite of Freemasonry.
> I forgive my family for opening me up to the curses and
> afflictions of this Degree.

I renounce the self-curses of this Degree:

- "If I ever violate my obligation, I consent to have my head cut off, and stuck on the highest pole or pinnacle in the eastern part of the world, as a monument to my villainy."
- "the sins of the person whose skull this once was be heaped upon my head in addition to my own; and may he appear in judgment against me, both here and hearafter, should I violate or transgress in Masonry, of Orders of this knighthood."

I renounce the false communion and the "spiritual self-crucifixion" of this Degree.

I renounce the black cross of crucifixion on the robes of this Degree.

Prayer partner speaks:

I witness and stand in agreement with these renunciations of (name of brother/sister). In Jesus' name, I forgive you for all of these sins and separate you from these sins of (yours and/or) your family in the Order of the Knights of Malta Degree of the York Rite. In Jesus' name, I command the curses of this Degree to come off (name of brother/sister). All evil spirits sent to bring self-criticism and self-hate, murder, vilification, decapitation, dismemberment, and to cause the judgment and sins of someone else to fall on you must leave (name of brother/sister) now. In Jesus' name, I break the curses of inviting a familiar spirit to come and persecute (name of brother/sister). [Wait a moment for God to cause them to leave. Check with the Holy Spirit to be sure that all necessary deliverance has taken place. If you need to, continue to command the spirit(s) to leave.

Include in this command the name(s) of any spirit(s) the Holy Spirit indicates.] Holy Spirit, please come and cleanse (name of brother/sister) and fill him/her where the enemy previously had rights. Please bring Your healing now to (name of brother/sister) where he/she was affected by these curses.

Please remember to thank Jesus for His release and healing in these matters.

Prayer Sequence—General Release (Renunciation) from Other Related Degrees

Your prayer:

I renounce (my and/or) the sins of my family in the rituals, oaths taken, and the curses and penalties of all other ungodly indoctrinations entered into, pronounced by or received by (me and/or) my family and I forgive them for every other Degree. I claim the shed blood of Jesus between (my and/or) their sins in these including the Allied Degrees, the Red Cross of Constantine, the Masonic Royal Order of Scotland, the Order of the Secret Monitor, the Knights of Malta, and the Knights Templar.

I also renounce (my and/or) the sins of my family in the rituals, oaths taken, and the curses and penalties of all other ungodly indoctrinations for every other group or organization entered into, pronounced by, or received by (me and/or) my family and I forgive them (and/or myself) for this. I claim the shed blood of Jesus between (my and/or their sins) with these groups, associations or organizations, including:[66]

- Prince Hall Freemasonry
- Mormonism
- The Order of Amaranth
- The Royal Order of Jesters
- The Druids
- Foresters
- The Manchester Unity
- Order of Odd Fellows
- The Orange, Buffalos, Elks, Moose and Eagles Lodges
- The Ku Klux Klan
- The Grange
- The Woodmen of the World
- Riders of the Red Robe
- The Knights of Pythias
- The Mystic Order of the Veiled Prophets of the Enchanted Realm

- The women's Orders of the Eastern Star, of the Ladies' Oriental Shrine, and the White Shrine of Jerusalem
- The girls' Order of the Daughters of the Eastern Star
- The International Orders of Job's Daughters, and of the Rainbow
- The boys' Order of DeMolay

Included with the above are all the ungodly indoctrinations and pledges in school (i.e. college/university) fraternities and sororities (including allegiance or homage to gods like Neptune and other Greek gods and goddesses). I renounce all the allegiances, agreements, and false deities associated with these, and their effects on me and all my family.

> I renounce the pagan ritual of the "Point within a Circle" with all its bondages and phallic worship. I renounce the symbol "G" and its veiled pagan symbolism and bondages in Freemasonry.

I renounce and utterly forsake the Great Architect of the Universe who is revealed in the higher Degrees of Freemasonry as Lucifer, and his false claim to be the universal fatherhood of God.

I also renounce the false claim that Lucifer is the Morning Star and Shining One and I declare that Jesus Christ is the Bright and Morning Star of Revelation 22:16.

I renounce the All-Seeing Third Eye of Freemasonry (or Eye of Horus) in the forehead and its pagan and occult symbolism.

I renounce all false communions taken, all mockery of the redemptive work of Jesus Christ on the cross, all unbelief, confusion, depression, and all worship of Lucifer as God.

I renounce and forsake the lie of Freemasonry that "man is not sinful but merely imperfect," and so can redeem himself through good works. I rejoice that the Bible states that I cannot do a single thing to earn my salvation, but that I can only be saved by grace through faith in Jesus Christ and what He accomplished on the cross of Calvary.

I renounce all fear of insanity, anguish, death wishes, suicide, and death in the name of Jesus Christ. Death was conquered by Jesus Christ; He alone holds the keys of death and hell. I rejoice that He holds my life in His hands now. He came to give me life abundant and eternal, and I believe His promises.

I renounce all anger, hatred, revenge, retaliation, murderous thoughts, pride, spiritual apathy, false religion, all unbelief, especially in the Bible as the Word of God, and all compromise of God's Word.

I renounce all spiritual searching into false religions and all striving for acceptance by God through works, and all legalism. I rest in the knowledge that I am in my Lord and Savior Jesus Christ and He is in me.

Prayer partner speaks:

I witness and stand in agreement with these renunciations of (name of brother/sister). In Jesus' name I speak forgiveness to you (name of brother/sister) for any of the sinful practices which you just now renounced and repented of, for yourself and for the family members in your generation line. I claim the shed blood of Jesus between you and these sinful practices.

In Jesus' name, I command the curses of these orders, groups, and organizations (associations) to come off (name of brother/sister). All blasphemy, death, witchcraft, unbelief, violence, dismemberment, murder, and other spirits rooted in the sinful practices of these, leave (name of brother/sister) now. [Wait a moment for God to cause them to leave. Check with the Holy Spirit to be sure that all necessary deliverance has taken place. If you need to, continue to command the spirit(s) to leave. Include in this command the name(s) of any spirit(s) the Holy Spirit indicates.] Holy Spirit, please come and cleanse (name of brother/sister) and fill him/her where the enemy previously had rights. Please bring Your healing now to (name of brother/sister) where he/she was affected by these curses.

Please remember to thank Jesus for His release and healing in these matters.

Prayer Sequence—General Closing Prayer for Chapter 12

Your prayer:

Lord Jesus, thank You for all You have given me throughout this chapter and this book. I continue to renounce (my and/ or) my antecedents' willingly entering into the various agreements with Satan as documented herein. As I have been faithful to pray through these issues, I declare that none of these covenants now belong to me and I ask that you would remove the effects from my family, including my descendants. These things were spoken onto our generational line. And now, Heavenly Father, in the Name that is above all other names, the Name of Jesus Christ, I continue to speak and affirm my new position of freedom in Christ Jesus. I continue to hold my antecedents (ancestors) in forgiveness for opening me up to the curses and afflictions of Freemasonry.

Jesus Christ is my Lord, and I proclaim that I come under the New Covenant of the precious blood of the Lord Jesus Christ and that covenant negates and totally obliterates every other contract, covenant, agreement, choice, decision, allegiance or oath given to Satan.

I ask that you would continue to cleanse and deliver me from all the after-effects of Freemasonry and the related Degrees and associated organizations as named in this chapter.

Amen.

APPENDICES

Salvation and Lordship

Introduction

It Isn't Free and It Isn't Masonry is a unique book providing ordinary believers with the pathway to freedom from Freemasonry. But typical churchgoers rarely have the training, understanding, and spiritual strength to escape Freemasonry by themselves. Going through the exercises in the first seven chapters will both strengthen and cleanse you in preparation for your journey through the last five chapters, where you will be addressing Freemasonry directly. This appendix is designed to augment the teaching and exercises presented in Part I of the book.

To receive the freedoms offered in this book you must be a Christian, knowing the Lord Jesus Christ as your personal Savior. (See "Salvation" paragraphs in Section 1.0, below.) We hope to assist you with a further working awareness of God and His Kingdom, and an understanding of yourself. Having said that, as you come to understand more, it may be that you will wish to pray the Salvation Prayer to God, as it is written in the following paragraphs (see

Section 1.0, "Salvation"). Making this commitment can help you begin or strengthen your walk with God through His Son Jesus Christ. Confirmation of your faith is vitally important when entering any level or form of spiritual warfare, including the removal of Freemasonry from your life.

Appendix I covers some of the basic building blocks for understanding both the natural and spiritual realms. Here we will discover our relationship to those realms and to our Creator. Without this knowledge, we cannot easily understand who we are, how we are made, or our relationship with God. Knowledge is power. Without knowledge of the spiritual realm, of God Himself and His spiritual laws and principles, we will perish. But there is a difference between worldly knowledge and godly knowledge—(Genesis 12:17 vs. 1 Corinthians 12:8), the latter bringing the purposes of God and life, the former separating us from God.

Later in Appendix I, we will explore our roles and responsibilities, both here on earth and in heaven. We will examine some basic parameters of the structure and makeup of people and of the earthly and heavenly realms. While these concepts are presented in the Bible, they are summarized here to give you a conceptual overview. Please join us as we begin our exciting journey into freedom and healing through the knowledge of God. The first step is salvation!

1.0 Salvation

In this section, we will look at the concept and doctrine of salvation and what it means to ordinary people like you and me. The concept of salvation is universal to Christianity. It is the doorway through which every man, woman, and child must pass in order to enter a relationship with God.

Salvation is a bit like the process of walking through the doorway to our home. We insert our key into the lock in order to enter into all the safety, comfort and provision inside our house. We are thankful for the door that keeps the world out. In salvation we enter our Maker's house, where we find a relationship with Him! Jesus is the door, and the Holy Spirit, like a lock, seals us for heaven. Let's now see exactly what God's gift of salvation is, and how to obtain the keys to receiving it for ourselves.

The word "salvation" gives us some clues to what it might be. The Greek word *sozo*, as it first appears in the earliest texts of ancient Bible manuscripts, means "to be saved." So, the most reasonable question is, "From what must I be saved?" The answer is simply "Hell." This is the final destination for all those who do not know God and are disobedient to His ways. This is where they will go when their earthly bodies die!

> ... the Lord Jesus will be ... dealing out retribution to those who do
> not know God and to those who do not obey the gospel of our Lord
> Jesus. These will pay the penalty of eternal destruction, away from
> the presence of the Lord and from the glory of His power... [i.e. in
> hell].

> 2 Thessalonians 1:7–9

The process of entering salvation is further examined in the Engle Scale (see paragraphs and table in the next section). The Engle Scale explains the route a person takes from unbelief to full salvation. The first step is becoming aware of something more than the natural world, or natural realm. Then we begin to discern good and evil. Progressively, we come to know about God. We then move on to discover our own sinful condition. Eventually heaven and hell, i.e. the eternal realms, are brought into our understanding. Finally, the Doorway to Heaven (Jesus) is revealed to us, that we might be saved from hell—if we so choose!

So, what must we do to be saved, to escape from having hell as our ultimate destination? We must enter into a relationship with the Living God and receive eternal life, to live with Him in heaven, when our earthly bodies die. Let's examine several Scriptures that explain how we might be saved. The first Bible verse we need to examine is

> *For God so loved the world, that He gave His only begotten Son, that whoever believes in Him shall not perish, but have eternal life.*

> John 3:16

So, the first key to salvation is to believe in Jesus. He is God's only begotten Son, who came to earth to take upon Himself the penalty of death that is due us for all of our sins. As we come to recognize Jesus' sacrifice for us, we may then acknowledge Him as Lord.

The second key is realizing that we must turn from our sinful (ungodly) ways, at which point we may receive salvation. Let's look at a second scripture to give us understanding of how to use these keys to salvation. The Bible tells us,

> *... if you confess with your mouth Jesus as Lord, and believe in your heart that God raised Him from the dead, you will be saved; for with the heart a person believes, resulting in righteousness, and with the mouth he confesses, resulting in salvation,*

> Romans 10:9–10

By now you might be asking, "Exactly how can I be saved?" Talk to God (i.e. pray) about it and tell Him you want to be saved. You may begin by using the Salvation Prayer provided in this section. Perhaps you've been attending church for many years, but you cannot ever remember saying the salvation prayer. Now would be a good time to pray through it. Going to church does not bring salvation. It only happens through personally receiving Jesus Christ as your Savior, in prayer.

Salvation Prayer

If you have come to a belief in Jesus Christ as Lord and Savior, the next step is to use these salvation keys to acknowledge your belief in testimony and prayer. Enter the doorway to salvation by praying the following model prayer aloud:

Dear Heavenly Father, I come to You now in the name of Your only begotten Son, Jesus.

- I acknowledge that I have not known You and lived my life according to Your righteous ways. Therefore, I have been headed on a course away from You, towards hell.
- I ask that You would forgive me for my sinful ways.
- I choose to change my ways and live my life according to Your ways.
- I confess today that Jesus is Lord and choose to make Him my Lord.
- I gratefully accept the work Jesus did in suffering the penalty of my sins in His body and dying on the cross, that I might live.
- I believe that You, Heavenly Father, raised Jesus from the dead.
- I ask that You would receive me now as Your child, through the precious blood that Jesus shed for me.
- I ask that You would reveal Yourself to me further, and that You would strengthen me to be able to walk in Your ways, Amen.

Salvation -
Like Receiving
Our Heavenly Citizenship

When you have prayed this prayer with a sincere and believing heart, you become a Christian. You will now have the privilege of knowing God here on earth and will join Him in heaven when your earthly body dies. You have just passed through the gateway to eternal life. However, it is necessary to understand that your salvation (new earthly life in Christ), while it has a beginning point in time, is not completed until you have entered heaven.

The initiation of your new life as a child of God is similar in concept to receiving a new passport, one that identifies you as a citizen of heaven. Similarly, you effectively receive a ticket for your future journey to your new country, heaven. We may further understand salvation as a process when we examine the Salvation Chart in the following section.

2.0 Salvation Scale

In the latter part of the twentieth century, missiologist James Engel devised a simple graded scale of measure for the salvation process, which now bears his name: The Engel Scale. To his credit, Dr. Engel did not end his scale with receiving Jesus as Savior, but continued it to show the general progression of discipleship and relationship with God required as we mature in God's family. In a similar way, the salvation scale we're presenting here progresses upward through twenty-one steps beginning with −10 and ending with +10. As you look at the Salvation Chart provided in this section, which was inspired by the Engel Scale, consider where your position is. The Salvation Scale illustration gives us a graphical illustration of the

Step Rating Relative to Initiation of Salvation	SALVATION CHART Qualitative Spiritual Category of Christian Faith
+10	Knowing God and doing the works of Jesus
+9	Developed prayer life
+8	Kingdom stewardship of resources
+7	Developing Christian lifestyle
+6	Discovery and use of spiritual gifts
+5	Initiation into the church as a functioning member
+4	Baptism in the Holy Spirit
+3	Growth of Christian character and Bible knowledge
+2	Water baptism
+1	Growth in understanding of the faith—Jesus' Lordship
0	Receive Christ as Savior—discipleship initiated
−1	Repentance and faith
−2	Challenge and decision to act
−3	Awareness of personal need; conviction of sin
−4	Positive attitude to the Gospel
−5	Grasp of implications of the Gospel
−6	Awareness of basic facts of the Gospel
−7	Interest in Christianity
−8	Initial awareness of Christianity
−9	No effective knowledge of Christianity
−10	No awareness of the supernatural

SALVATION SCALE

**INCREASED DISCIPLESHIP -
BODY AND SOUL ENTERING KINGDOM OF LIGHT**

DISCIPLE - SOUL ENTERING KINGDOM OF LIGHT

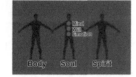

SAVED - SPIRIT UNDER KINGDOM OF LIGHT

UNSAVED - UNDER KINGDOM OF DARKNESS

pre- and post-salvation process in regard to our body, soul and spirit. (See Section 8, "The Makeup of Mankind," for a description of the function and relationship between these parts of our lives.)

While this section helps us understand the process of salvation, it also introduces the concept of discipleship—progressively becoming more like Jesus. A question we might ask is, "How do I travel upwards on the Salvation Scale?" The answer lies in both God and in us.

All spiritual progress is a combination of our choices and the actions of God influencing us. As we travel the road from unbelief to knowing Jesus and salvation, the scripture tells us we are drawn to Him (externally) by the Father (John 6:44). Once we are saved, we must be led by the Holy Spirit to make further progress. This is called discipleship.

Now let us consider the second most important decision that you will ever make in your life here on earth, the decision to make Jesus Lord over every aspect of your life. It is a decision that most who call themselves Christians have yet to intentionally make.

After choosing salvation and receiving the assurance of eternal life, the most important thing you can do is to bring your earthly existence under the power and holiness of God. This is done by allowing Him to express Himself through you. This is an important part of our progress up the Salvation Scale.

In the next section, "Lordship," we'll see how we may live our lives for Jesus, impacting others, and our surroundings, for God through the influence of the Holy Spirit.

3.0 Lordship

When we enter into salvation, God's Holy Spirit comes to live in our human spirit (see Section 8.0, "The Makeup of Mankind"), and we receive the assurance of heaven when our earthly body dies. However, something additional happens. As God's Holy Spirit takes residence in our human spirit, our spirit comes alive to God. It is now able both to hear Him and to bring His influence to bear upon our soul, so that we act in godly ways.

As our thought-life and actions begin to manifest the influence of God through the activities of the Holy Spirit within us, we can see ourselves following some of the steps noted above the zero point in the Salvation Scale chart. Changing our behavior from the way it was, to reflect what God wants for our life, is part of the discipleship process. It is not easy; our soul has practiced other ways and, at least in habit, wishes to have its own way, the way of the past.

Effectively then, we have an internal conflict between our spirit, under the influence of the Holy Spirit, and our soul, which is accustomed to having its own way. How then will we be able to walk at the level of obedience and holiness to which God has called us? How do we appropriate the healing and wholeness that God has to offer us as part of our salvation package?

Let's explore this further. Jesus Christ is Lord over everything in heaven and on earth. He declared:

All authority has been given to Me in heaven and on earth.

Matthew 28:18

We can sing songs about Jesus being Lord and confess with our mouth this truth. But, at the initiation of salvation, while our spirit becomes filled with God's Spirit, the Holy Spirit, our soul and body remain largely under another lord, the god of this world. The soul and body have had a long-standing habit of sin—sinful habits, thoughts, dreams, behavior patterns; corrupt use of emotions; and wrongful decisions. Our soul has been under the influence of our previous father, the devil, and our body has carried out his desires. Declaring this truth is not a matter of condemnation, but rather a statement of fact.

If we are going to overcome the past practices of our sinful nature, we are going to need some help. We don't know how to "be good." In many cases, we are woefully ignorant of what is right and wrong because we were not imprinted as children with the image of God upon our souls. All of our reasoning and habits were influenced by the world in which we grew up. One of the characteristics of the Spirit-filled human spirit is conscience, and our consciences will help us realize something of right or wrong, but frequently the soul/body partnership will override the Spirit's quiet voice.

Our body and soul retain residual ways of operating from times past when we were not in God's family. And the enemy still has earthly rights to access our soul and body gained by our partnership with him in sin, and granted to him by the sins of our ancestors. In this unhealed condition we do not have the strength to change and to sustain a holy lifestyle. We need God's help to "be good." But where can we get this help? Let's recall that another name for the Holy Spirit is the Helper.

> *I will ask the Father, and He will give you another Helper, that He may be with you forever ...*

John 14:16

"But don't we already have His help? Doesn't the Holy Spirit come to live within my human spirit when I receive salvation?" Yes, the Holy Spirit does live within those of us who have received salvation. However, He is in charge of our spirit and not our soul, which is a separate entity. Many Christians miss this important fact. Salvation deals with our future, our destination, either heaven or hell. As Christians we are saved from an eternity in hell. But the initial impact of salvation is not as dramatic an influence on our earthly lifestyle as it is on altering our destination in the heavenly realms.

Perhaps a simple illustration will help. We can buy a horse to ride. When we've paid, the horse belongs to us. However, if it has never been ridden, there is a behavior modification process that the horse must pass through for it to be suitable for riding. Various techniques can be used to bring the horse into submission so that it may be ridden. But, until the horse gives over its will, it is of no use to its master; it will not obey and serve his purposes and pleasure.

Many Christians are like the horse that cannot be ridden. Although they have been bought by the blood of Jesus, and have acknowledged Him as God (see Section 1.0, "Salvation"), they have never given the Lord full access to their lives. Although we may have acknowledged Jesus as Lord in His position as Deity, we may never have submitted ourselves and all that we have and are to Him personally; He is, in fact, not our Lord. You are invited to change from that position to enter a deeper relationship with God, to fully live your life for Jesus, by praying the "Lordship Prayer" of dedication and submission found below.

Lordship Prayer

Lord Jesus, I acknowledge my need of You and I accept You as my Savior, my Redeemer, my Lord, and my Deliverer.

I invite You to be Lord of my whole life:

- Over my spirit—my prayers, my worship, my spiritual understanding, my creativity, and my conscience
- Over my mind—my thoughts, my memories, my dreams
- Over my emotions—my feelings and emotional expressions and responses
- Over my will—all my decisions and purposing.

I invite You to be Lord over my body:

- Over my eyes—all that I look at and over every look that I give outward
- Over my ears and all that I listen to

- Over my nose and all that comes into it
- Over my mouth and all that goes into it and every word that comes out of it
- Over my sexuality
- Over all my physical activities.

I invite You to be Lord over all my relationships: past, present, and future.

I invite You to be Lord over my resources: time, energy, finances, property, and all that I have.

I invite You to be Lord over the time and manner of my death.

Come, Lord Jesus, and take Your rightful place in all the areas of my life.

Thank You that Your blood was shed that I might be set free from the influence of selfishness and Satan.

Amen.

4.0 Baptism

4.1 WATER BAPTISM

Water baptism is part of being born again (see John 3:1–21). In His conversation with Nicodemus, Jesus reveals two important pieces of information about entering His Kingdom—we must experience the process of being born into the Kingdom through both the medium of a) water and b) Spirit. Since God is Spirit, if we are going to encounter Him and do His works (i.e. carry out our life assignment from God) we must be able to meet Him in the spiritual realm. We need to see, hear, and operate both in the natural earthly realm and in the spiritual realm where He dwells (the Kingdom of God). To enter the Kingdom we must be "born again."

Jesus answered and said to him, "Truly, truly, I say to you, unless one is born again he cannot see the kingdom of God."

John 3:3

The word "see" in this verse is translated from the Greek word ὁράω (horaō); which means to see, recognize, perceive, or attend to.

4.2 ENTERING THE KINGDOM—THE FIRST KEY: BEING BORN OF WATER

In this section of Appendix I, we are examining the first key: being born of water. Unless we are born again (into His Kingdom), we cannot really know God because we cannot hear, see or perceive what He is doing. Further, if we can't sense what He is doing, we cannot enter into His works as Jesus did.

In the following verse Jesus shows us the first "Kingdom key" to being born again: water baptism.

Jesus answered, "Truly, truly, I say to you, unless one is born of water and the Spirit he cannot enter into the kingdom of God.

John 3:5

A wonderful, but sometimes confusing, tension exists in Scripture concerning the "Kingdom of God." Sometimes this phrase refers to the coming heavenly age, to both that which is in heaven and that which will be manifest when Jesus returns to the earth. But there is even a third concept—the Kingdom both being seen, understood and breaking through into this present evil age, being made manifest by those who have entered into the "Kingdom of God" by becoming born again—Those who are born again (initiated into salvation) will do the works of Jesus.

In the previous section we saw that making Jesus Lord of every area of our life means we must die to our personal desires where they clash with those of Jesus. This is because they are not founded on furthering the wishes of God the Father. In the "Lordship Prayer" we gave Jesus Lordship of every area of our life. Now we will link this dying to self with water baptism.

In Scripture we find two progressive revelations in regard to water baptism. The first is the baptism of repentance introduced and performed by John the Baptist.

> ... and they were being baptized by him in the Jordan River, as they confessed their sins.

Matthew 3:6

This baptism for repentance from sin was both a public confession of sin and an outward declaration of an inward change in attitude away from sin. As Jesus' ministry increased, John's decreased, but Jesus' disciples continued what John initiated.

The second revelation regarding water baptism begins in the last chapter of Matthew. After Jesus' resurrection, He commands His disciples to baptize each new convert (beginning disciple) into the three Persons of God:

> Go therefore and make disciples of all the nations, baptizing them in the name of the Father and the Son and the Holy Spirit ...

Matthew 28:19

Again, this baptism commanded by Jesus incorporates confession and repentance for sin. But something more is added to what we see John the Baptist and Jesus' disciples doing at the beginning of the Gospels. Jesus introduced a new element here: being baptized into the Father, and the Son and the Holy Spirit—the complete Godhead.

The Bible explains that:

• As we go under the waters of baptism, we are making a break with our former worldly and self-oriented lives. We are being baptized

300

into Jesus' death as we die to ourselves. Going under the water symbolizes death (Romans 6:4–5; Colossians 2:12a).

• As we arise from the water, we are being raised into the family of God the Father and into the life of Jesus (Romans 6:4–5; Colossians 2:12b).

It is important to understand that Jesus commanded the sacrament of water baptism. It is more than a symbolic exercise; something spiritual happens to us when we obey His directive. To some, the results are dramatically noticeable and to others they are not immediately, experientially obvious. But something always occurs in and for us in the spiritual realm. Baptism is an act of faith on our part.

4.3 A CLOSER LOOK AT THE PROCESS OF BAPTISM

Having been born of water, we are now nearly ready to look at the second key to the Kingdom of God: being born of Spirit. Before we progress further, though, we need to examine more closely the underlying Greek word that is translated (transliterated) into our

word "baptize." This word, associated with both of the keys (by water and Spirit) to the Kingdom of God, is the Greek word βαπτίζω, baptizō: to dip, sink.

Conceptually, this word means to totally immerse and saturate in. It also means a ceremonial washing or cleansing in which all of the body is dipped or immersed. It does not mean to be sprinkled or poured upon, nor does it mean to be touched or dampened by a wet object. If we were to baptize a ship, for example, we would need to push it under the surface of the water. When the ship was finally covered by the waters, then we could say it had been baptized.

Baptism is a physical act that has spiritual consequences. We are not saying baptism must drown us, only that we go under the water for a moment. We must be obedient to the commands of the Lord. All that is within us of our fleshly (soul-controlled) life is to be spiritually put to death, to rise again in Christ Jesus to the purposes and plans of God.

4.4 ENTERING THE KINGDOM—THE SECOND KEY: BEING BORN OF THE SPIRIT (BEING BAPTIZED IN THE HOLY SPIRIT)

Let's revisit the discussion with Nicodemus from John 3. Here, Jesus tells him, in outline form, how to enter the Kingdom of God. The context of this Scripture is Nicodemus' inquiry into how Jesus was able to perform Kingdom (of God) works.

Jesus' answer draws Nicodemus from his natural, worldly thinking into a deeper mystery. But Jesus reveals the mystery to us:

> Jesus answered and said to him, "Truly, truly, I say to you, unless one is born again he cannot see the kingdom of God."

> John 3:3

Jesus is answering him in light of John 5:19, explaining that He (Himself, who has been born of both water and Spirit) is only doing what He sees the Father doing. Let's remind ourselves how Jesus later explains a healing miracle to a group of Jews:

> Therefore Jesus answered and was saying to them, "Truly, truly, I say to you, the Son can do nothing of Himself, unless it is something

He sees the Father doing; for whatever the Father does, these things the Son also does in like manner."

John 5:19

Nicodemus did not understand Jesus' answer, sounding more puzzled in his next question. So Jesus gives him (and us) the keys we began discussing in the last section:

Jesus answered, "Truly, truly, I say to you, unless one is born of water and the Spirit he cannot enter into the kingdom of God."

John 3:5

The explanation of the mystery is as follows. To do the works of God requires that we be born again. Part of that process is being baptized into Christ, His death, and resurrection, in the baptism sacrament known as baptism in water. But the first baptism (in water) needs to be followed by a baptism of another kind. This second medium is the Holy Spirit. How does this baptism occur? While we can pray for someone and even lay hands on them to be baptized in the Holy Spirit, ultimately it is Jesus who has to manifest His presence and clothe them in the power of the Holy Spirit as on the day of Pentecost (Acts 2). Let's look at what Jesus has to say about being baptized in the Holy Spirit:

... for John baptized with water, but you will be baptized with the Holy Spirit not many days from now.

Acts 1:5

And behold, I am sending forth the promise of My Father upon you; but you are to stay in the city until you are clothed with power from on high.

Luke 24:49

Nicodemus puzzled over how Jesus was able to do His amazing works, but we now have understanding. Both Jesus and those who do the works of Jesus today are empowered to do them through baptism in the Holy Spirit. This knowledge helps us with another mystery. How are we personally going to be able to fulfill Jesus' expectation for us? He said,

> Truly, truly, I say to you, he who believes in Me, the works that I do, he will do also; and greater works than these he will do; because I go to the Father.

John 14:12

Most of us, when we first read this scripture, have trouble believing it. But the apostle Paul's letter to the church at Ephesus tells us that God made us for that purpose: to do the works of Jesus:

> For we are His workmanship, created in Christ Jesus for good works, which God prepared beforehand so that we would walk in them.

Ephesians 2:10

James helps us understand that the works of born-again believers are the hallmark of their faith and salvation:

> What use is it, my brethren, if someone says he has faith but he has no works? Can that faith save him?

James 2:14

> For just as the body without the spirit is dead, so also faith without works is dead.

James 2:26

So, we begin to understand that a born-again (of water and the Spirit) disciple (Christian) will manifest the works of Jesus in his or her life. Those who are moving upward into increased intimacy with God (remember the Salvation Chart in Section 2) can expect to see the works of the Father, and, by means of the Holy Spirit, join Him in what He is doing. These works are the supernatural outcome of knowing God as our Father through Jesus Christ.

Now that we know *why* we need to be baptized in the Spirit, let's take a look at *how* we are born of the Spirit. Earlier we read in Luke that Jesus will send forth the promised baptism in the Spirit:

> *And behold, I am sending forth the promise of My Father upon you; but you are to stay in the city until you are clothed with power from on high.*

Luke 24:49

This promise was first voiced by John the Baptist, who heralded Jesus as the Messiah:

> *I baptized you with water; but He will baptize you with the Holy Spirit.*

Mark 1:8

Jesus is the one who baptizes us in the Holy Spirit. Therefore, in our seeking this baptism we need to ask Jesus to come flood, bathe, and overwhelm us with the presence of His Holy Spirit.

As at Pentecost (Acts 2) and at Cornelius' house (Acts 10), we may be overwhelmed, clothed in power, and flooded with the presence of the Holy Spirit without anyone visibly or discernibly touching us. However, Jesus may use also a person to pray over and lay hands on us. This experience can somehow impart the presence of the Spirit and initiate a Spirit baptism experience:

> [Peter and John came down] *and prayed for them that they might receive the Holy Spirit. For He had not yet fallen upon any of them; they had simply been* [water] *baptized in the name of the Lord*

Jesus. Then they began laying their hands on them, and they were receiving the Holy Spirit.

Acts 8:15–17

Two practical questions about baptism in the Spirit need to be addressed: a) How will I know if I have been baptized in the Holy Spirit? and b) What would keep me from being baptized in the Holy Spirit? Let's take a look at some answers.

4.5 SENSATIONS OF HOLY SPIRIT BAPTISM

Baptism in the Holy Spirit is usually both a spiritual and natural (i.e. physical) experience. Therefore, when it happens to us, most will know we have been baptized in the Holy Spirit. However, the effects and sensations will vary from one person to the next.

You may be filled with joy and laughter, feel the power of God upon you (which could cause you to temporarily physically collapse or fall to the ground), become very weak, feel heat or tingling sensations, see visions, hear the voice of God, speak in tongues (a language not known to you), etc. Following baptism in the Holy Spirit, God's spiritual gifts (for which you need this empowering) will begin to manifest in your life.

If you haven't experienced something physically / spiritually and have not received any of the Spirit's supernatural gifts, then you probably have not yet been baptized in the Holy Spirit. Keep seeking and ask God about any blockages that you have to receiving Him in this necessary step.

4.6 BLOCKAGES TO HOLY SPIRIT BAPTISM

A number of factors may delay your being baptized in the Holy Spirit. The first consideration is whether you are actively seeking God for this blessing. He comes to those who are seeking Him with all their heart (Jeremiah 29:13). Another factor that hinders receiving

Holy Spirit baptism is permission. Have you given God permission to do anything that He wants with you, at any time and in any situation? Trusting Him is necessary. Of course, you need to have received Jesus as your Savior and to have made Jesus the Lord of your life—normally you would have been baptized in water first, but sometimes God does things in the opposite order (Sections 1–4 of this appendix). Certain spiritual blockages can also prevent our being baptized in the Holy Spirit, for example:

- Unconfessed sin—personal and generational occult practices such as hypnotism, astrology, water witching, séances to speak or commune with the dead, spiritism, and/or babka (or witch doctor) healing;
- Un-renounced claims of false religions—personal and generational practices including oaths, dedication rituals and invitations to false gods who inhabit or act in and through you (may come from participation in martial arts or Freemasonry, the Communist Party and youth groups, and other organized spiritual activities or groups, including Satanism and witchcraft);
- Involvement in astrology, soul travel, and/or heavy metal (hard rock and other occult-based) music.

5.0 Purpose of Our Life on Earth

God forms us physically in our mother's womb similarly to how all mammals are formed. But there the similarity ends (see Section 8 below, "The Makeup of Mankind"). God has a much higher plan and purpose for us than for members of the animal kingdom. Let's begin by looking at a few concepts about ourselves.

5.1 THE GENESIS MANDATE

The book of Genesis provides an overview of God's plan for humankind. In the first twenty-five verses of chapter 1, we receive an overview of creation, as God permits us to watch while He forms the natural universe. The focus quickly moves to planet earth and all that it contains, both its environment and its inhabitants. In the last five verses of chapter 1, God begins to reveal His plans for mankind, His supreme creation. The rest of the Bible is then filled with God's revelation of Himself, His planned relationship with mankind, and an understanding of who we are.

5.1.1 *Image*

The first thing God shows us about mankind is that He will treat us differently from the rest of creation. We are the only species made in His image, i.e., like Himself (Hebrew selem: likeness, image, form—Genesis 1:26). (However, He never expressly stated our physical shape would be exactly like His.)

5.1.2 *Relationship and destiny*

In studying the Bible, we may come to realize that God's purpose in making mankind like Himself was to encourage relationship, like to like. One could easily conclude that God's main purpose in creating all of mankind, including you, was for relationship. He wants to have relationship with us, in some sense similar to the way He relates among the three Persons of the Godhead. This role places a high and special calling on us as men and women.

God has designed a destiny for us to gather all the Earth to Himself. He begins the process by first bringing us into relationship with Him. Then, as His partners, we are to introduce godly order to the earth by our obedient actions. We are to subdue it, including the wild flora and fauna that He created. He made us to be like Himself and to rule. During our time on earth, our first assignment is to shape and organize the planet, ruling over it, as we exercise free will and allow God to rule over us (Genesis 1:26).

5.1.3 Fruitfulness versus multiplication

Further, He gave us an assignment to rule over the earth and everything in it (Genesis 1:28). God knew the first man and woman He created could not subdue the earth all by themselves, so He fashioned in them the ability to have offspring. In Genesis 1:28, God then commanded them to be fruitful and multiply. Through interrelationships with each other and with God, these offspring eventually would be numerous enough to fulfill God's plan.

We might be tempted to view the two words, "fruitful" and "multiply," as meaning the same thing; however, they are different. "Fruitful" (Hebrew *parah*) means "to produce," while "multiply" (Hebrew *rabah*) means "to make more of the same kind." What's the difference?

God made us similar to Himself in character and internal nature. But, when Adam and Eve drew their first breath, this was not an accomplished fact. Although Adam and Eve were physically complete, their instruction and character shaping was missing. God, as Father, needed to impart to them something of Himself. He did this through spending time with them. If mankind is to fulfill God's objectives, we need to be fathered so that we carry within ourselves His image. In our biological fruitfulness, babies are automatically produced in every physical detail to be like us. But their character, like Adam and Eve's, is unformed at birth. Children do not come into this world expressing the nature and character of God; imprinting is a post-natal process.

In multiplying, we are to help form Christ (God's image) within each of our children (Galatians 4:19; Proverbs 22:6). We must obey God, both in being fruitful and in making our children the "same kind" as God. That is, reproducing His image in ourselves and in our children.

5.1.4 The biblical model

We can see this process at work in Genesis chapter 2. First God was fruitful in forming and creating Adam. Then He began to infuse His ways into him. He gave him a model of godly order (an already formed garden) and a godly work process (cultivate and maintain the godly order). God also spent time with Adam to personally reproduce (multiply) the image of Himself (God) through imprinting, by relating and working together with him in the model garden.

God gave Adam his first assignment to maintain the Garden of Eden which He Himself had established. Although mankind had the ultimate assignment to subdue the whole earth, God first organized a small area of the planet (the Garden of Eden) according to His wishes. He then put Adam into it so that he could see God's ways of organizing earthly territory. Man had to understand this model so that it could later be used outside the garden to subdue the whole earth.

It was in this context of on-the-job training that God began to instill His ways into newly created man. In the Garden of Eden, God shaped His image in Adam, and later in Eve, through direct discipleship as He walked and talked with them. As they were thus shaped (after being physically made), they were to reproduce (multiply) this image in their children, who were also to reproduce (multiply) this image in their children.

It is significant to observe that, when it comes to children, there is always the issue of free will. Even in the first family, Abel chose to receive the godly imprinting and Cain did not.

There are, therefore, three express purposes of God for our individual earthly lives:

1. To be fruitful and produce children;
2. To get to know God and His ways so that we continue to grow and develop into the spiritual image of God, reflecting His ways, attitudes and behavior. If we reflect God's ways,

then as our lives impact the earth, we will be doing our part in bringing His order to His planet.

3. To instill God's image into our children so they, too, reflect Him.

5.1.5 Fruitfulness outside the family

As the apostle Paul expressed it, we are to be ambassadors of God. In John 15:8 Jesus explains that His (and our) Father is glorified when we bear much fruit. In this context, Jesus is referring to our spiritual impact on the world.

In the "Great Commission" (Matthew 28:18–20), Jesus commands us to go into all the world, making disciples and teaching them to do all that He had commanded the first disciples to do. We are to preach the Gospel, declare the Kingdom, raise the dead, heal the sick, cast out demons, pray for the lepers (Matthew 10:7–8). As we obey these commands of Jesus, we will certainly bear much fruit. We will multiply God's image across the face of the earth, in and among those who come to belief in the Living God and who act in accordance with His ways.

There is, therefore, a fruitfulness and multiplication God intends for us to participate in, both inside the family and outside of it. We can be fruitful if we know God, have been born again, filled with the Spirit, and live a life submitted to Jesus as our Lord.

6.0 Heavenly Destiny

Our life and destiny are not limited to earthly time and location. We have a heavenly destiny beyond our earthly one. Many of us act as if heaven is merely a destination—the place we would like to go when our body dies. But there is more to our life than waiting for our arrival in heaven. Yes, how we will live out our life in heaven is our ultimate destiny, as we will see in the next section. However, something of our heavenly destiny is established by how we live our lives here on earth.

As we have already seen, God made us in His image. He planned and purposed to prepare us for dominion, just as He is equipped for dominion. This earthly life is where we may get to know God as our Father and Lord (see 1.0, "Salvation," and 3.0, "Lordship," above) and to become like Him through the process of a life submitted to Him. However, even though our earthly bodies will eventually cease to function here on earth and we die an earthly death, our being does not end.

We have been designed and built after the fashion of God Himself, who exists in the continuum of the heavenly realms. There we will continue to exist in the spiritual realms, either in heaven or hell. Our destination is determined by the choices we make and how we live our life here on earth. God has a planned destiny for us in heaven, to continue as His sons and daughters in loving intimacy with Him as our Father, but we can choose not to enter into it.

There is great activity in heaven. Those who have chosen to follow God shall share with Him, as part of the King's family, dominion over the spiritual realms and all that they contain (Ephesians 2:4–7). That's what royal families do! We will examine the spiritual realms, or dimensions, in the next section.

The word "dominion" incorporates the concept of ruling. God has dominion everywhere—in the heavenly realms, here on planet earth, and over the whole universe. This should make you more than just a little excited. He has planned and purposed that we should be like Him, not just in this life here on earth, but also in the heavenly realms after our earthly life is finished. In Revelation 3:21, we glimpse God's plan for us in heaven. Jesus tells us if we overcome the adverse circumstances in our earthly life, when we get to heaven we will be able to sit down with God on His throne, just as the Father granted Jesus the right to sit on the Father's throne.

Sitting on a throne is reserved for rulers, those with dominion. All authority in heaven and earth has been granted to Jesus and He sits ruling at the right hand of the Father in heaven. If we practice godliness here on earth, developing a loving and obedient relationship with God, He will grant us the right to join Him on His throne, sharing in His dominion or rule over the heavenly realms and all that they contain.

Again, we are only receiving a glimpse into our heavenly future, but it is a compelling and encouraging promise. God intends for us to learn about Him, His ways and His heart, through relationship with Him here on earth. As we develop and practice our Father's ways as his sons and daughters in our natural life, He develops us into princes and princesses, able to join Him in heaven, ruling as part of His family.

> ... godliness is profitable for all things, since it holds promise for the present life and also for the life to come.
>
> 1 Timothy 4:8

7.0 Natural and Heavenly Realms

As we continue to strengthen our understanding of salvation and Lordship, we need some knowledge of both the natural and heavenly realms. If we were learning about spectator sports such as soccer, basketball or ice hockey, we would need knowledge of both the players and the playing field. In this and the next section we will be looking first at the "playing field" of life, the stage upon which the drama of all life is carried out in the created and heavenly realms. Then, in the next section, we will learn about the players in the "game of life" or, perhaps more aptly, the characters in the drama of life (i.e. mankind and his makeup).

7.1 THE FIRST HEAVEN

In this section we want to introduce a conceptual view of the relationship between the natural realm, particularly about the earth, and the spiritual (supernatural) realm. As you understand the concept of heavenly realms, you will be more solid in your beliefs and knowledge of the revealed Word of God. This foundational knowledge will help you to operate in the spiritual gifts with more confidence.

In the Scriptures we receive little didactic teaching about the heavenly realms and their relationship to the physical earth and its heavens (i.e., earth's sky and atmosphere plus the observable universe). But there are a few scriptural anchor points that will enable us to construct a working model. To do this we will have to understand the Hebrew word *shamayim*. The Hebrew word *shamayim* occurs 392 times in the Bible and is translated variously as "sky," "heaven" and "heavens." In Genesis 1:17, God is speaking about the natural universe, outside of the earthly reams, where he placed the stars in the heavens (*shamayim*). In Job 28:21, we see this same word indicating where birds fly—the natural sky. But in many other verses (e.g. Psalm 115:3), *shamayim* indicates the spiritual heavenly realm where God lives. Clearly, this word is used to indicate both the natural realms and the supernatural realms; context tells us which it is. We can now begin to make our model.

There are three realms that we want to consider in this appendix. The first realm (or heaven) is that which belongs to the earth, its natural sky. In Genesis 1:26, God gave mankind authority over the earth, including the birds that fly in the sky. Clearly, mankind's dominion extended into the earth's heavens (sky).

We know from numerous verses that God lives in his holy heaven (*shamayim*). But Paul, having been caught up to God's holy heaven, gives testimony in 2 Corinthians 12:2–4, introducing us to its name as the "third heaven." By inference then, there also exists a "second

Schematic view of the created and heavenly realms
in relationship to earth

heaven" and a "first heaven." We are going to call the earth's
atmosphere (sky) the first heaven.

7.2 THE THIRD HEAVEN

The Greek word for heaven used in 2 Corinthians 12:2, ouranos,
occurs 256 times in the New Testament. One distinctive of the third
heaven, where God has His throne, is that it encompasses the other
two heavens, as we shall see.

Genesis 1 shows God making the heavens and the earth. In this
case, "heavens," or firmament, refers to the physical universe, where
the stars and other planets are, as well as the atmosphere surrounding
the earth.

Let's use a simple example to illustrate God's creation. Think of
blowing up a toy balloon. We could imagine ourselves standing at
home in our parlor with an empty balloon in our hands. In this
illustration we represent God, and the parlor, although limited in
size, symbolizes God's holy heaven, which, in reality, is limitless. The
balloon represents the whole created universe. As we inflate it with
our breath, it takes a shape and function that it did not have before.
It is both in our hands to do with as we please, and it remains within
the realm of our dwelling place, the parlor. It contains our breath,

**HEAVENLY REALMS
(ETERNITY)**

BEGINNING
OF TIME

END
OF TIME

α   Ω

BALLOON OF TIME AND SPACE

All our time and space dimensions exist, but only
as part of creation inside the balloon.

Our Universe Suspended in The Heavenlies

and nothing can escape from it into the parlor unless we decide so. Furthermore, if we wished, we could even put something else into the balloon at any time, perhaps a small button or paper clip.

So it is with the earth and the entire natural universe—it is in His hands and surrounded by God's parlor (i.e., God's dwelling—limitless heaven). God's breath went forth as He spoke (Isaiah 55:11) and formed the universe (Genesis chapter 1). God can do with it as He pleases, interacting, putting things into it, or removing them.

> *But our God is in the heavens* [shamayim];
> *He does whatever He pleases.*

Psalm 115:3

There are two qualities of the created realms (our life inside the balloon) that we should note. One, no one can go in or out of the balloon unless God causes it. And two, the time scale in the created universe (inside of the balloon) is not the same as time in the heavenly realm—it is a separate system. Time as we know it does not exist in God's holy heaven.

7.3 OUR UNIVERSE SUSPENDED IN THE HEAVENLIES

Let's look a little more carefully at these two points. First, God, who is in the higher order realm (third heaven), can see into and reach downward into our lower order realm, but we cannot see into or travel upward into the third heaven of our own free will. Therefore, heavenly beings such as angels and God Himself (inhabiting the upper realms) can penetrate or reach into, interact with, or override conditions on the earth. Secondly, all of time exists complete before God, and is contained in creation's balloon. He is the Alpha and the Omega, the beginning and the end. He is before all things, and in Him all things are held together.

In the New Testament, the first place the word "heaven" (Greek *ouranos*) occurs is Matthew 3:2 (NIV): *"Repent, for the kingdom of heaven is near."* This scripture could be interpreted to say that something of the goodness of God, from the third, holy, heaven where He rules and reigns, has penetrated into the fallen realm of earth.

We may ask, "How far away is God's holy heaven?" This question is unanswerable in terms of natural measurement, because the spiritual realm surrounds and permeates the natural environment. In Hebrews 12:1, it is written that we are surrounded by a cloud of witnesses. Just who are these witnesses? I believe they are all the people listed in Hebrews 11 who died and are no more walking the face of the earth as mortals. But they dwell in the heavenly realms, which contain the natural realm; therefore, they surround us. The heavenly realm is greater than the earthly realm.

We hope that you now have a better understanding of what happens when we declare the Kingdom of God. As we do that at God's request, He reaches into our realm to do what He wishes. He is not far away and can come in a moment (Jeremiah 23:23).

7.4 THE SECOND HEAVEN

In the last part of this section we will examine the second heaven, the one that so far has been missing. If there is a first and a third, then where is and what is the second heaven? In Revelation 12:7–9 we read that the devil and his angels were thrown out of heaven (the holy or third heaven), down to a lower order realm, the earth. However, these spiritual beings have no physical bodies; they live in a spiritual realm in and about the earth. This realm extends to the limits of earth's heaven (atmosphere). It is helpful to recall that Satan is known as the "prince of the power of the air," as well as the "ruler of this world." We will call this supernatural realm, away from God's presence, the second heaven.

Living in the second heaven, the devil and his "angels," without God's permission, cannot penetrate, see, or affect what happens in the next realm above (i.e. the third heaven). They were ejected for disobedience (Isaiah 14:12–15; Ezekiel 28:12–17), having lost the privilege of residence with God. These spiritual beings can, however, reach downward through the spiritual order or realms into the first heaven and earth. Here they have dominion, spiritual rulership, through the rights given to them as a result of Adam's original sin and mankind's continuing sin. It is our continuing sin which has given the enemy of our souls more and more freedom to interact in the affairs of this planet (within or under the first heaven).

The last question is, "Where is hell?" Hell is a place set apart by God in the spiritual realms, a place that does not enjoy His fellowship. It is directly mentioned thirteen times in the New Testament. Jesus Himself introduces the topic and teaches about it the first eleven times. The word "hell" is translated from the Hebrew word *geenna*, which is derived from the name of the Valley of Gehenna, located southwest of Jerusalem. In biblical times refuse was dumped and burned in Gehenna. In Jesus' teaching, we understand that "hell" is a symbolic name for where the ungodly will be finally punished. It is a place of fire, pain, and sorrow located in the spiritual realms, away from the fellowship of God and separated by Him from everything else.

We have learned that both godly influence from the third heaven and ungodly influence from the second heaven may be exerted upon the earthly realm and all that it contains. With this knowledge, we are prepared to look at mankind to see how we are both made and prepared to interact with the natural and spiritual realms within which we are immersed.

8.0 The Makeup of Mankind

The objective of this section is to understand the composition of man, both physically and spiritually. It is this working knowledge of mankind that will serve as one of the building blocks of our faith. This understanding will help us relate more easily to God our Creator, understand the Scriptures, and enable us to pray, receive, and give ministry with greater effectiveness. We will also begin to understand how we interact with, or can be influenced by, our natural and spiritual environment.

The Scriptures tell us that we are made with a spirit, a soul, and a body:

> Now may the God of peace Himself sanctify you entirely; and may your spirit and soul and body be preserved complete, without blame at the coming of our Lord Jesus Christ.

> 1 Thessalonians 5:23

The soul and spirit were created by God to live within the body, to give life to it and cause it to operate. The illustration shows schematically the basic component makeup of a person.

8.1 THE BODY

Our human body is an amazing biological machine crafted by God, made up of common earthly materials, mostly water and salt. But although it is closely associated with us as a person, our body is not actually who we are. While the brain controls such activities as speech, movement, recognition, and perception, the brain is not the initiator of activity in the body. That is done by the soul.

8.2 THE SOUL

Our identity, who we are as a person, is expressed by the soul. The soul directs the body's activities, processing sensory input from the body and spiritual input from the spirit. The soul synthesizes responses that it deems to be in the best interest of the whole person, or what he or she believes to be proper under the circumstances. These responses may take into consideration family, society, the environment, God, or possibly false deities worshiped by the person. The soul has three parts: the mind, the will, and the emotions.

The mind, will, and emotions are not made up of physical, but spiritual material. Somehow, God has anchored something of eternity (the spiritual realm) within our earthly bodies. When our earthly body dies and disintegrates, the soul that resided there, incorporating our personality and life-gifts, does not cease to exist. It only loses its attachment or assignment to the created realm of planet earth.

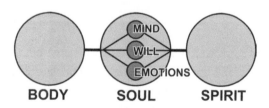

BODY   SOUL   SPIRIT

The soul interfaces with the physical body through the brain, which is part of the physical body. The brain receives input or direction from the soul, causing the body to respond appropriately from the soul's complex input. Soul-initiated actions are then combined with actions operated autonomously by the brain stem— breathing, the heart beating, the eyes blinking for lubrication, etc. In some areas, the soul can temporarily override the brain's autonomic operation, for example holding our breath when we dive under water, or choosing to not blink when we stare.

8.2.1 The mind

Although the brain is often believed to be the source of our thoughts, it is not. It is directed in all of its cognitive processing by the mind. Without the mind, no thoughts can enter our brain. That is not to say the brain has no cerebral or mental function. Rather, the brain is the connection between our mind and our body.

Our mind reviews and processes information from three sources. Input about our physical environment is obtained through our body's sensory organs. Past information is stored as short- and long-term memories. And spiritual information is obtained through our human spirit (see Section 8.3, "The human spirit"). Based on this information, our mind determines what is in our best interest and/ or that of our belief systems, and forms a plan of action. Execution of this plan or purpose is carried out through the will.

8.2.2 The will

The will, often associated with purpose, is the driving force of our soul and body. When the will receives instructions from the mind and/or emotions, it commands the body to respond through the agency of the brain. We could say that someone's personality or character is weak- or strong-willed depending upon how often they can carry out the plans of their mind. Another aspect of the will, where it seems to overlap with the functions of the mind, is in the area of decisions. The mind and the will appear to function together in making decisions or planning to carry out an action, but the function of the will operates more in the area of plan execution.

8.2.3 The emotions

The emotions overlap with both the will and the mind, coloring and influencing their activities. The emotions also feed into the brain directly, eliciting responses like laughing, crying, trembling, and more. In the purest sense, where our emotions are not overlapping in function with our mind and will, they are a qualitative evaluation of our feelings about someone, something, or a situation (real or imagined). We express these internal reactions, either in cooperation with the mind and will or nearly autonomously as emotions feed directly into the body. Thus, emotions can cause changes in action, speech, muscular tension, posture, facial expression, tears, blood circulation, breathing rate, etc.

Expressed emotions are what we might call the language of relationships. They tell how we feel inside, communicating that feeling outwardly into our situation. Since emotions, with their autonomic aspect, are tied directly into our physiology, they can have a powerful influence on the health and well-being of our body. When combined with our will and mind, emotions result in attitudes, emotionally inspired formulas for behavior that will influence or shape our relationships with others.

God has given our emotions a temporal quality. He requires that they be expressed daily before sleeping. If they are not some-how expressed within that waking period, three major types of problems arise—one physical, one spiritual, and one soulish. Physically, unexpressed emotions begin to have a toxic influence on the body. God did not create our bodies to live with the constant pressure of stored emotions. Our bodies begin to break down in health and function. Spiritually, unexpressed emotions begin to cause a breach in God's protection around an individual, giving the devil an opportunity to visit us through this spiritual vulnerability. Finally, stored emotions begin to pollute the mind and will, parts of the soul, causing them to devise and execute strategies that will alleviate the emotional pressure being experienced. Unfortunately, unexpressed emotions somehow seem to multiply and build, creating even more pressure than when first experienced.

8.3 THE HUMAN SPIRIT

In the simplest sense, the human spirit gives life and animation to the body through communicating to the soul what God wants done (Exodus 35:21). In James 2:26 we read that the body without the (human) spirit is dead. The human spirit is the center of creativity and as such reflects the character of God, who is creative. At the time of salvation (see the illustration in Section 2.0, "Salvation"), the human spirit is brought into communication with God. This is sometimes expressed as "being made alive to God." At this time, the Holy Spirit comes to live within our human spirit. It is not the soul or the body that is indwelt by the Holy Spirit at salvation. Rather the human spirit is God's place in our person.

In redeemed individuals, God communicates His feelings, thoughts and will directly into the human spirit. It is then the job of the human spirit to pass on God's communication to our souls. As we read in the Bible (Romans 7), we can see the struggle between the soul and spirit. Looking carefully at the soul-versus-spirit confrontation, it is possible to observe the human spirit mirroring the areas of activity (or functions) of the soul (i.e. mind, will, and emotions), as it champions God's ways. While the human spirit can and does communicate or express God's heart to the individual, the soul still has free will to act either autonomously or in concert with the heart of God. The human spirit also contains the functions of conscience, worship, discernment, and, once we have been saved, the knowledge of God.

God's Commandments and Spiritual Laws

Introduction

In Chapter 2, in the section on spiritual laws, we examined the spiritual laws that affect our lives here on earth. These spiritual laws come into action when we sin. Under temptation, stress, and pressure, we may have opened ourselves up to the effects of these laws, either intentionally or in ignorance.

In this appendix, we will step back from the close examination of the Scriptures we studied in Chapter 2 and look at general principles. To be equipped for Christian living, the detail of the law establishes behavioral boundaries for us. But to avoid becoming legalistic Pharisees, we need the perspective of God's heart. While details and specifics are important, sometimes we cannot see the forest of our lives because of the tangle of trees in the way. If we have a conceptual understanding, we can begin to untangle our lives from sin and its overwhelming consequences.

To obtain an overview, we must cut back some of the underbrush of confusion, particularly regarding God's laws. We need an understanding of two terms: **command** and **law**. Many of us are influenced, or even led astray, by contemporary use of the word "law."

We often hear a person talk about someone who has broken the law. Nothing could be further from the truth. If someone's behavior is outside the statutory limits for "behavior," they have not broken the law that prescribes the punishment for misbehavior. They have exceeded the statutory limitation and the law tells us what they will pay for their misbehavior. If the law is broken, then indeed, it was not a law at all. Spiritual, natural, and governmental laws tell us what will happen if certain actions are taken. The law of gravity tells us that if you step off a cliff, you will fall—every time! Commandments, on the other hand, can be broken through disobedience. As you can see, the words "command" and "law," while interlinked, describe two completely different things.

Now, let's look more generally at how God's commandments are linked to His spiritual laws. As this topic is developed, we will discover how to use this information to bring ourselves and others out of the area of curse and judgment, and into the blessings of God. We will examine:

- God's standards for our lives, which may be expressed as commandments
- God's spiritual laws, which reward our behavior with either blessings or curse
- The way to move from God's disfavor into His favor through confession, repentance, and forgiveness in Jesus' name.

1.0 God's Commandments

At Sinai, the Israelites experienced thunder, a whirlwind, darkness, gloom, blazing fire, and words like a trumpet sound that were so powerful they begged to hear no more. God was shouting at His people as they were about to step off a spiritual cliff. Their lives and attitudes were completely out of order; He was calling them back to safety. He graciously gave them a spiritual boundary to keep them from falling to their deaths—a behavioral plumb line called the Ten Commandments (Exodus 20:1–17).

Our fleshly human nature always wants to do things our way, but our way only leads to death. We need God's perspective:

> *There is a way which seems right to a man,*
> *But its end is the way of death.*

Proverbs 16:25

Since God's ways are not our ways, we tend to view His behavioral boundaries as restrictive or controlling. Rather, they are a lifeline thrown down from heaven to rescue us from spiritual, and often physical, death.

When we hear about God's commands, we immediately think of the Ten Commandments. But there are many other prescriptive commands throughout the Bible; all are guidelines for our life here on earth. Some are directly and imperatively stated as standards for our behavior. Others are taught in parable form. Yet others are found in the biblical narrative of national histories, with stories of cities, villages, individuals, and families. However they are stated, the goal is always to help us emulate our Heavenly Father. He is holy, just, righteous, and loving. We describe our deviation from God's ways as sin.

2.0 Speed Limits of Life

It may be helpful to think of a natural parallel to God's commandments. We are familiar with roads and motor vehicles. To protect lives and property, governments have decided how fast you may drive on the roads. The speed limit for each portion of road, according to the conditions of the area, may be posted on signs along the road or it may be assigned according to the type of driving environment (countryside, city, school or hospital zone, etc.).

These speed limits are commands: you shall not exceed this speed. Compliance with the command allows you the privilege of driving on the roads. If you do exceed the speed limit, governmental laws and codes require a penalty to be paid. Often you will pay a certain sum of money for breaking the speed limit (command). This punishment for misbehavior, a fine, is designed to make it sufficiently painful that you will obey rather than endangering yourself and others.

God has also posted His spiritual "speed limits"—His commands for our behavior. They are written both in the Bible and upon our hearts. And when in doubt, we can pray and ask God directly about a situation in our lives.

3.0 Spiritual Laws

Let's now look more carefully at God's spiritual laws to see how they work, either in our favor or against us. In a negative sense, spiritual laws, like traffic laws, come into effect when we transgress the behavioral standards (commandments) of God. Our disobedience takes us out of the circle of God's blessings and protection and into the land of trouble:

> But it shall come about, if you do not obey the LORD your God, to observe to do all His commandments and His statutes with which I charge you today, that all these curses will come upon you and overtake you ...

Deuteronomy 28:15

However, our personal conformance to God's standards (obedience) also assures us of His blessings:

> All these blessings will come upon you and overtake you if you obey the LORD your God ...

Deuteronomy 28:2

4.0 Laws and Commands: A Parable Picture

Here's a parable illustrating how the spiritual commands and laws work together.

As the story opens, we are looking down on the most beautiful green pasture. Our attention is caught by the overwhelming richness of the green grass that undulates gently in the soft hint of a fresh breeze. Even at our height, the air carries the fragrance of meadow flowers and something deep and reassuring—a full-bodied aroma coming from the earth itself.

Gradually we become aware of a brook gurgling and singing as crystal-clear waters play over the smooth pebbles and larger stones. Now we notice that the meadow gently climbs until it becomes rather steep, finally giving way to a breathtaking mountain covered with alpine meadows and the most aromatic cedars and pines.

By degrees, we recognize something amazing about the light. In one sense it appears to be luminescent, a clear transparent light at once pure and bright, and yet, for all the brightness, it does not hurt the eyes but rather gives an unusual clarity and brilliance. It is unlike anything experienced here on earth.

As our eyes wander, following the incline, we begin to notice the light becoming stronger and the colors brighter; the intensity grows as we gaze towards the top of the mountain, so bathed in light that its whole top is lost in it.

Oh, how could we have missed noticing? Everywhere are the most contented sheep, grazing, frolicking, resting, and sleeping: separately, in ones and twos, and in flocks—contented, woolly, white, well fed, and beautiful. And then we notice a most amazing thing. Even though they turn and wander, somehow they are always facing the mountain and its glorious light. It's not something that can be explained in geometric terms, for what we are seeing is not possible in earth's three-dimensional spaces.

Finally, we spot a beautiful white fence running as far as the eye see, to the right and to the left. We presume that somehow it surrounds the whole mountain.

Now here is something puzzling. On the outside of the fence the light immediately and rapidly begins to dim. The expanse of grass, as it passes under the fence, can be seen turning brown. Not that it is already dead, but it is actively turning brown as if it is in the act of dying. You would think that if it is dying, then it would have a final state—dead and brown. The best way to describe it is something like a waterfall. The water is continually falling, and if you look at the bottom of the fall, indeed it has dropped. Yet, at the same time, the water continues to fall over the precipice. Here at the fence line, between the land of life and death, life seems to be falling continually into death. The further we look past the fence, the more rapid is the descent into death, and darkness falls with the swiftness of an executioner's sword.

But wait, here at the edge, some of the sheep have actually managed to turn their backs on the mountain of light and life. The foolish things are straining to eat that horrible dying grass just on the other side of the fence. It is so confusing. Why would they eat that stuff?

We ask this question out loud and suddenly we're there, standing beside one of the animals that strains to eat the meal of death. We plead with this sheep and tug at its great woolly coat, but it does not listen. Now, strangely, we notice that from this perspective, you cannot see that the dying grass is brown. If anything, it looks more succulent, more sumptuous and inviting. Those sheep that turn their backs on the mountain of life and light are deceived and cannot see the trap of death. As the animal that we are trying to save breaks through the fence and disappears into the darkness, great sobs rise up in our breasts, shaking us to our very core.

As we cry bitter tears of loss and helplessness, we realize we will never be the same. In this powerful moment, we ask for understanding. And as suddenly as we descended, we're once again looking down on the scene from above.

We continue to see sheep eating through the fence. Tasting of death, they fall into a frenzy. Becoming increasingly excited, they push against the fence for more. Finally, they push right through, the fence restoring itself behind them as if the breach was never there.

As these wayward sheep consume more and more of the dying grass, they too begin the dying process. "No, no," we cry, "turn back," but they do not hear. Their once white wool begins to turn yellow and fall out in great patches. Their sure-footed steps turn into a faltering walk. Some begin to fall down. Others already lie there twitching, with their sides heaving. In the twilight we see a great black wagon pulled by hideous beasts. Shadowy figures stop to collect the dead carcasses and the procession moves on.

4.1 MEANING OF THE PARABLE

The explanation of the parable is simple. The fence represents God's commands and precepts for righteous living. On one side of the fence are God's presence, His blessings, and life. Outside of the fence and away from God's ways is the outer darkness, death, Satan's domain. When we turn our backs towards God and disobey His commands for living, we push through His fence of protection. The commands are boundaries set by God, marking where life and light end and death, both spiritual and physical, begins. When we turn our backs on God, sin may be appealing, but it's deceiving. In truth, it is the doorway to death. In our disobedience to God's commands, we discover that we've breached His hedge of protection—not that darkness flows into the Kingdom of Light, but that we fall into the darkness.

The spiritual laws of God tell just what will happen to us and our families as we turn away from God and push into sin. The general, overarching law is that as we transgress, we separate ourselves from the life-sustaining presence of God. He is perfect, holy, filled with love and life; He is light. Therefore, when we travel where He does not dwell, we enter the land of opposites. There is imperfection, un-holiness, hate, death, and of course, darkness. His commandments are a fence to keep us safe.

In one sense, it doesn't matter which command we've disobeyed. We will find ourselves beyond God's barrier of protection and outside of His blessings. When we exceed the statutory speed limits for safe driving, the laws prescribe our punishment. Likewise, the punishment for disobeying some of God's commands is written very clearly in the Bible. However, not all of God's laws are so obviously stated. Furthermore, the time between our disobedience and the enforcement of the law (i.e. when the law takes effect), may be years or even generations later. But know this, the Scriptures tell us that God is not mocked. Whatsoever we sow, we will also reap (see Galatians 6:7).

The commands, precepts, and statutes of God set down the protective boundaries for our lives. God's laws, whether they are written, understood and observable or not, will decide whether we enjoy blessings or curse, life or death (see Deuteronomy 30:19).

5.0 Moving from Death to Life

Here on earth, both Christians and non-Christians alike may elect to travel between the land of life and the land of death, between blessings and curse. The choice is ours. Anyone who obeys God, who lives his life within God's standards, may enjoy His blessings. Those who disobey God, living outside of His standards, will find that death of some kind will enter their lives. It could be death to finances, marriage, relationships, mental acuity, or emotional stability. Or it could manifest as sickness, infirmity, accidents, tragedy, and more. God's commands, precepts, and laws are universal for all mankind.

Since His laws are universal, all mankind is subject to them. Both those going to heaven and those going to hell are governed in like manner. Here on earth, both the saved and the unsaved will receive the consequences of their obedience to, or non-compliance with, God's standards for behavior.

We can decide to live according to God's ways, turning from our previous, unacceptable ways of life. Historically, most countries with a Judeo-Christian heritage have systems of laws that reflect God's standards for behavior. Ungodly behavior is punished by the government, encouraging godly lifestyles. Both believers and non-believers alike are led, in many ways, to change from the ways of death to the ways of life. By being a law-abiding citizen, you can enjoy the benefits and privileges of that behavior.

However, some sinful behaviors remain legal in many countries. For example, it is not against the law to become an alcoholic, as long as we do not endanger others by our behavior. Yet drunkenness is still against God's ways and we, our families, and future descendants will suffer for our disobedience. If we are privileged to recognize the error in our ways, it is possible to set our will against our past behavior and decide to stop drinking alcohol.

A good example of someone deciding to make a change was Jules Marine, a very successful motivational speaker in the 1980s. He had been an alcoholic for years. At some point, he decided to stop drinking. To reward himself for staying sober, he decided to save all the money that he would have spent on alcohol and buy himself a Rolls Royce. When I met Jules, he was still sober and driving the Rolls. He, an unbeliever, decided every day to stand against his addiction. By not drinking, he could continue to own and drive his dream car. Alcohol would have eaten up his fortune, as well as his privilege to drive—and many other things in his life.

Not all of us have the willpower and ability to generate wealth like Jules Marine, but we also can become free from besetting sins by choosing to change (repent). When we were unbelievers, we had to fight daily against our addictions and sin natures in order to hold to godly ways of life.

God offers another way for Christians. It begins in a similar manner, with the realization that our behavior is wrong. This realization leads to a decision to change, with repentance in our hearts, resulting in turning away from our sin.

For the Christian in relationship with God, an apology to our Heavenly Father is in order, with an admission of guilt for breaking His commandments. This step is called confession of our sin. We are calling sin what God calls it. We admit that He prescribed the proper way to behave and we disobeyed. Then the Christian asks for forgiveness through the blood of Jesus, who died on the cross, taking the penalty for our sins on Himself so that we would not have to suffer our deserved punishment.

You may legitimately ask why this second approach is important, since both the Christian and non-Christian may enjoy the fruits of godly behavior. The answer is, all sin (ungodly behavior) carries with it the punishment of death. And death means separation from God, both in an earthly, temporal sense and in a spiritual, eternal sense.

When we come out of a life of walking in sin, it is something like walking out of a boggy, muddy field and stepping onto a nice paved road. While we were walking in the field, it was extremely hard to make progress. The mud resisted our movements and clung to our feet in a mass inches thick. However, even when we get out of the field, the mud still clings to our feet, making walking very difficult— until we cleanse our boots. Sin clings to us in the same way.

Here's a more concrete example. If we robbed banks for a living, we would be owed punishment. Even if we decided to never rob another bank (i.e. repented) and turned from our past practice, what we did deserves punishment. Until we received our just punishment by going to prison, we would have to live our lives in hiding. Just as our path through the boggy field impeded our walk on the paved road, our past sins spiritually cling to us, holding us in the disfavor we deserve. We may begin to receive the benefits of walking on God's righteous pathway as soon as we change. But these benefits may be difficult to see, enjoy, or maintain since we are still reaping what we sowed in sin. Being set free (cleansed or healed) from our past sin is impossible for an unbeliever. He (or she) does not know Jesus and has no right to have his sin and its effects removed through the verbal application of His precious blood.

6.0 Practical Application

Escaping the temporal punishment of sin (the kingdom of death) and being free (cleansed) to walk in righteousness involves three elements:

- Confession
- Repentance
- Forgiveness.

In confession we admit to God, and usually another Christian, that we sinned. We name the sin as God describes it and agree with God that we were wrong. It is important to confess one to another, since God has commanded us to do it this way.

> *Therefore, confess your sins to one another, and pray for one another so that you may be healed. The effective prayer of a righteous man can accomplish much.*

> James 5:16

In repentance, we choose to change from our past behavior and to walk in God's way of righteousness. God tells us that a necessary step in restoration to His blessings is to change our ways.

Therefore repent and return, so that your sins may be wiped away, in order that times of refreshing may come from the presence of the Lord …

Acts 3:19

Now therefore amend your ways and your deeds and obey the voice of the LORD your God; and the LORD will change His mind about the misfortune which He has pronounced against you.

Jeremiah 26:13

In forgiveness we are receiving a judicial pardon that frees us from the due penalty of God's law. This pardon is only possible through verbal application of the blood of Jesus. It is calling upon, or invoking, God's provision of the sacrifice Jesus made both on the cross and through the abuse He suffered beforehand.

If you forgive the sins of any, their sins have been forgiven them; if you retain the sins of any, they have been retained.

John 20:23

7.0 Summary

In review, God in His wisdom and love has revealed His ways to us through the Bible, and commanded us to live in accordance with them. When we obey His commands, we enjoy His benefits. When we disobey, it is called sin and we find ourselves open to death, destruction, and slavery to the kingdom of darkness.

Without confession, repentance, and forgiveness through the blood of Jesus, we may somehow, through circumstance or willpower, begin to behave in a more godly way. However, death, destruction, and harassment from the kingdom of darkness will continue to cling to us. All sin ultimately brings the punishment of death to the one who did it. This spiritual law is just as certain as getting muddy feet when crossing a muddy field. The only way to escape the encumbrance of our past sins is to confess them individually and specifically. Failure to do so will result in temporal problems (trouble on earth) and loss in the eternal realms (of heavenly reward or privilege).

Another wonderful blessing comes from bringing our sins to the Lord in confession and repentance, along with a petition for forgiveness. We may ask the Holy Spirit, whose name is the Helper, to strengthen us and help us not fall again in the area of the sin we are leaving behind.

We must be mindful that this section of the appendix is not dealing with salvation—the receiving of Jesus' forgiveness that results in a relationship with Him, and ultimately in our entrance to heaven. Rather, we're looking at the process of sanctification, the cleansing from our previously unconfessed sin. Neglect of sanctification brings personal loss in our earthly lifetime as well as the loss of reward in heaven. If we clean our boots when leaving the muddy field, our walk home will be much easier. In any case, we will have to clean our feet at the door of our home. Walking in muddy boots will not keep the believer out of heaven; it just makes the journey more difficult.

Spiritual Ties That Bind

1.0 Oaths, Rituals, and Pledges

Oaths, rituals, and pledges are the core elements that are used to develop strong relationships between individuals in both the natural and spiritual realms. Between human beings, these actions establish an interdependence that can be either good or evil, depending upon the individuals, the intent of their hearts, and what they agreed upon. We can also make oaths, participate in rituals, and pledge ourselves to supernatural beings, either to God or to powers of darkness. Whether we are pledged to human beings or to spirit beings, the cords of power tying one individual to another are supernatural. These cords are empowered by God's spiritual laws.

We are examining these supernatural ties fabricated in oaths, rituals, and pledges because they remain long after we have made them. Our words and deeds have spiritual power to either bless us or curse us. God tells us that every word we speak, and everything we do, while in our earthly bodies has spiritual consequences. At the end of the age we will be held accountable for them. This accountability is because words and actions have power to damage or to bless.

But I tell you that every careless word that people speak, they shall give an accounting for it in the day of judgment.

Matthew 12:36

For we must all appear before the judgment seat of Christ, so that each one may be recompensed for his deeds in the body, according to what he has done, whether good or bad.

2 Corinthians 5:10

Oaths, rituals, and pledges are used in false religions and cults, in Satanism, witchcraft, and occult groups, to tie each participating individual into both the powers of darkness and to each other. These ties give the spirit world under Satan legal rights an administration of darkness over each individual who has participated, willingly or unwillingly. Furthermore, this administration of darkness places individuals under the control of other human beings and earthly organizations.

Oaths, rituals, and pledges are used to bind the participants into the spiritual forces behind organizations like Freemasonry and Mormonism.

In my book *Widows, Orphans and Prisoners*, we see that the power of Communism was established through the oaths, rituals, and pledges that were initiated in children's youth groups at school: *Kisdobos* (October Group), *Úttörők* (Pioneers), and *KISZ* (*Komsomolsk*) for the nation of Hungary (and the Russian-speaking nations). It was further extended by these same means in the Party, armed services, civil services, and in factories, collectives and other organizations.

1.1 BREAKING THE POWER OF OATHS, RITUALS, AND PLEDGES

Four initial steps can be used to release us from the enemy's legal claim (curse) on our lives that we have put ourselves under through our oaths, rituals, and pledges. The initial steps towards freedom from wrongful relationships with individuals, groups and evil spirits are:

1. Renunciation of the oaths, rituals, and pledges;
2. Confession of the sins involved;
3. Repentance from these sins (includes asking God for forgiveness for these transgressions);
4. Receiving forgiveness in the name of Jesus (this forgiveness is usually pronounced by the born-again believer who is helping you pray through these issues).

If you forgive the sins of any, their sins have been forgiven them; if you retain the sins of any, they have been retained.

John 20:23

The above process releases us (through the blood of Jesus) from Satan's power, but it may or may not bring any immediate personal relief. Three additional steps are usually needed:

5. Release from ungodly soul ties to the individuals in a group to which you belonged (see Section 2.0, "Soul Ties");
6. Deliverance from any evil spirits associated with your sinful involvement, through indoctrination, and with the group's sinful activities, goals, and purposes (see Appendix VI, "Deliverance Ministry," Section 4, "Spiritual Realm Basics");
7. Inner healing of memories, emotions, and damage to the soul and spirit from any abuse suffered because of your

involvement in the group may also be needed. These issues would often follow release from the bondages formed by our oaths, rituals, and pledges. Invite Jesus to come into each of the areas of damage and to bring His healing through the Holy Spirit.

2.0 Soul Ties

Soul ties are a special form of spiritual connection or binding between individuals. They involve the knitting or tying together of the souls of separate individuals. As in the previous discussion, these ties can be either for good or for evil. In the case of Jonathan and David, for example, the tie was a godly one.

> *Now it came about when he had finished speaking to Saul, that the soul of Jonathan was knit to the soul of David, and Jonathan loved him as himself.*

1 Samuel 18:1

We also see that there was a powerful soul tie between Jacob and Benjamin.

> *Now, therefore, when I come to your servant my father, and the lad is not with us, since his life* [soul; Hebrew *nepes*] *is bound* [bound/knitted; Hebrew *qashar*] *up in the lad's life* [soul; Hebrew *nepes*] ...

Genesis 44:30

2.1 ESTABLISHING A SOUL TIE

There are a number of ways that soul ties can be initiated. Each produces a strong spiritual connection between individuals, resulting

342

in either blessings and help, or curses and control. A few of the ways in which soul ties are established are:

- Strong godly relationships—between parents and children, between siblings, and between other special family members, including grandparents;
- Through strong shared experiences—such as disasters, accidents, torture, and violence;
- Through sexual handling and intercourse—both inside and outside marriage;
- Through the shared experience of rituals—for example, between the person being indoctrinated and the ones who preside over or administer the rituals, oaths, and pledges.

2.2 SEXUALLY ESTABLISHED SOUL TIES

The Word of God tells us that when a man and woman come together in sexual union they establish a "one flesh" condition— being spiritually connected (tied together) in their souls.

For this reason a man shall leave his father and his mother, and be joined to his wife; and they shall become one flesh.

Genesis 2:24

This spiritual connection, established in sexual union, is the platform beneath the deep level of commitment and interdependence necessary for marriage. It facilitates cooperation between a man and woman over a lifetime to make them successful as partners in raising children unto the Lord, taking care of each other, and carrying out the various assignments the Lord has for them.

We establish and/or deepen lifelong soul ties each time we have sexual intercourse (including other strongly sexual acts or interaction) with another human being, whether we have made a marriage commitment or not.

We are told that Shechem, the son of Hamor the Hivite, had his soul knit to Dinah, the daughter of Jacob, whom he raped (Genesis 34:3).

> *Or do you not know that the one who joins himself to a prostitute is one body with her? For He says, "THE TWO SHALL BECOME ONE FLESH."*
>
> 1 Corinthians 6:16

Sexually founded soul ties established within the boundaries of marriage are a source of blessings from God. However, sexually developed soul ties with sinful origins will open a lifelong supply line of curse and may bring demonic influence into each of the individuals joined in this way.

Marriage following immoral sex with the same individual will not remove, break, or convert the ungodly sexual ties that we have established outside of marriage. In this instance, the marriage will only result in a second, but now godly, soul tie with the same individual with whom we have also an ungodly, curse-producing, soul tie.

Many ancient pagan or mystery religions included sexual acts as part of their indoctrination. Worship rituals increased the power of control over individuals. These practices are still in effect for Satanism, witchcraft, and other occult activities today.

2.3 GETTING FREE FROM UNGODLY SOUL TIES

All this may sound like bad news; however, it is just one of the many costs of sin. On the other hand, the fact that Christ died for our sins is surely good news. The blood of Jesus offers redemption from this sin trap. It is available to born-again believers in Christ Jesus. As the Holy Spirit convicts us of our sexual sins, we have the opportunity to be set free, if we are willing to walk away from them and renounce the pleasure that we got from them. The process to remove the legal basis for sexual sin curses is as follows:

- We become aware of our sexual sin.
- We are convicted in our spirit and agree with what God says about our sexual sin.
- We renounce the pleasure we received from our sexual sin.
- It is often necessary to forgive both ourself and our sexual partner for our sin.
- For each partner we've had, we confess our sexual sin.
- We repent for each instance or partner with whom we've engaged in sexual sin.

With the preceding steps genuinely accomplished, the prayer counselor speaks forgiveness for each sin confessed through the shed blood of Jesus Christ on the cross—His atoning death at Calvary.

The last four steps above are best done in a discipleship/counseling session with at least one, or preferably two, trustworthy born-again Christians who know how to minister the Word of God in the gifting of counsel and prayer. As such, they will understand and operate gracefully in their authority in Christ. At least one of your counselors should be of the same sex as you are (i.e. men ministering to men and women ministering to women).

2.4 REMOVING THE UNGODLY SOUL TIE

Once the first seven steps have been performed, we are then ready to ask Jesus to remove the ungodly soul tie and to drive out any demons that have taken advantage of the opportunity and legal right given them by the sexual sin. The following steps may be used to bring the freedom desired:

- The prayer counselor asks Jesus to release every part of the sexual partners' souls that are sinfully tied together, to be returned to the person from whom it came. In heterosexual relations, we would be asking Jesus[1] to return everything of the woman to herself and everything of the man back to himself (but we would follow the same model for the partners when dissolving homosexual relationships).
- Then the prayer counselor commands every evil spirit that came into the person whom he or she is counseling, through the ungodly soul tie, to leave now (see Appendix VI, "Deliverance Ministry").
- In releasing someone from soul ties established from other sins (for example, control and domination, abuse, or rituals, oaths, and pledges), the ministry format is nearly the same as with sexual sin. The counselee needs to forgive himself or herself, and those who were part of their sin or who caused their damage. They will also need to renounce any ungodly oaths and rituals in which they participated and destroy any materials in their possession as a result of the indoctrination they underwent.

---

1   Please note: While we might describe this process as **breaking ungodly soul ties,** we ourselves cannot manipulate or move someone's soul from one place or position to another. Doing so is what is defined as witchcraft! What God has empowered us to do in ministry is to forgive sins, bring counsel and healing, and to cast out demons. Therefore, we ask Jesus to restore the sinners' souls into the same condition as before the sexual sin (which is being resolved) was committed.

Idolatry

In this appendix we will explore the sin and the law of idolatry. The objective of this brief conceptual study is to help make us aware of other deceptions that we may have been under. If we are going to escape from the power of idolatry, we must first see it. If we are to avoid it in the future, we must be able to recognize it in its many forms. When we don't see or recognize idolatry, we may fall prey to it. Let's now examine some basic concepts.

The first two of the Ten Commandments (Exodus 20:3–4) refer to idolatry. God is saying, Don't do it; it's not good for you. But idolatry seems to be the number-one problem worldwide. As Christians we may recognize that bowing down to a statue, image, or false deity is idolatry, but we can be drawn into much subtler forms of this sin. We can be deceived, lured into it, and ultimately come under its influence. The core issue with Freemasonry is that it incorporates idolatry.

1.0 What Is Idolatry?

In the classical sense, worshiping a statue or image that represents a personality who lives in the spirit world is idolatry. But idolatry can involve more than asking a false god (evil spirit) for your crops to grow, a wife for your son, good health, profitable business, etc.

Idolatry in its many forms can move stealthily into our lives. Spirits of idolatry always operate with spirits of deception and mockery. God wants us to come to Him, rather than to them, to supply all of our needs.

Since idolatry can be deceiving, to be safe we need to ask, "What is idolatry?" One of the reasons we can get caught up in idolatry is that we don't know what it is. It could be worshiping other gods, perhaps statues of wood or metal, but this form of idolatry is quite obvious to most Christians.

Taking other forms, idolatry can ensnare us by leading us to **something** or **somebody**, or to **a process** or **substance**, to obtain that which God Himself wants to give us. A broad-brush, basic core definition for the practice of idolatry would be: to look to anything other than God for something God wants to give. Here are several examples:

- **A substance:** Tobacco, alcohol, narcotics, etc. Going to cigarettes for comfort is idolatry. God is the God of all comfort, and another name for the Holy Spirit is the Comforter. Substance abuse also leads to physical death. So the wrongful use of substances also leads to the sin of self-murder!
- **A process or activity:** If the goal of participating in any activity is primarily to bring comfort or peace to areas of our lives that are anxious, in pain or in stress from past or present difficulties, there is a high probability this activity is idolatrous.

One such idolatrous practice is masturbation. Most Christians, by the conviction of the Holy Spirit, realize that masturbation is wrong. If you are engaged in this process, it is something you usually do in secret without mentioning it to others. If you feel it's wrong and you do it in secret, it should be a clue that it is a sin. The problem is that the church has not addressed this problem very well since there is no specific scripture mentioning masturbation.

We once were counseling a young woman who asked if masturbation is wrong. While we felt that it was, we didn't know what to tell her. Desperately we cried out to God in silent prayer for the correct answer. Immediately He told us that indeed it is wrong and that it is the sin of idolatry. It is comforting oneself rather that coming to Him for the comfort and peace that He wants to bring us.

There is a further sin problem in masturbation. Most people visualize/imagine a partner of the opposite sex while performing this act. This practice brings us also into the related sin of pornography, which involves physical images. The Bible tells us that even looking at someone you are not married to, with the imagination of having sex with them, is the same as adultery. So there are at least two sin areas in this activity: idolatry and adultery.

- **Materialism:** If having or obtaining things or money begins to overshadow our relationship with God, our spouse, or our family, we need to examine ourselves. We might be trying to meet a need within ourselves that God wants to resolve. We could easily be engaging in idolatry. The secondary sin in this area is the wrongful spending of time and money to the detriment or neglect of our families (both personal and church) to whom we have responsibilities, as commanded by God.
- **Person or group:** It is also possible to make an idol of our spouse, children, family, university, job, or favorite sports team. The test for all these possible idols-in-disguise is always the same. Are they displacing God in our attentions and are we going to them in place of God for our needs and satisfactions? If we are, then we need to renounce this sin, confess it as idolatry and cry out to God for

forgiveness through the blood of Jesus (see also Appendix VI, "Deliverance Ministry").

- **False gods:** Worshiping idols or images, either two-dimensional or three-dimensional, or just worshiping their names and the spirits that are behind them, is idolatry. These idols can be individuals who live only in the spirit world (second heaven, see Appendix I), animals, living persons, and those who lived such as Buddha, Confucius, Lenin, Stalin, Chairman Mao, or even now-deceased Bible characters such as (Saint) Mary or (Saint) Peter.

2.0 The Curses of Idolatry

Idolatry occupies the first two positions in the Ten Commandments. When we practice idolatry, we place ourselves under a curse. In addition, we bring this curse onto our family members, even to the fourth generation after us (Exodus 20). The outworking of idolatry's curses can take various forms in our lives.

Psalm 135:15–18 details some of the curses that will come upon us and our family for practicing idolatry. These curses will also affect cities and nations.

> The idols of the nations are but silver and gold,
> The work of man's hands.
> They have mouths, but they do not speak;
> They have eyes, but they do not see;
> They have ears, but they do not hear,
> Nor is there any breath at all in their mouths.
> Those who make them will be like them,
> Yes, everyone who trusts in them.

At first reading, these verses appear to be a description of the idols themselves. But verse 18 tells us that idolaters will display these same characteristics. These characteristics take two forms we need to look at here:

- We carry a long-term effect in our physical bodies.
- We also reap spiritual effects from the curse of idolatry.

The physical effect can result in:

- Speech difficulties, both in ordinary language expression and in the gift of tongues;
- A diminishing of physical and spiritual sight;
- A diminishing of physical and spiritual hearing;
- Many breathing difficulties, including asthma, allergies, emphysema, lung cancer, etc;
- Walking problems (i.e. foot, ankle, and leg) and problems with hands (see Psalm 115:7).

Frequently, the physical problems affect areas that were involved with the idolatrous practice—knees that were bowed to idols; lips that kissed statues; fingers, hands, wrists and arms from rings, bracelets, and amulets; feet from which shoes were removed to visit a temple of false religion (even during sight-seeing).

Some of idolatry's spiritual effects that we may experience today could include the following:

- We read the Bible but we don't really connect.
- We are sleepy in church or don't understand very well.
- Perhaps we are really having a hard time hearing God.
- Although we want to, we cannot speak in tongues.
- We do not seem to be able to exercise the spiritual gifts.
- We want to be baptized in the Holy Spirit, but somehow it doesn't happen when we are prayed for.

During prayer ministry there may be noticeable reactions, whether it's the person, or someone in their family, who has been involved in idolatry. As we begin to pray for healing, the spirits of idolatry reveal themselves and their power, and the person may be unable to move, see, or hear us. Once again, these spirits are allowed to exercise this power over an individual because of idolatrous sins and their attendant curses. All of these effects, both physical and spiritual, may be removed through prayer ministry.

Today, in our personal past and in the recent generational past of our families (within four generations), there are many possible sources of organized idolatry, particularly from religion:

- Overt religions, for example: Buddhism, Hinduism, Mormonism, other cults
- Freemasonry
- Worshiping dead saints or holding séances for deceased friends or family
- Communism—maybe we didn't believe what party members said, but if we cooperated then we bowed down to the idols of Communism.

3.0 Basic Steps to Eradicate Idolatry

Here are steps to take towards freedom from idolatry and its curses:

- Recognize the idolatry, what it is, or that it is there.
- Confess that we and/or our family were in idolatry.
- Repent of the idolatrous practice(s).
- Receive forgiveness from God, in the name of Jesus, through the prayer minister who is ministering to us.
- Any spirits of idolatry must be cast out (commanded to leave).

Temporal versus Eternal

Who, What, Where, and When

Many misunderstand the Scriptures, forming faulty belief systems, because they do not understand the context into which God is speaking. If we are going to follow Jesus as His disciples, we need to understand the Scriptures, as God intended for them to lead, restrain, correct, encourage, and train us in righteousness.

God speaks of things pertaining to both the natural creation (universe) and the heavenly, eternal realms (see illustration in Appendix I, Section 7.2, "The third heaven"). Understanding God and the context into which He is speaking is not always easy; it can take prayer, training, experience (with God) and determination. Sometimes, because of our own damages and limitations, it is easy to miss what He is saying. In this appendix, we are going to address two common, contemporary points of confusion in regard to some Bible texts:

- We can misunderstand the earthly time period that God is speaking about.

- We can misunderstand the location that God is speaking about, believing it to be in the earthly realms when He is speaking about heavenly (eternal) things.

> ... we look not at the things which are seen, but at the things which are not seen; for the things which are seen are temporal, but the things which are not seen are eternal.

2 Corinthians 4:18

1.0 Earthly Orientation

Because we are earthly people, we see through the eyes of our earthly experience. This experience leads us to misapply statements from God's Word that pertain to the heavenly realms, believing them to be about earthly life.

God has placed us on earth, a minuscule planet orbiting a small star in the Milky Way galaxy, amid a vast universe. Time, in our material universe, progresses in an orderly procession with each second following the last. But surrounding, enveloping, and permeating (overlaying) the material universe with all its God-given physical laws are the spiritual realms where both time and distance are measured differently and do not correspond in any discernible way to the created, material, universe.

Comparing the spiritual realm with the earthly, 1,000 years is like a day and a day is like 1,000 years (2 Peter 3:8). They are very different places.

All too often, without understanding, we attempt to "help" God by giving a natural explanation for supposed "conflicts" in Scripture. There are no conflicts in God's Word, only conflicts in our understanding.

God has provided us with His Word, the Bible, to help us understand both the material world and the heavenly realms by revealing Himself in person, character, purpose, plans, and principles. His hope and plan is to prepare us for our future life in the heavenly realms with Him. This preparation is to occur here on planet earth:

If you address as Father the One who impartially judges according to each one's work, conduct yourselves in fear **during the time of your stay on earth** ...

1 Peter 1:17

Some of God's declared truths apply to present-day conditions here on earth and some are for future times. Others apply, not to this present earth, but to the future new earth. And there are yet other biblical statements that apply not to the earth at all, but to the heavenly realms. Most importantly, we want to see how God explains our present and future condition, and how we are to become more like Him. His Word is intended to be a lamp unto our feet for our present calling and a light unto our path (future walk towards Him) (Psalm 119:105). Let's now examine a few passages of Scripture, with an emphasis on avoiding earthly thinking.

2.0 Prophetic Future

In Scripture, God's prophetic men and women speak about events that will take place in the future. One example of such a man is Jeremiah. In Chapter 5, "Sins of the Family," in the section headed, "Contradictory Scriptures?" we discovered that in Jeremiah 31:27–34 God was not speaking about the present conditions of Jeremiah's day (earth time/calendar). In a vision, the prophet was transported forward in time to see what Israel would someday be like. He saw a future time, "in those days," which was beyond both his time and ours as well. These things have yet to happen in earth time.

3.0 Prophetic Past

A prophet may speak about future events as if they happened in the past. As they occur, they become the past. Over 500 years before Christ, Isaiah wrote as if Jesus had already been born and died for our transgressions. In vision, Isaiah was transported into the future, to stand with us today and look back at what Christ did for us 2,000 years ago:

> But He was pierced through for our transgressions,
> He was crushed for our iniquities;
> The chastening for our well-being fell upon Him,
> And by His scourging we are healed.

Isaiah 53:5

Because God is both inside and outside of time, He can give us any viewpoint He desires. He sees it all, from beginning to end, inside and outside of time.

4.0 Heavenly versus Earthly View

We can mistake the place and time that God is talking about in some of the Scriptures. Ephesians 2:6 offers an example that we might view as prophetic future (on earth), but we are actually seeing into the heavenly realm where all has been accomplished:

> ... and raised us up with Him, and seated us with Him in the heavenly places in Christ Jesus.

Ephesians 2:6

This verse is a heavenly statement. In sequential earth time, we are not yet gone to heaven to be seated with Christ in the heavenly places. However, God, in the heavenly realms outside of earth time, can see the whole of time stretched out before Him and all is accomplished (see illustration in Appendix I, Section 7.2). The heavenly realms are a parallel, but overshadowing, kingdom. From God's perspective, we are already seated with Him in the heavens. From our perspective, we are yet living here on earth with no perception or experience of heaven, except what we have read in the Bible.

To help imagine this duality of time and space, let's imagine a fiction author who wrote a book about events beginning in the past and extending into the future. This author's manuscript lies on the table before him. In terms of the story, the past, present and future have already occurred because time in the book is not connected to our time. The author knows everything from the beginning through to the end. He is the creator of the story. If he wishes, he can alter events, the outcome of the story, the timing of events, even the length of lives and rewards for each character. The characters cannot break out of the story or pages of the book and interact by their free will with the world of the author. Neither can we earth-dwellers visit heaven of our own free will.

5.0 The Process of Salvation

Many believe that salvation is a finished work upon accepting Christ (see Appendix I, Sections 1–2). Many also believe that upon salvation, we are immediately filled with the Holy Spirit. Both of these beliefs result in a stunted growth in Christ. Yes, it is true that upon belief we are justified, credited with righteousness in the heavenly realms (Romans 10:9), so that from that moment on, we have an assurance that we will be saved (Romans 10:13)—that we will spend eternity with God. However, from His and our earthly perspective, salvation is a process that lasts for our entire earthly life (2 Corinthians 2:15; Philippians 2:12). This process applies whether our life lasts a few minutes, as in the case of the thief on the cross (Luke 23:42–43), or for over a century.

Salvation, from an individual's point of view, is something like the process of urban renewal. A prospective developer chooses a piece of property to build upon—one on which an old derelict building houses all kinds of illegal activities. The developer buys the property and seals it off with a high fence. Then he begins to demolish the old structure before building a new one. The old wreckage is removed, some foundations rebuilt, other new foundations dug, then they are poured full with concrete and reinforcing steel. Finally, building construction can begin.

Like the derelict building, when we first believed, we were full of sin and wrongdoing. But prior to that, Christ died (paid the price) for us while we were yet dead in our trespasses and sins (Ephesians 2:1–10). As soon as we believed the message of salvation, God sealed us off as His own with a fence of His presence and protection in the form of His Spirit. Then He began the redemptive demolition and renewal project in us:

> In Him, you also, after listening to the message of truth, the gospel of your salvation—having also believed, you were sealed in Him with the Holy Spirit of promise, who is given as a pledge of our inheritance, with a view to the redemption of God's own possession, to the praise of His glory.
>
> Ephesians 1:13–14

This sealing of our lives is not the same thing as being filled with (baptized in) the Holy Spirit (Appendix 1, Section 4.3), in which He comes to fill (or clothe) us with power from on high.

6.0 Temporal Effect of Sin on the Believer's Life

Many have been taught in church, or have come to believe in some other way, that their sins (past and present) have no effect on their lives if they have received Jesus as Savior. This error, if believed, will have grave consequences in our lives and will also result in loss of heavenly rewards. In this section we will explore the Word of God to bring light into this misconception.

Repenting of our past sins lets God know that we are sorry for them, and that we wish to change our ways to lead a godly life (agreeing that Jesus' death on the cross was personally needed).

But sin does more than preclude us from heaven (before we receive forgiveness through Jesus's death on the cross); there are temporal effects that continue after we receive Jesus as our Savior. The temporal effects of each individual sin do not stop until we confess each sin and turn in our heart from it, asking Jesus to forgive it.

First, let's look at the spiritual condition of the apostle Paul's disciples. He wrote to the believers at the church at Ephesus who had proved faithful, staying in God's discipleship program.

> *So then you are no longer strangers and aliens, but you are fellow citizens with the saints, and are of God's household, having been built on the foundation of the apostles and prophets, Christ Jesus Himself being the corner stone, in whom the whole building, being fitted together, is growing into a holy temple in the Lord, in whom you also are being built together into a dwelling of God in the Spirit.*

Ephesians 2:19–22

Paul also wrote to the church at Corinth. He and his apostolic team had spent well over a year there, personally discipling the believers. He exhorted them to act like, and treat each other, according to what God had made them to be through knowing Christ, not according to what they were before:

> *Therefore if anyone is in Christ, he is a new creature; the old things passed away; behold, new things have come.*

2 Corinthians 5:17

This is a heavenly statement about the heavenly identity (or condition) of earthly disciples. Although they look the same in their flesh (read the whole chapter), in their heavenly identities they have been changed. Paul is exhorting the disciples at Corinth to both be encouraged and to behave as God's children (reminding them that there are heavenly consequences for their behavior, verses 9 and 10).

He was not saying that we've completed sanctification (or the salvation process) here on earth (which is a lifelong process). Nor was he saying that we've been healed here on earth of all our diseases. Nor that the earthly effects of all our unconfessed sins have gone away. Rather, it was just the opposite in verses 9 and 10.

Later in the same letter, Paul continues to write to these heaven-bound, spirit-filled "new creatures in Christ" (believers) who had begun to walk in the power of God, but had not yet made peace with God over issues from their past (i.e. before their salvation):

I am afraid that when I come again my God may humiliate me before you, and I may mourn over many of those who have sinned in the past and not repented of the impurity, immorality and sensuality which they have practiced.

2 Corinthians 12:21

Paul was deeply troubled. The enemy had blinded these disciples to the curses (demonic access) they were under because of their life choices in the past! Apparently the Corinthians were so excited about their (assurance of) salvation and spiritual gifts, that many of them did not want to consider that the enemy still had access to them.

Receiving Jesus as our Savior brings us into God's family and changes our destination in the eternal realms from hell to heaven. Upon our arrival in heaven, we can proclaim, "I have been saved (from hell)!" But, even for believers, those who will be saved, the process of removing punishment, curse, and blame from their lives still needs to occur here on earth (1 Thessalonians 5:23).

Finally, all people, Christians and non-Christians alike, will suffer here on earth for their sins of the past, present, and future, but only Christians will reap rewards for godly behavior both in heaven and on earth. There is an eternal (heavenly) system of reward and punishment for our behavior here on earth:

> ... godliness is profitable for all things, since it holds promise for the present life and also for the life to come. It is a trustworthy statement deserving full acceptance.

1 Timothy 4:8–9

See Appendix VI, "Deliverance Ministry," for more information on removing the enemy's access to our lives.

Deliverance Ministry

1.0 The Road to Freedom: Introduction

Throughout this book, we have discovered that many things our ancestors and we have experienced have opened us to the influence of evil spirits. If we are to receive any significant measure of healing and release from the damage we received in our lives, we can expect that deliverance will be needed. The road to freedom from demonic influence requires both confidence in Christ, who will set us free, and some knowledge of the enemy's schemes of enslavement. We will be looking at these keys in this appendix. The basic principle is: when we sin, we give the enemy opportunity to enslave us.

> *Jesus answered them, "Truly, truly, I say to you, everyone who commits sin is the slave of sin."*

John 8:34

The questions that immediately spring to mind are: what were the sins that have opened me up to demonic influence, and how can I become free from their enslavement? Answers to these questions were explored in Chapters 2–6 of this book and were looked at more extensively in Chapter 7.

Let's move forward now and examine some of the elements of deliverance, in order to establish a basic working knowledge of how to be set free, as well as how to set others free from demonic influences. Without this knowledge, the enemy of our souls will continue to take advantage of us, defeating us in our attempts to walk in holiness, damaging our health, robbing us of prosperity, and stopping us from becoming workers of righteousness and justice. Without a basic understanding of the material presented in this appendix, we are extremely vulnerable to the enemy.

> *My people are destroyed for lack of knowledge ....*

> Hosea 4:6

2.0 Who May Minister Deliverance

If we were to examine all the documented healings that Jesus accomplished, we would find that about one-third of them were directly and obviously connected to casting evil spirits out of afflicted people. This aspect of healing is what we refer to as the deliverance ministry. Jesus told us that, as believers, we would do likewise.

> *Truly, truly, I say to you, he who believes in Me, the works that I do, he will do also; and greater works than these he will do; because I go to the Father.*

> John 14:12

Again, those who believe in Jesus will cast evil spirits out of the afflicted, just as Jesus did. They will do it in the name of Jesus and through the power of the Holy Spirit. God wants us to do this ministry.

Jesus summoned His twelve disciples and gave them authority over unclean spirits, to cast them out, and to heal every kind of disease and every kind of sickness.

Matthew 10:1

In Matthew 28, Jesus has extended this authority to all believers who have chosen to walk as His disciples in obedience to His commands.

3.0 Know Your Enemy: The Enemy's Plans

Our first impression may be that deliverance is frightening or intimidating. We may wish to never have an encounter with an evil spirit. However, we probably already have had encounters with demonic spirits acting through others or ourselves—we just didn't realize it. As we develop this subject further, you will feel more comfortable, safe, and perhaps even excited about removing Satan's influence from your own life and the lives of others.

The first thing we need to know is that evil spirits (demons) exist and that they oppose God's Kingdom, and therefore God's purposes and God's people. Secondly, as we saw in Section 2 of this appendix, we, as born-again believers who are submitted to Christ, have authority over them, not the other way around. To walk in that authority, we need a bit more knowledge about evil spirits and how they function independently and in groups.

Put on the full armor of God, so that you will be able to stand firm against the schemes of the devil.

Ephesians 6:11

For our struggle is not against flesh and blood, but against the rulers, against the powers, against the world forces of this darkness, against the spiritual forces of wickedness in the heavenly places.

Ephesians 6:12

Demons are spiritual beings that live in the second heaven (see Appendix I, Section 7.4). They are able to extend their evil influence into the earthly realm based upon the rights given them by mankind through the Fall and because of our continued sinful behavior throughout the ages—down to and including this present day. Their job is to bring Satan's influence into the natural realm by using people who have open spiritual gateways into their lives through sin, abuse, or damage done to them.

3.1 HOW THE ENEMY WORKS

Because demons are spiritual beings, they can reach into any physical or spiritual place in our lives. They can bring influence into our bodies and souls. They are a source of much infirmity and illness in our bodies, and they also continually attempt to influence us to do Satan's work for him.

When we are least in control of ourselves (e.g. overtired, under stress, in an argument, or under emotional pressure), we are more likely to be influenced by demons encouraging us to say or do something wrong. It is not so much that they control us, but that we choose to do what they suggest, or pressure us towards doing. The problem is that we usually do not recognize we are being manipulated by an evil spirit and mistake the influence for our own reasoning and understanding. In stronger cases, when more of our will has been given over to the demonic, we may develop compulsive behavior that is no longer under the control of our conscious will and mind.

3.2 HOW TO REMOVE THE ENEMY'S DIRECT ACCESS

Satan's servants, the demons, have direct access to our lives through the sins we and our families have committed. They can walk right into our workplace, past our secretary, and into our private office without asking or prior announcement. They step into our flat at their will and stride directly into our bedroom. As we're standing before a group to speak at work, in church, or elsewhere, they can step right up on the platform and accuse us, confuse us, or shame us; we cannot stop them because our sin has invited them into our lives.

Demons have rights, not only to our minds, but to our bodies—our skin, hair, internal organs, bones, joints and marrow, blood, muscles, fat, and sinew. They come freely into our emotions and thought-processes. They squeeze their way into our decisions and plans.

Each place where we've chosen to disobey God provides an opening to the influence of the enemy. Even though we are saved from hell and our ultimate destination is heaven, here in the earthly realms the enemy can bring early death, ruin our lives, and incite us to sin.

When we come to a saving knowledge of Jesus Christ, it is like the Lord raises a sail on the small boat of our life and His Holy Spirit begins to blow us in the directions He wishes. But, if we look closely at our boat, we can see many holes where we've sinned, where we've run our boat aground in the past. Water continues to leak into the boat through these holes, slowing us down and endangering our lives. Our course is affected by this unwanted, shifting weight and as the boat sinks lower in the water, deeper shoals are struck, making more holes. Then, when we try to control the course of our life without consulting the Holy Spirit, we find ourselves going aground again and again, each time making more weakness and holes in our lives.

Many have been taught that when they receive Jesus as their Savior, the effect of their past lives has passed away. While this concept is true insofar as our eligibility to enter heaven is concerned (see Appendix V, "Temporal versus Heavenly"), all sin, even that which occurred before our salvation, gives the enemy the right to come in, just as in the preceding illustration every hole in the boat allows water to enter.

The question is: how do we patch up the holes in our boat? How do we remove the enemy's access to our lives? First, we need to recognize that areas of our life are open to demonic influence and intrusion because of sin. Then, we need to use the blood of Jesus to close these access points (gateways), both the ones we've put there, as well as those established by the sins of our families (i.e. through generational sin, see Chapter 4, "Sins of the Family").

3.3 REMOVING THE LEGAL RIGHT OF INHABITATION/INFLUENCE

The process of removing the enemy's right of access to our lives is very simple:

- Confess our sin (and/or the sin of our family) one to another.
- Forgive ourselves and our ancestors who opened us to the enemy's intrusion through this (these) sin(s).
- Repent of our named sin and that which came from our direct ancestral bloodline.
- Receive forgiveness in the name of Jesus.

Removing the enemy's right to our lives is the first step. The second step is to remove his presence from us. If a demon has a right to our lives through sin, we will not successfully evict him from our body and soul. However, once we have canceled those rights through the blood of Jesus, it is not very difficult to drive him from our presence. Relief comes when, finally, the evil spirit is caused to leave our presence.

3.4 EVICTING THE ENEMY FROM A CHRISTIAN'S LIFE

- Command the demon to leave in Jesus' name.
- Keep your eyes open and watch what happens next.

- You must receive some kind of witness that something has happened. We must have evidence that something left. Our evidence will ultimately be from the Holy Spirit through spiritual discernment, seeing physically, or hearing testimony from the person receiving deliverance. If God doesn't provide us with a witness that deliverance has taken place, then we have no assurance that it has.

4.0 Spiritual Realm Basics

In the previous paragraph we were introduced to the concept that, while Jesus has given us authority over evil spirits, they may not immediately leave us when we command them to go. Let's look at this concept a little further to discover why this might be true and what to do about it.

Generals over armies and teachers over classrooms must know both the extent of their authority and the characteristics of those under them: how the individuals operate separately and collectively. It is not enough to be a brilliant military strategist or to be well versed in a teaching subject. We must have knowledge of those under us to be successful. But having authority and knowledge is still not enough. We also must understand the realm in which we are attempting to operate. Let's take a look at some basic concepts about demons and how things work in the spiritual realms.

4.1 CHARACTER AND NATURE OF EVIL SPIRITS

Demons are spiritual beings who have intelligence, knowledge, experience, and emotions. They know the Scriptures and understand that Christians can exercise authority over them. These evil spirits are under assignment (authority) that ultimately leads back to Satan, but usually their authority is administered down through layers of higher-ranking demons in something that resembles military organization. Failure to carry out their assignment against a person, church, denomination, etc., will lead to their punishment.

Demons are created beings with their origin as angelic individuals that chose to follow Satan in his rebellion. While it's true that they were thrown out of God's presence and their heavenly assignments were canceled, they still retain much of their spiritual power.

4.2 IDENTIFYING THE ENEMY

Demons assigned to afflict those in the earthly realms have particular job functions (e.g. lust, perversion, lies, deception, death, idolatry, confusion, infirmity, blindness, heresy, murder, addiction and many more). While they may have personal names as spiritual individuals, their names do not concern us. When addressing a demon to command it to leave or to bind it (i.e. forbid it to act in a certain situation and time frame), the easiest and best practice is to use the name of its job function; for example, "Spirit of Death," or more simply, "Death."

Sometimes we are not really sure what spirits entered through a particular sin. This makes it more difficult to address the demon by name. In this case, without the Holy Spirit revealing its name, we can address the demon(s) by designating the doorway or sin through which they came. For example, "Every spirit that came in through this lie, I command you in the name of Jesus to leave now!" With systematic demonization that occurs through involvement in false religions, cults, and systems like Freemasonry or Communism, deliverance becomes more complex. It is not possible to remove every demon at once by "batch ordering" all those that came in through that practice to leave at once.

We must deal with them either individually or in smaller groups by category or function name and by entry point; for example, in Communism, those that came in through the wearing of the red scarf of the Pioneers. But, if we wanted to remove the demons that came in through the indoctrination into Pioneers, we would need to walk through each element of the indoctrination, confessing and repenting for each sinful thing; then we could cast out the demons for each step. This practice may seem contrary to when Jesus cast many spirits out of the demonized man in Mark 5:9, but they were all operating under one name, "Legion." Further, these demons recognized the authority of Jesus, the "Son of the Most High God" (the sinless one).

A system of demonization like Freemasonry or Communism is ruled by controlling spirits that help coordinate the efforts of the various demons involved. Jesus called the ruling spirits "strong men," since they have the collective power of the group under their authority and at their disposal. And such ruling spirits, along with the group they rule, can exist within an individual, making the deliverance procedure a little more complicated than simply ordering out the demon. Since more than one spirit may be present, it is often easier for them to resist eviction with the aid of their colleagues. Jesus has given us a strategy to deal with cases of organized evil spirits.

> *Or how can anyone enter the strong man's house and carry off his property, unless he first binds the strong man? And then he will plunder his house.*

> Matthew 12:29

During the process of deliverance, we may use our authority to bind up the spirits that have a higher rank or authority than the one we are casting out. The strong man is a spirit whose strength is multiplied when commanding other spirits to join in resisting eviction. By binding up these higher-order spirits, we are forbidding them from helping the lower-order ones to resist expulsion.

In general, for systems of spirits like those built up under Freemasonry and Communism, there is a simple deliverance strategy: bind up the higher-order spirits to prevent them from defending their group and then cast out the demons that have no helpers beneath them. This process usually means beginning with demons that came into the person first (earliest). In the case of Communism, we would begin with those that entered through the earliest oaths and rituals (i.e. October Group, then Pioneers, etc. For Freemasonry we would start with the 1st Degree).

When we become more familiar with how evil spirits work in particular situations, we can begin to identify the strong men (ruling spirits) present in a typical demonic system. In Communism, there are a number of strong men, some of which are described below.

One demonic kingdom or grouping is Jezebel, the strong man, with lesser demons under it:

- Deception and lies
- Confusion
- Unbelief
- Mockery
- Idolatry, etc.

Another kingdom is Death as a strong man, with lesser demons under it:

- Infirmity
- Murder, etc.

Another kingdom is Anti-Christ as a strong man, and lesser demons under it:
- Blasphemy
- Anti-Semitism
- Atheism
- Evolution (Darwinism), etc.

5.0 Summary of Deliverance Ministry Procedure

5.1 PREPARATION—REMOVING THE ENEMY'S LEGAL RIGHTS

These steps remove the demonic right to trouble us because of our personal sin:

- Confess our personal involvement in the sin (sinful practice).
- Repent of our personal sin.
- Receive forgiveness in the name of Jesus.

These steps remove the demonic right to trouble us because of our family sin.

- Confess the sins of our direct bloodline antecedents.
- Repent (renounce) the sinful practice.
- Forgive the family members who did these things.
- Claim the blood of Jesus between yourself and those who sinned.

5.2 MINISTRY—DELIVERANCE PROCEDURE

- Bind up any strong man (ruling spirit above the one you are casting out).
- Command the evil spirit that entered through the sin (by name—job function) to leave the person in Jesus' name.
- Watch to see what happens. If you have no direct witness from the Lord or from what you see, ask the person what happened or how they feel. Be looking for an improvement.
- If you have witness that deliverance took place, then thank God for His kindness and mercy.
- Ask God to close the spiritual doorway that allowed this spirit (or grouping) to come into the person.
- Ask the Holy Spirit to come, cleanse and fill the person from what left their life.

- (If you have no confirmation that the demon has left, then you will need to ask the Lord why. There are a variety of reasons, including other hidden sins, wrong attitudes, missed ancestral sin, etc. The areas that the Holy Spirit brings to your attention will need to be ministered into. Following that ministry, you will need to again address the spirits that would not leave earlier.)

The deliverance ministry steps outlined above are best done in a discipleship / counseling session with at least one, or preferably two, trustworthy born-again Christians who understand and operate gracefully in their authority in Christ; they need to know how to minister the Word of God in the gifting of counsel and prayer. At least one of the counselors should be of the same sex as the person receiving ministry.

Please note that the above deliverance ministry steps apply to each sinful area of our lives. Therefore, when we have been bound by a succession of oaths, rituals, and indoctrinations, we may need to go through the steps above several times until we have cleared out all these areas of sin.

This appendix is not an exhaustive teaching on deliverance. It is intended only to provide the reader of this book with a practical, scriptural method of casting out demons. If the born again, Spirit-filled Christian reader follows the prayer guidelines for each subject developed in this book, there is enough information presented to be able to be personally set free.

This book is meant to be a self-help text to aid you in getting free from the spiritual damage and pollution that came from exposure to Freemasonry. There are many other things that could be explained about demons and the deliverance ministry. Complete books are written on the subject.[67,68,69]

References

1 Campbell, Ron G., "From Darkness to Light," *Free From Freemasonry* (Ventura, California: Regal Books, Gospel Light, 1999), p. 127.

2 Shaw, Jim and Tom McKenney, *The Deadly Deception* (Lafayette, Louisiana: Huntington House, 1983), p. 157.

3 Campbell, Op. cit., p. 13.

4 Pike, Albert, "The Fellow-Craft," *Morals and Dogma of the Ancient and Accepted Scottish Rite of Freemasonry* (Richmond, Virginia: L.H. Jenkins, Inc.), Kindle Edition, p. 22.

5 Mackey, Albert G., *An Encyclopedia of Freemasonry, Vol. II* (New York and London: The Masonic History Co., 1916), p. 497.

6 Pike, Op. cit., "Royal Arch of Solomon," p. 180.

7 Ibid., "Grand Elect Perfect and Sublime Mason (Perfect Elu)," p. 185.

8 Ibid., "Knight of the Sun, or Prince Adept," p. 603.

9 Ankerberg, John and John Weldon, *The Secret Teaching of the Masonic Lodge: A Christian Perspective* (Chicago: Moody Press, 1990), pp. 23–24.

10 Lawrence, John, *Freemasonry: A Way of Salvation* (Bramcote, Nottingham: Grove Books, 1988).

11 Knight, Stephen, *The Brotherhood* (London: HarperCollins, 1994).

12 Ibid., pp. 75, 76.

13 Decker, Ed. *The Dark Side of Freemasonry* (Lafayette, Louisiana: Huntington House, 1994), pp. 70–72.

14 David Barton, *The Question of Freemasonry and the Founding Fathers* (Aledo, Texas: Wallbuilders, 2005).

15 Decker, Op.cit., pp. 103–105.

16 Kitchen, Yvonne, *Freemasonry: Death in the Family* (Mountain Gate, Victoria, Australia: Fruitful Vine, 1997), pp. 126–140.

17 Ibid., p. 70.

18 Martin, Walter, *The Kingdom of the Cults* (Minneapolis: Bethany House, 1985).

19 Larson, Bob, *Larson's Book of Cults* (Wheaton, Illinois: Tyndale House, 1984), p. 156.

20 Enroth, Ronald, et al., *A Guide to Cults and New Religions* (Downers Grove, Illinois: InterVarsity Press), p. 117.

21 Martin, Op. cit., p. 38.

22 Larsen, Op. cit., p. 146.

23 Enroth, Op. cit., p. 103.

24 Martin, Op. cit., p. 126.

25   Larson, Op. cit., p. 130.

26   Shaw and McKenney, Op. cit.

27   Larson, Op. cit., p. 293.

28   Larson, Op. cit., p. 356.

29   Bixler, Op. cit.

30   Martin, Op. cit., p. 351.

31   Larson, Op. cit., p. 71.

32   Burnett, David, *The Spirit of Hinduism* (Crowborough, East Sussex: Monarch).

33   Martin, Op. cit., p. 364.

34   Larson, Op. cit., p. 103.

35   Morey, Robert, *The Islamic Invasion* (Eugene, Oregon: Harvest House, 1992).

36   Musk, Bill, *The Unseen Face of Islam* (Crowborough, East Sussex: Monarch, 1989).

37   Larson, Op. cit., p. 293.

38   Larson, Op. cit., p. 356.

39   Pike, Op. cit., "Royal Arch of Solomon," p. 180.

40   Ibid., "Grand Elect Perfect and Sublime Mason (Perfect Elu)," p. 185.

41   Ibid., "Grand Elect Perfect and Sublime Mason (Perfect Elu)," p. 188.

42   Ibid., "Prince of Mercy or Scottish Trinitarian," p. 441.

43   Ibid., "Grand Elect Perfect and Sublime Mason (Perfect Elu)," p. 185.

44   Ibid., "Knight of the Sun or Prince Adept," p. 524, and "Elect Perfect and Sublime Mason (Perfect Elu)."

45   Storms, E.M., *Should a Christian Be a Mason?* (Kirkwood, Missouri: Impact Christian Books, 2014), Chapter 7, "Freemasonry and Christianity," p. 90.

46   Stevens, Selwyn, *Freemasonry: Removing the Hoodwink* (Wellington, New Zealand: Jubilee Publishers, 1996), p. 13.

47   Ibid., pp. 13, 14.

48   Storms, Op. cit., Appendix 1, "Lecture of the 32nd Degree," pp. 97, 98.

49   Pike, Op. cit., "Royal Arch of Solomon," pp. 172, 521.

50   Storms, Op. cit., Chapter 5, "Self-Destructive Oaths," pp. 65, 66.

51   "The Masonic Fairy Tale Known as the Leo Taxil Confession," Freedom Ministries International, 20 Jan. 2016: https://www.freedom-ministries. com/catalog/confession-leo-taxilm-and-albert-pike.html

52   "Lucifer is the god of Freemasonry," Secret Societies, 20 Jan. 2016: http:// www.amazingdiscoveries.org/S-deception-Freemason_Lucifer_Albert_Pike

53   "Freemasonry Data Bank," Christian Restoration, 20 Jan. 2016: http://www. christian-restoration.com/fmasonry/lucquotes.htm

54   Pike, Op. cit., "Grand Elect Perfect and Sublime Mason (Perfect Elu)," p. 185.

55   Ankerberg, Op. cit., p. 42.

56   Storms, Op. cit., pp. 19–53.

57   Ankerberg, Op. cit., pp. 178–182.

58   Lawrence, Op. cit., pp. 12–19.

59   Lawrence, John, *Freemasonry: A Religion?* (Eastbourne, East Sussex: Kingsway, 1987), pp. 82–91, 143–147.

60   Ibid., pp. 93–100, 148–176.

61   Stevens, Op. cit., pp. 41–45.

62   Lawrence, Op. cit., pp. 92–107.

63   Ankerberg, Op. cit., pp. 182–191.

64   Shaw, Op. cit.

65   Kitchen, Op. cit.

66   Ibid., pp. 155–171.

67   Gibson, Noel and Phyl, *Evicting Demonic Intruders: Guidelines for Pastors and Counsellors on Ministering Freedom to the Oppressed Christian* (Chichester: New Wine Press, 1993).

68   Horrobin, Peter, *Healing through Deliverance: The Foundations and Practice of Deliverance Ministry* (Grand Rapids: Chosen Books, Revised and Expanded Edition, 2008).

69   Subritzky, Bill, *Demons Defeated* (Ellel, Lancaster: Sovereign World, Second Edition, 1996).